AN ORFF MOSAIC
FROM CANADA

ORFF AU CANADA:
UNE MOSAÏQUE

A collection of music, accompaniments, poems,
dances, essays and teaching suggestions
contributed by teachers from across Canada

Edited by Lois Birkenshaw-Fleming

SMC 80

SCHOTT

Mainz · London · Madrid · New York · Paris · Tokyo · Toronto

Acknowledgements

The publishers are grateful for permission to reproduce the following copyright music and text:

p. 20, Leslie Bricker and Dover Publications Inc.; p. 51, Crown Vetch Music, a division of Stompin' Tom Ltd. Administered by Morning Music Ltd.; p. 60, From *Songs to Play, Games to Sing,* by Ada Vermuelen; Gordon V Thomson Ltd, a division of Wamer/Chappell Music Canada Ltd.; p. 78, Myra Stillbom; p. 79, Wade Hemsworth, Peer Music (UK) Ltd; P. 89, Barabara Cass Beggs; p. 94, Stanley Triggs and Ean Hay, p. 98, From *Don't Eat Spiders,* Stoddart Publishing Ltd; p. 104, Courtesy of the Estate of Robert Service; p. 117, From *Jelly Belly* by Dennis Lee; p. 131, J Reaney; p. 142, From *Jelly Belly* by Dennis Lee; p. 148, From *Don't Eat Spiders,* Stoddart Publishing Ltd; p. 155, From *Alligator Pie* by Dennis Lee; p. 191, From *Don't Eat Spiders,* Stoddart Publishing Ltd; p. 214, From *Primary Rhymerry* by Sonja Dunn; Pembroke Publishers Ltd; p. 225, From *Don't Eat Spiders,* Stoddart Publishing Ltd; p. 226, From *Primary Rhymerry* by Sonja Dunn; Pembroke Publishers Ltd; p. 235, From *Tales of nokomis,* Stoddart Publishing Ltd; p. 240, From *Mortimer* by Robert Munsch; Annick Press Ltd; p. 266, From *Don't Eat Spiders,* Stoddart Publishing Ltd; p. 267, From *Don't Eat Spiders,* Stoddart Publishing Ltd; p. 318, From *Jelly Belly* by Dennis Lee

The following pieces are all copyright of Waterloo Music Company and are reproduced by permission:

p. 15, From *Folk Songs of Canada* by Edith Fowke and Richard Johnston; p. 16, From *Let's Sing and Play* by Keith Bissell; p. 54, From *Chansons de Québec* by Edith Fowke and Richard Johnston; p. 57, From *Chansons de Québec* by Edith Fowke and Richard Johnston; p. 66, From *Chansons de Québec* by Edith Fowke and Richard Johnston; p. 68, From *Folk Songs of Canada* by Edith Fowke and Richard Johnston; p. 76, From *Folk Songs of Canada* by Edith Fowke and Richard Johnston; p. 79, From *Touch the Pioneers* by Tim Rowat, Joe Grant and Bob Wogan; p. 83, From *Folk Songs of Canada* by Edith Fowke and Richard Johnston; p. 173, From *Songs for Today* volume 4 by Richard Johnston et al.; p. 175, From *Songs for Today* volume 4 by Richard Johnston et al.; p. 221, From *Singing and Playing* by Keith Bissell; p. 296, From A *Medieval Feast* by Carolyn Ritchey and Ursula Rempel.

Every effort has been made to contact copyright holders. The publishers would be pleased to hear from owners of copyright material not acknowledged here.

SMC 80
ISBN 0 946535 63 9
© Schott Music Corporation, New York, 1996

Designed and typeset by Musonix
Cover by Økvik Design
Printed in England

Contents

Foreword

Welcome to *An Orff Mosaic from Canada*

Orff friends around the world welcome this new publication from Canada. We know the important role Canada plays in the diffusion of Orff-Schulwerk stimuli on the North American continent. The efforts of Doreen Hall and Arnold Walter will always be remembered and we are fortunate to have so many competent teachers and artists carrying on the task of presenting the basic ideas of Carl Orff and Gunild Keetman in the world of music and education today.

May the *Mosaic* stimulate music and dance education in Canada and other parts of the world. The etymological root of the word "mosaic" is to the Muses, the nine daughters of Zeus and Mnemosyne, whose thoughts were of singing and dancing, who inspired composers and poets and who relieved the pains and sorrows of man.

Prof. Dr. Hermann Regner
Orff Institute, Salzburg

… But it will happen that the words we need will come of themselves. When the words we want to use shoot up of themselves … we get a new song.

Songs are thoughts, sung out with the breath when people are moved by great forces and ordinary speech no longer suffices.

Orpingalik
(as told to Knud Rasmussen)

Faster
the drum sounds
as the spirits move closer

The rattle shakes
and we dance.

Chief Dan George

Preface

Carl Orff Canada exists to encourage the development of a holistic music education evolved from the pedagogical philosophy of Carl Orff.
Mission statement of Music for Children – Carl Orff Canada – Musique pour enfants

And what a philosophy it is!

People still refer to the Orff approach as a "new" method in spite of the fact that Carl Orff and Gunild Keetman were formulating their ideas close to a half century ago, and Doreen Hall introduced the approach to Canada in the 1950s.

The timeless nature of the Orff philosophy owes much to its holistic and elemental approach. It is a philosophy that is close to the child, that grows from the elemental roots of child behaviour and learning. It is an approach that is never static but which incorporates new ways of teaching material that is current and relevant while retaining the basics tenets of the philosophy. Thus it is appropriate for all times.

Orff and Keetman based their approach on the following principles:

1   Start at the developmental level of the child, in rhythm, melody, movement and speech and build sequentially, and in a spiral fashion, following the path that human kind is thought to have followed in the development of music.

2   Always integrate movement, speech, rhythm and melody in every activity. The child in his or her own world does this, moving, speaking, chanting and singing little melodies all at the same time – very seldom in isolation. We teachers must build upon this "playful" behaviour and incorporate it into our teaching.

3   Use material from the child's own world, culture and traditions – folk songs, nursery rhymes, poems, chants and stories. These contain all the basic rhythmic and melodic patterns used in the beginning musical studies of childhood. In addition, the use of this material naturally involves movement (both creative movement and traditional dances and games), and through its use the rhythms and cadences of language are experienced. When music other than folk is used, it should be of high quality.

4   Always encourage the children to create their own rhythms, melodies, speech patterns and dances. Creativity is the central core of the Orff approach to music education.

As movements and trends in education come and go, Orff-Schulwerk appears not only to be holding its own, but indeed to be gaining ground. The basic principles of the philosophy have often been used as the basis for other approaches to music education. In many places Orff-Schulwerk is taught as a supplement to methods such as Yamaha and Suzuki, and the Schulwerk has long provided the framework for music experiences in early childhood, kindergarten and infant school classes. Almost every article written in music-education journals about creativity in general mentions the Orff instrumentarium, and if pictures accompany the article, these most often show children playing Orff xylophones and drums, even if the Orff approach is not named.

In the school music curricula of Canada, the United States, England and other countries, the Orff approach, more than any other, has changed the way music is taught. Gone (we hope forever) is the time when everyone had to sit quietly, not moving, and "have" singing. "Having singing" began with modulator drill (singing sequences of *do*, *re*, *mi* that were printed on one of John Curwen's modulators) and then progressed to the learning of the one or two songs prescribed by the music department each month.

This approach produced some very good singing but did not follow sound principles of child development. The movement component that is so necessary for full understanding and enjoyment of music was entirely lacking.

And what of the child who was never able to sing in tune? I am afraid that he or she was relegated to sitting in the back row, being called a "blackbird" and being told "just to mouth the words" especially when the supervisor or principal visited the class.

We now know that we learn best by participation. We learn music by making music, and the Orff approach does precisely that. Its many and varied activities encourage everyone to participate on his or her own level and above all the approach gives a place for everyone to succeed on that level. A "blackbird" could have a phenomenal sense of rhythm and could become indispensable by playing a complicated instrumental part that would hold the rest of the group together. (The instruments that were designed to be used with Orff-Schulwerk sound beautiful, are easy to play, and are irresistible to children. They add yet another dimension to the music experience by enlarging the pallet of sound and leading to a deeper understanding of timbre.)

Above all, children who work in the "Orff way" experience the joy of creating something uniquely their own. This is a fundamental and basic part of the Orff approach. Through these creations come competence and growth in self-confidence.

The schools of today have a mix of children from many cultures and traditions, with many and varied abilities and disabilities and from many different economic backgrounds. An approach that uses the philosophy of Carl Orff can include *all* these children in the music programme and encourage each and every one of them to develop to their fullest their love and knowledge of music.

In the educational philosophy of the 1990s the emphasis is not only on including everyone in the learning process but also on integrating different subject areas. Integrating the Orff approach with the regular curriculum assists all children to develop co-ordination and motor-sensory skills, listening skills, creative thinking, and proficiency in speech and language. The learning of basic skills such as counting and recognizing colours can be made easier and more pleasurable by using appropriate songs and chants, and by coming together to dance and make music the students develop social skills. Music can tell much about the history and geography of other lands and can even become part of science classes with the study of sound and vibrations. Many years ago Carl Orff stated that music should be fundamental to all other subject areas:

It then becomes not only exclusively a question of music education, it is rather a question of developing the whole personality. This surpasses by far the so called music and singing lessons found in the regular curriculum ... [1]

In this, of course, he joins scholars such as Plato who said:

Musical training is a more potent instrument than any other, because rhythm and harmony find their way into the inward places of the soul and take the strongest hold there, bringing that grace of body and mind which is only to be found in one who is brought up in the right way.[2]

Brain researchers today are validating these truths. They are finding that *taking part* in all facets of music making from an early age builds and helps retain synaptic connections in children's brains, and can lead to vastly more efficient abilities, particularly in the area of spatial relationships and reasoning. The thinking is also that, in old age, by using the brain in challenging ways, people will be far less likely to succumb to confusion and dementia. Learning to play a musical instrument is cited in this research as one of the very best ways to challenge and exercise the brain.[3]

So it would seem that the Orff approach is yet again an idea "whose time has come". Because it is based on the fundamentally correct and eternal principles of child development it will not only endure, but will always seem "new" for each person discovering it, whether as a teacher, a pupil or a parent.

Carl Orff Canada existe pour encourager le développement d'une éducation musicale dite holistique qui découle de la philosophie pédagogique de Carl Orff.
Mission statement of Music for Children – Carl Orff Canada – Musique pour Enfants

Et c'est toute une philosophie!

Même si Carl Orff et Gunild Keetman ont formulé leurs idées il y a près d'un siècle et que Doreen Hall a introduit cette approche d'enseignement de la musique au Canada à la fin des années 50, les gens continuent de penser que cette approche d'enseignement de la musique est une "nouvelle" méthode.

La philosophie Orff doit cette qualité d'apparence éternelle à son approche holistique enracinée dans les éléments essentiels de la musique. C'est une philosophie qui est proche de l'enfant, qui évolue selon les principes de base du comportement de l'enfant. C'est une approche qui n'est jamais statique mais qui intègre de nouvelles façons d'enseigner qui sont actuelles et pertinentes tout en gardant les principes fondamenteux de la pédagogie. Dès lors, c'est une méthode d'enseignement appropriée à notre époque.

Orff et Keetman ont façonné leur approche à partir des principes suivants:

1   Commencer là où l'enfant se situe dans son développement rythmique, mélodique, moteur et verbal, et l'amener progressivement, de façon spiralée, à poursuivre un cheminement propre en régard de la musique.

2   Introduire le mouvement, l'expression verbale, le rythme et la mélodie dans chaque activité. L'enfant le fait constamment dans son propre monde, il bouge, parle, chante de petits airs et cela en même temps. Nous, les enseignants, devont bâtir notre enseignement sur ce comportement "enjoué" de l'enfant.

3   Utiliser le matériel venant du monde de l'enfant, de sa culture et de ses traditions – chansons folkloriques, comptines, poèmes, chansons et histoires. Ce matériel contient tous les modèles rythmiques et mélodiques de base utilisés pour les jeunes enfants

débutant leurs études musicales. De plus, l'emploi de ce matériel entraîne naturellement le mouvement (le mouvement créatif, les danses traditionnelles et les jeux). C'est à travers l'utilisation de ce matériel que les rythmes et les cadences de la langue sont appris. Lorsque l'enseignant fait appel à une musique autre que le folklore, elle devrait toujours être de haute qualité.

4   Encourager constamment les enfants à créer leurs propres rythmes, mélodies, danses et parler-rythmés. La créativité est le noyau fondamental de l'éducation musicale selon l'approche Orff.

Alors que les mouvements et les orientations en éducation ont tendance à fluctuer, Orff-Schulwerk non seulement semble tenir bon, mais aussi se met à gagner du terrain. Les principes de base de sa philosophie ont souvent été utilisés par d'autres approches en éducation musicale. Ils sont enseignés comme supplément dans diverses méthodes telles que Yamaha et Suzuki. Le Schulwerk a depuis longtemps fourni une structure pour les expériences musicales des classes pré-scolaires et des jardins d'enfance. Presque tous les articles parus dans les périodiques en éducation musicale à propos de la créativité en général, mentionnent l'instrumentarium Orff. Et si des images accompagnent l'article, souvent ces photographies illustrent des enfants jouant des xylophones et des tambours "Orff".

Dans les programmes d'étude des écoles, l'approche Orff, plus que toute autre philosophie a changé la façon dont la musique est enseignée au Canada, aux États-Unis, en Angleterre et en d'autres pays. Disparue (espèrons pour toujours) l'époque où tout le monde devait s'asseoir sans bruit, sans bouger, et "avait" de la musique. "Avoir de la musique" commençait par des exercices de solfège (chanter des exercices de *do, ré, mi* imprimés dans un des cahiers à moduler de John Curwen) et de là, progressait vers la mémorisation d'une ou deux chansons prescrites chaque mois par le département de musique.

Cette approche avait comme résultat du beau chant mais ne suivait pas des principes valables quant au développement de l'enfant. L'élément du mouvement si nécessaire pour la compréhension et l'appréciation de la musique dans la joie, était totalement absent.

Et de que dire de l'enfant qui ne pouvait jamais chanter juste? On le renvoyait s'asseoir dans la dernière rangée en lui demandent de prononcer les mots en silence particulièrement lors des visites de l'inspecteur ou du directeur.

Nous savons maintenant que la connaissance s'acquiert par la pratique. Nous apprenons la musique en faisant de la musique et l'approche Orff nous le permet justement. Ses activités multiples et variées encouragent chacun à participer selon son niveau. Par-dessus tout, cette approche permet de réussir. Un/e élève moins doué/e pourrait avoir un sens phénoménal du rythme et pourrait devenir indispensable s'il apprend à jouer une partie instrumentale plus compliquée. (Les instruments conçus pour le Orff-Schulwerk sont agréables à entendre, faciles à jouer et sont irrésistibles pour les enfants. Ils ajoutent une autre dimension à l'expérience musicale en élargissant la palette sonore et favorisent une meilleure connaissance du timbre.)

De plus, les enfants qui travaillent avec la "façon Orff" éprouvent la joie de créer quelque chose qui leur appartient. C'est une base fondamentale de l'approche Orff. A travers ces créations se développent la compétence et la croissance de la confiance en soi.

Les écoles d'aujourd'hui comprennent un mélange d'enfants venant de plusieurs cultures et traditions, avec des habilités et des handicaps variés, et de classes économiques différentes. Une approche qui utilise la philosophie de Carl Orff inclut tous les enfants dans le programme de musique et encourage tous et chacun à développer du mieux qu'ils peuvent leur amour et leur connaissance de la musique.

Dans la philosophie éducative des années 1990, l'emphase est mise non seulement sur l'inclusion de tous dans le processus d'apprentissage mais aussi sur l'intégration de différentes matières à l'étude. L'intégration de l'approche Orff dans le programme du cours régulier aide les enfants à développer la coordination et les habiletés motrices et sensorielles, la capacité d'écoute, la pensée créative, et la compétence dans l'étude de la langue. L'apprentissage des habiletés de base comme le calcul et la reconnaissance des couleurs peut devenir plus facile et plus agréable en utilisant des chansons et des comptines appropriées; le fait de se retrouver ensemble pour une danse et pour faire de la musique permet aux jeunes de développer leurs habiletés sociales. La musique peut nous raconter beaucoup sur l'histoire et la géographie d'autres pays et peut même faire partie des classes de science en étudiant le son et les vibrations. Il y a de cela plusieurs années, Carl Orff mentionnait que la musique devait avoir une place fondamentale dans tous les autres champs d'étude:

It then becomes not only exclusively a question of music education, it is rather a question of developing the whole personality. This surpasses by far the so called music singing lessons found in the regular curriculum … [1]

Suivant le cours de cette pensée, il se joint aux érudits comme Platon qui dit:

Musical training is a more potent instrument than any other, because rhythm and harmony find their way into the inward places of the soul and take the strongest hold there, bringing that grace of body and mind which is only to be found in one who is brought up in the right way.[2]

Aujourd'hui les chercheurs du cerveau sont en voie de prouver ces vérités. Ils reconnaissent que prendre part, dès le jeune âge, à l'activité musicale sous tous ses aspects, construit et aide à retenir les synapses nerveuses chez les enfants, et peut conduire à des habiletés intellectuelles plus vastes et efficaces particulièrement dans le domaine des relations spatiales et du raisonnement. De la même façon, dans l'âge avancé, on pense maintenant qu'en utilisant le cerveau de façon stimulante, les personnes seront moins portées à succomber à la confusion et à la démence. Cette recherche cite "qu'apprendre à jouer un instrument de musique est une des meilleures façons de stimuler le cerveau"[3]

Il semblerait donc que l'approche Orff est, encore une fois, une idée "dont le temps est venu." Parce qu'elle est basée sur des principes éternels et fondamentaux du développement de l'enfant, non seulement va-t-elle persister, mais semblera "nouvelle" à toute personne qui la découvre, qu'elle soit enseignant/e, étudiant/e ou parent.

Notes

1   Bellflower Symposium, Bellflower, California, 1967
2   Plato, *The Republic*, bk III
3   Daniel Golden, "Building a better brain", *Life Magazine*, July 1994

About *An Orff Mosaic from Canada / Orff au Canada: une mosaïque*

The book was compiled in answer to a need expressed by many teachers for a collection of songs, poems and activities from our own great country. Orff teachers in many communities have long been using Canadian songs, working out sound effects to Canadian poems and writing original material. Some of this material had been published but most had not and we felt that it was time to make our "Canadian Orff" available to a wider audience.

The intent was to have selections from every part of Canada – not only folk material from the entire country but also lesson plans, accompaniments, poems and songs written by educators, poets and musicians in every province, the Yukon and the North-West Territories.

Appeals for material were printed in *Ostinato* (the journal of Music for Children – Carl Orff Canada – Musique pour enfants), letters were written to the presidents of every Orff chapter in Canada and many, many individuals were contacted. In addition, a great amount of research into possible material was undertaken, including the works of the "Pioneers" – the men and women who taught in the "Orff way" in the early years.

All this was done in the hope that it would be a representative, interesting, lively and useful mosaic of Canadian material. Some 300 items were contributed by teachers from right across the country!

There was a panel of readers who reviewed the submitted material. These people were chosen because of their knowledge and experience in the Orff approach. In addition *An Orff Mosaic from Canada / Orff au Canada: une mosaïque* was reviewed by the editorial board of Schott Music in London.

While most of the folk selections come from the British and French traditions, music from other cultures has been included. But because of the tremendous numbers of ethnic groups in Canada today (one school in Toronto has children whose parents were born in 72 different countries) it would be impossible to include songs and poems from all the countries. Many songs from different lands have been included and we are grateful to all those people who shared their heritage with us. The content is in no way a reflection on all the other cultures which have also enriched Canada with their distinctive contributions, but rather a result of what material was submitted for inclusion.

Canada is a young nation and, as such, is a nation of immigrants. Indeed, the only peoples who have been living here longer than 390 years or so are the First Nations who came at least 10,000 years ago (some think as many as 20,000 years). Needless to say, their music is well represented.

Most of the songs and poems have written lesson plans. Those that do not were for the most part written for the older grades or for Orff withdrawal groups.

The songs and activities include suggested age or grade levels. But they are just that: suggestions. Each teacher will have to make selections based on the needs of his or her group.

Organization of the book

The first chapter discusses the history of Orff-Schulwerk in Canada. Then follows "Hello!", a series of introductory exercises. The next chapters include selections from every region in Canada, mostly folk material.

The next part of the book is organized around themes: weather and seasons; animals; transportation; our world; the Canadian mosaic; holidays; basics; stories, fables, music and drama; students' work; move and dance; instruments; listening awareness and music appreciation, and "Good-bye!"

The book ends with a glossary and a chapter of tips for teachers. The latter gives ideas of how to work with the material in the "Orff way" but is in no way intended to supplant formal Orff training. There is a bibliography, a list of recordings, and an index of songs, music, poems, chants, speech patterns and stories.

Acknowledgments

Heartfelt thanks go first to those who gave so generously of their "treasures" for the book. It is an act of great courage to allow one's work to be included in a publication such as this and these contributions are gratefully acknowledged.

Thanks to the reading committee who reviewed most of the work prior to publication: Sœur Marcelle Corneille of Montréal, Donna Otto of Vancouver, Susan Knight of St. Johns, Judy Sills of Edmonton, and Ruth Wiwchar of Winnipeg. As you can imagine, the time commitment for this task was considerable. These busy people are owed a debt of gratitude from us all for agreeing to participate. Sœur Marcelle Corneille in particular gave tremendous help and encouragement in all stages of the book's development and was a valued resource in the selection of the French material.

Many thanks to John Harper, the retired Managing Director of Schott, London, who initiated the project, and to the production team at Schott, especially Wendy Lampa, who inherited it and gave it such great support.

Lastly, thanks also to countless others who gave enthusiastic support to the project and in particular to my husband, Kip Fleming, for his constant and continuing encouragement.

It is our hope that you will find *An Orff Mosaic from Canada/Orff au Canada: une mosaïque* interesting and useful, and that the songs, poems and activities in the book will help you continue to bring joy and musical development to all children in the "Orff way".

Lois Birkenshaw-Fleming
Toronto, 1996

An Orff Mosaic From Canada / Orff Au Canada: une mosaïque

Le livre a été conçu pour répondre à un besoin manifesté par plusieurs enseignant/es de pouvoir disposer d'une collection de chansons, poèmes et activités nous venant de notre merveilleux pays. Les enseignant/es de diverses communautés qui se sont familiarisé/es avec la méthode Orff utilisent depuis longtemps des chansons canadiennes, adaptent des effets sonores aux poèmes canadiens et composent du matériel original. Une petite partie seulement de ce matériel a été publiée et nous avons pensé qu'il était temps de rendre notre "Orff Canadien" disponible à un auditoire plus vaste.

Au point de départ, nous désirons recevoir du matériel nous venant de partout au Canada – non seulement du répertoire folklorique de tout le pays mais aussi des plans de leçon, des accompagnements, des poèmes et des chansons écrites par des éducateurs, des poètes et des musiciens de chaque province, mêmes du Yukon et Territoires du Nord-Ouest.

Les demandes de matériel furent imprimées dans *Ostinato*, des lettres furent écrites aux président/es de chaque chapitre Orff au Canada et plusieurs individus furent contactés. De plus, on entreprit beaucoup de recherches de nouveau matériel tout en incluant le travail des "pionniers" – les hommes et les femmes qui ont enseigné "la façon Orff", au tout début.

Tout ceçi fut accompli dans l'espoir que le résultat représenterait une mosaïque fidèle, intéressante, vivante et utile du matériel canadien en français et en anglais. Quelques 300 écrits ont été offerts par des enseignant/es à travers tout le Canada!

Un jury de lecteurs revisa le matériel soumis. Ces gens furent choisis d'après leur connaissance et leur expérience de l'approche Orff. De plus, *An Orff Mosaic from Canada / Orff au Canada: une mosaïque* fut revisé par le conseil de rédaction de Schott Music, Londres, Angleterre.

La majorité des pièces folkloriques viennent des traditions britanniques et françaises. Plusiers chansons de pays différentes ont été retenues et nous sommes reconnaissants envers les gens qui ont partagé leur patrimoine avec nous. Toutefois, comme il y a aujourd'hui au Canada de nombreux groupes ethniques importants (une école de Toronto a une population d'enfants dont les parents viennent de 72 pays différents) il était impossible d'inclure des chansons et poèmes venant de tous ces pays. Le contenu découle du matériel qui nous a été soumis et ne réflète donc toutes les autres cultures qui ont aussi enrichi le Canada de leurs contributions distinctes.

Le Canada est un jeune pays et dès lors une nation d'immigrants. Les seuls peuples qui ont vécu ici depuis plus de 390 ans (ou à peu près) sont les nations amérindiennes qui sont arrivées il y a de cela au moins 10,000 ans (certains vont jusqu'à dire 20,000 ans). Il va sans dire que leur musique est bien representée.

La plupart des chansons et des poèmes ont des plans de leçons écrits. Ceux qui n'en ont pas sont, pour la plupart, écrits pour des classes plus avancées ou pour des groupes Orff en parascolaire.

Les chansons et les activités sont appropriées à un niveau d'âge suggéré. Ce ne sont que des suggestions. Chaque enseignant/e devra faire ses propres choix à partir des besoins de son groupe.

L'organisation du livre

Le livre est organisé de telle façon que le premier chapitre est un exposé sur l'histoire du Orff-Schulwerk au Canada. Les chapitres suivants comprennent un choix de pièces venant de toutes les régions du Canada, surtout du matériel de source folklorique.

La section suivante du livre est organisée autour de thèmes – les animaux, la température et les saisons, les vacances, le transport, notre environnement, la mosaïque canadienne, les connaissances de base, les histoires, les fables et la musique, le mouvement et la danse, les instruments, le travail des étudiants, l'écoute active et l'appréciation musicale.

Le livre se termine par un glossaire, un chapitre avec un choix de suggestions aux enseignant/es (donnant des idées sur la façon de travailler le matériel selon les procédés Orff, ce qui ne remplace pas une formation pédagogique Orff), une bibliographie, une discographie, et des listes en ordre alphabétique de chansons et musique, poèmes, chants, parler-rythmé et histoires.

Remerciements

Des remerciements sincères vont d'abord à ceux et celles qui ont si généreusement donné de leurs "perles" pour élaborer ce livre. C'est une décision courageuse que celle d'autoriser l'utilisation de son travail dans une publication telle que celle-ci; ces contributions sont grandement appréciées.

Des remerciements s'adressent aussi au Comité de lecture qui a passé en revue la majorité du travail avant la publication: Soeur Marcelle Corneille de Montréal, Donna Otto de Vancouver, Susan Knight de Saint Johns, Terre-Neuve, Judy Sills d'Edmonton et Ruth Wiwchar de Winnipeg. Comme vous pouvez l'imaginer, le temps consacré à ce travail à été considérable. Soeur Marcelle Corneille en particulier a largement contribué et encouragé le développement du livre dans toutes ces étapes. Son apport a été d'une valeur inestimable dans le choix du matériel français.

De nombreux remerciements vont à John Harper, le directeur général à la retraite de Schott Music, Londres, qui a promu ce projet, et à tous les autres membres de l'équipe de production de Schott, en particulier, Wendy Lampa, qui en a hérité et qui l'ont tellement appuyé.

Enfin, notre gratitude rejoint tous ceux qui ont donné leur appui enthousiaste au projet, en particulier mon mari, Kip Fleming, pour son constant encouragement.

C'est notre voeu sincère que *An Orff Mosaic From Canada / Orff au Canada: une mosaïque* soit des plus intéressants et des plus utiles et que les chansons, les poèmes et les activités du livre favorisent la poursuite de l'idéal Orff: apporter la joie à tous les enfants dans leur développement musical grâce à la "façon Orff".

Lois Birkenshaw-Fleming
Toronto, 1996

Introduction

The Orff Movement in Canada

Nancy Vogan

Through a colourful and varied program of music-making the child is carried through the centuries up to the contemporary music scene … ; the music is all first-class, with the emphasis placed on the folk song, which has through the ages been the chief source of the world's greatest music. I believe that Orff has pointed the way, and that in this direction lies the future salvation of school music.[1]

Thus wrote Keith Bissell in 1960, following a visit to Carl Orff in Germany. Bissell recommended that all teachers, supervisors and others genuinely interested in elementary music education undertake a serious study of this approach. Orff's concentration on improvisation and the development of creativity has indeed been welcomed as a means of introducing students of all ages to contemporary composition. Over the past forty years the Orff movement has made a most significant contribution to the entire field of music education in Canada, fostering the development of early childhood education in music, encouraging the integration of singing, movement and playing of instruments, kindling an interest in recorder playing, and supporting the interrelationship of the arts in education.

The Orff approach had its origins in Europe during the 1920s; Carl Orff's "Music for Children" as we know it developed following World War II. It was in 1954 that Arnold Walter, director of the Faculty of Music at the University of Toronto, and a European by birth, arranged for Doreen Hall to study in Germany with Carl Orff and Gunild Keetman. Upon her return in 1955, Doreen Hall introduced the Orff-Schulwerk to North America through classes at the Royal Conservatory of Music in Toronto and later at the University of Toronto's Faculty of Music. Doreen Hall and Arnold Walter collaborated to produce the first English adaptation of the Orff–Keetman five-volume *Orff-Schulwerk*, called *Music for Children*; Hall also wrote a teacher's manual outlining the basic philosophy and methodology of the approach.[2]

Over the next few years Doreen Hall gave workshops in various parts of Canada as well as in the United States. By the late 1950s the Waterloo Music Company had begun to place advertisements for the specially designed Orff instruments in music publications, and the Leeds Music Company was promoting the Hall–Walter edition of *Music for Children*, published by Schott. The National Film Board produced a documentary entitled "Music for Children"; a CBC radio series led by Joan Sumberland, "Living Through Music", featured the Orff approach.

School music departments in the Toronto area began this approach in some of their work. The way was led by Keith Bissell, supervisor of music for the Scarborough schools, followed by Harvey Perrin from the Toronto Board and Laughton Bird, who later became supervisor of music for the North York schools. The Orff movement spread to French-speaking Canada as well, primarily through the work of Sœur Saint-Armand-Marie,

CND (later Sœur Marcelle Corneille) at l'École Normale de Musique in Montréal. The approach has been incorporated into enrichment programs for gifted children and has also been used in programs for children with disabilities. In the mid-1960s Lois Birkenshaw was invited to use her Orff training with students at the Metropolitan Toronto School for the Deaf. She subsequently worked with students with many different special needs in institutions and schools with the Toronto School Board.

For many years Toronto remained the North America centre for Orff training. Classes were given regularly at the Royal Conservatory of Music and at the Faculty of Music at the University of Toronto. In 1962 a two-week summer course in "Music for Children" for both private and school music teachers was held in the new Faculty of Music building of the University of Toronto. Instructors included Lotte Flach and Barbara Haselbach from the Orff Institute in Salzburg in addition to Canadians Doreen Hall, Laughton Bird, Keith Bissell and Hugh Orr. A special three-day conference on elementary music education was included in this summer session; Carl Orff attended this conference and presented the keynote address. Other speakers included Arnold Walter, Vally Weigl (music therapy) and Richard Johnston (North American folk songs); demonstration classes were led by Doreen Hall. This conference and the Orff courses attracted many participants from both Canada and the United States and led to the spread of the Orff movement throughout North America.

In the fall of 1974 a Canadian Orff association was founded with Doreen Hall as its first president. The first convention of "Music for Children – Carl Orff Canada – Musique pour enfants" was held in Toronto in 1975. Since then, the organization has developed extensively, sponsoring national conventions and regional workshops, maintaining a publication for its members and offering scholarships for young teachers. National conventions have been held from coast to coast and have attracted participants from all parts of Canada as well as from the United States and abroad. Held first on an annual basis, these events are now held biannually. Over the years regional associations have been formed throughout the country, further fostering the growth of Orff activities.

In the spring of 1994 the national conference was held in Toronto for a third time. Entitled "Mosaic", this convention combined a mosaic of Orff activities for the 1990s with a retrospective look at the Orff movement in Canada. This featured a tribute to founder Doreen Hall and an honouring of the pioneers in the movement. A special musical tribute was given to the memory of Keith Bissell for his significant contribution to Canadian music education and particularly for his work as a composer and arranger of material for Orff ensembles.

Le Mouvement Orff au Canada

Nancy Vogan

Through a colourful and varied program of music-making the child is carried through the centuries up to the contemporary music scene … ; the music is all first-class, with the emphasis placed on the folk song, which has through the ages been the chief source of the world's greatest music. I believe that Orff has pointed the way, and that in this direction lies the future salvation of school music.[1]

Voilà ce qu'écrit Keith Bissell en 1960 après avoir visité Carl Orff en Allemagne. Bissell recommanda que tous les enseignant/es, coordinateur/trices, et autres personnes sincèrement intéressé/es à l'éducation musicale à l'élémentaire, entreprennent une étude sérieuse de cette approche. L'importance de l'improvisation et du développement de la créativité chez Orff a en effet été reçue comme étant une façon de présenter la composition contemporaine aux étudiants de tout âge. Durant les quarantes dernières années, le mouvement Orff a été un apport considérable dans le domaine de l'éducation musicale au Canada. Il a favorisé le développement de l'éveil musical au préscolaire, encouragé l'intégration du chant, du mouvement et du jeu instrumental, éveillé un intérêt pour la flûte et appuyé l'intégration des arts en éducation.

L'approche Orff tire ses origines de l'Europe dans les années 1920; "Musique pour les enfants" de Carl Orff, comme nous le connaissons maintenant, s'est developpée après la deuxième guerre mondiale. Ce fut en 1954 qu'Arnold Walter, directeur de la Faculté de musique à Toronto et européen de naissance, envoya Doreen Hall étudier en Allemagne avec Carl Orff et Gunild Keetman. A son retour en 1955, Doreen Hall introduisit l'Orff-Schulwerk en Amérique du Nord, grâce à des cours au Conservatoire royal de musique à Toronto et plus tard à la Faculté de musique de l'Université de Toronto. Doreen Hall et Arnold Walter ont collaboré pour la publication de la première adaptation anglaise d'Orff–Keetman en cinq volumes Orff-Schulwerk, intitulée "Music for Children" ("Musique pour enfants"); Hall a aussi écrit un "Teacher's Manual" / "Manuel de l'enseignant" soulignant la philosophie de base et la méthodologie de l'approche.[2]

Au cours des quelques années qui suivirent, Doreen Hall a donné des ateliers dans diverses parties du Canada ainsi qu'aux Etats-Unis. A la fin des années 1950, la Compagnie de musique Waterloo commençait à placer des réclames publicitaires pour les instruments spéciaux Orff dans des publications musicales, et la Compagnie de musique Leeds faisait la promotion de l'édition de Hall–Walter, *Music for Children*, publiée par Schott. L'Office national du film réalisa un documentaire intitulé "Music for Children"; une série d'émissions de radio sur les ondes de CBC, animées par Joan Sumberland, "Living Through Music" (vivre à travers la musique) mettait aussi en valeur l'approche Orff.

Les départements de musique des écoles aux alentours de Toronto commencèrent à adopter certains aspects de cette approche d'enseignement dans leur travail. Keith Bissell, coordonnateur du programme de musique des écoles de Scarborough, se révéla le pionnier, suivi de Harvey Perrin du Conseil scolaire de Toronto et de Laughton Bird, qui plus tard deviendra coordonnateur du département de musique des écoles de North York. Le mouvement Orff s'est aussi répandu au Canada français, surtout grâce au travail de Sœur Saint-Armand Marie, CND (qui plus tard deviendra Sœur Marcelle Corneille) à l'École Normale de Musique à Montréal. L'approche a été introduite dans les programmes enrichis pour les enfants doués et elle a aussi été développée dans les programmes pour les enfants handicapés. Au milieu des années 1960, Lois Birkenshaw fut invitée à appliquer sa formation Orff avec les étudiants de l'École métropolitaine de Toronto pour les déficients auditifs. Par la suite, elle travailla avec des étudiants aux handicaps multiples dans des institutions et des écoles attachées au Conseil scolaire de Toronto.

Pendant plusiers années, Toronto fut le centre de formation Orff en Amérique du Nord. Des cours furent régulièrement donnés au Conservatoire royal de musique et à la Faculté de musique de l'Université de Toronto. En 1962, un cours d'été de deux semaines pour les professeurs d'écoles publiques et privées intitulé "Music for Children", fut donné à la nouvelle faculté de musique de l'Université de Toronto. Parmi les chargés de cours on retrouve les noms de Lotte Flach et Barbara Haselbach de l'Institut Orff de Salzburg, en plus des canadien/nes Doreen Hall, Laughton Bird, Keith Bissell, et Hugh Orr. Une conférence spéciale de trois jours sur l'éducation musicale à l'élémentaire marqua aussi cet événement; Carl Orff y participa en tant que conférencier responsable du discours d'ouverture. Parmi les autres conférenciers, on retrouvait Arnold Walter, Vally Weigl (musique et thérapie) Richard Johnston (la chanson folklorique en Amérique du Nord) et des démonstrations données par Doreen Hall. Cette conférence et les cours Orff attirèrent plusieurs participants du Canada et des Etats-Unis et marquèrent l'expansion du mouvement Orff à travers l'Amérique du Nord.

A l'automne 1974, l'association canadienne Orff fut fondée; Doreen Hall en devint la première présidente. La première conférence, "Music for Children – Carl Orff Canada – Musique pour enfants", eut lieu en 1975 à Toronto. Depuis, cette organisation s'est grandement développée, parrainant des conférences nationales et des ateliers régionaux, appuyant un périodique pour ses membres et offrant des bourses d'étude aux jeunes enseignants. Les conférences nationales ont eu lieu d'un océan à l'autre et ont attiré des participants de tous les coins du Canada ainsi que des Etats-Unis et de l'étranger. Organisées annuellement au début, ces évènements ont maintenant lieu à tous les deux ans. Au fil des ans, des associations régionales se sont formées à travers le pays, encourageant encore davantage le développement des activités Orff.

Au printemps 1994, la conférence nationale eut lieu pour la troisième fois à Toronto. Intitulée "Mosaic/Mosaïque", cette conférence combina une "mosaïque" d'activités Orff pour les années 1990 avec un regard rétrospectif sur le mouvement Orff au Canada. Ce retour au passé a été l'occasion de rendre hommage à la fondatrice Doreen Hall et de faire connaître les pionniers du mouvement. On a souligné la mémoire de Keith Bissell en mettant la lumière sa contribution considérable à l'éducation musicale canadienne et tout particulièrement son travail de composition et d'arrangements pour des ensembles Orff.

Notes

1   Keith Bissell, "A Visit to Carl Orff", *Canadian Music Educator*, vol. 2, no. 2 (December 1960), p. 20
2   For details regarding the early development of the movement,/pour plus de renseignements concernant le développement du mouvement à ses débuts, see/voir Doreen Hall (ed.), *Orff-Schulwerk in Canada* (Schott, 1992)

A Canon for Canada

Grades

3 and 4

Leslie Bricker

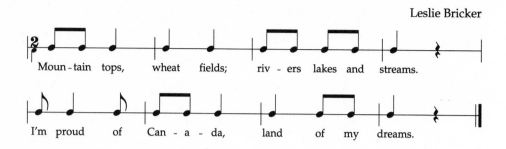

Moun - tain tops,   wheat   fields;   riv - ers   lakes   and   streams.

I'm   proud   of   Can - a - da,   land   of   my   dreams.

Body percussion *

snap
clap
stamp

sn
cl
st

Process

1   Learn speech and perform in a four-part round (canon).

2   Transfer speech to body percussion (they are the same rhythm). Perform them together.

3   The body-percussion part can be performed on unpitched percussion instruments. Let the children choose the instruments, matching the strong (stamp), medium (clap) and weak (snap) sounds to the sounds of the various instruments.

*   When stems go up use the right hand and/or foot. When stems go down use the left. Stems up and down mean use both hands and feet. (The exception is when clapping. Stems can go up or down because one has to clap with two hands.)

Places in Canada

Leslie Bricker

Grades

2 and 3

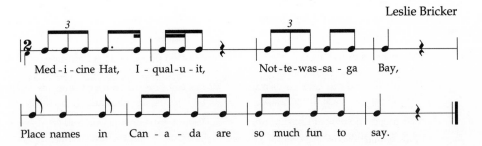

Med - i - cine Hat,   I - qual-u - it,   Not-te-was-sa - ga   Bay,

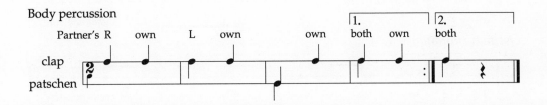

Place names   in   Can - a - da   are   so much fun   to   say.

Body percussion

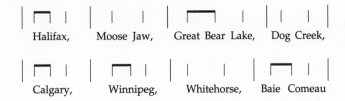

Partner's R   own   L   own   own   both   own   both

clap

patschen

Process

1   Learn the speech, add body percussion and unpitched percussion instruments as above. The example given is for working in pairs.

2   Use it as the A section of a rondo (ABACADAEA), creating interludes (C, D, E, and so on) using other place names in Canada. Accompany with body percussion and/or unpitched percussion instruments or speech rhythms.
    An example of a speech interlude follows:

Halifax,   Moose Jaw,   Great Bear Lake,   Dog Creek,

Calgary,   Winnipeg,   Whitehorse,   Baie Comeau

Les valeurs musicales de chez-nous

"Les valeurs musicales de chez-nous" est un parler-rythmé ayant comme thème le multiculturalisme qui invite à la promotion de la bonne entente, de l'acceptation et du respect de toutes les cultures. Plus qu'un parler-rythmé, c'est un pourparler mettant en évidence les valeurs de notre Mosaïque, de notre beau pays.

Viva la musica oui, oui, oui!
C'est l'âme, le feu de notre pays.
On chante et on danse en s'amusant;
On fête et on crie, c'est divertissant.

Le rythme, la mélodie et l'harmonie,
C'est le seul langage des gens d'ici.
On connaît très bien tous les tons;
On accepte aussi tous les sons.

Tout est possible dans l'amitié;
Il s'agit d'écouter et de respecter
Les diverses croyances, toutes les nuances,
La gamme des couleurs, les différences.

Viva la musica oui, oui, oui!
C'est un langage qui nous unit.
Il nous invite à prendre la main,
D'accepter tout l'monde comme un copain.

Vivianne Panizzon

Ostinati rythmiques

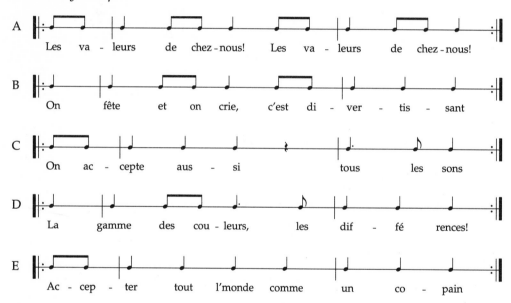

Démarche pédagogique

A   ostinato de base: peut être employé seul comme introduction;

B   transition entre les couplets 1 et 2: accompagné de l'ostinato de base;

C   transition entre les couplets 2 et 3: accompagné de l'ostinato se base;

D   transition entre les couplets 3 et 4: accompagné de l'ostinato de base;

E   message final accompagné de l'ostinato de base:
      graduellement ajouter les autres ostinati en crescendo.

CHAPTER ONE

Hello!

Hello

Grades

K and 1

Concepts

☐ Socialization;

☐ creativity;

☐ co-ordination.

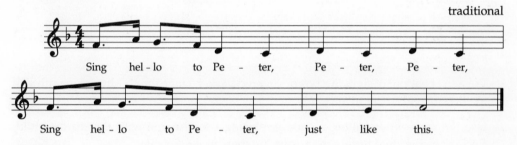

Process

1 The children sit in a circle. Sing "hello" to everyone in turn asking what action each would like for their "special" hello.

> Clap hello to Johnny …
> Wave hello to Karim …
> Blink hello to Emily …

2 Place three or four percussion instruments in the centre of the circle. The child whose turn it is chooses one and plays it while the others mimic the playing action.

> Play the drum with Monica …
> Play the triangle with Tony …

3 The original song is an action song. The words are as follows:

> Everybody do this, do this, do this,
> Everybody do this, just like me.

4 Each child in turn creates an action – clapping, stamping, jumping, blinking. The others copy.

Special learners

● Make sure that actions are included that everyone can do such as nodding, blinking, waving and so on.

Friendly Bear

Age

2 to 3

Concepts

☐ Tone matching;

☐ socialization.

words and music Birthe Kulich

Process

1 Put a toy bear out of sight in a box or covered basket. Have the children sing with you to encourage the bear to appear.

2 Use the song while calling a child, replacing Bear's name with that of the child. Encourage the child to sing the answer by matching your pitch.

3 Use different pitch placements: high, low, medium.

4 If the child has difficulty matching your pitch, sing in the child's range a few times, gradually trying to get the child's pitch to equal yours.

Extensions

● This song might be used to introduce a mascot such as a toy bear, dog or other soft, cuddly animal, or a puppet – something that can act as a catalyst for singing. Indeed, a whole music program could be built around a toy such as this:

"Friendly Bear is going to sing a song with you today. Help him by singing with him," or "Listen with Friendly Bear while I tell you a story."

● This is a useful device to use with very young children or with others who need extra help in focusing.

Welcome

Grades

K and 1

Concepts

- [ ] Names;
- [ ] beat;
- [ ] word rhythm;

- [ ] rondo;
- [ ] listening;
- [ ] social interaction.

Angela Elster

Wel - come, wel - come all of you are wel - come.

Wel - come, wel - come. Please play your name.

Bienvenue, bienvenue,
Tout le monde, bienvenue,
Bienvenue, bienvenue,
Dites-moi votre nom.

Process

1 Say everyone's name and play each rhythm on a drum.

2 Teach the song by rote.

3 Everyone sings the song and after each repetition, one child says his/her name and plays the rhythm on a drum. The rest of the children in the class repeat the name and clap the rhythm four times.

4 The drum is passed to the next child as the song is sung again. This will create a rondo form.

5 Repeat until everyone has had a turn. If there are too many children in the class, make sure each has a turn during the next lesson.

6 Use body percussion in as many ways as possible to keep the beat.

7 Try the song in French (see above) or other languages that the children speak in class. The rhythm of the words and music, of course, will have to be changed:

Bi - en - ven - ue, bi - en - ven - ue.   Tout le monde bi - en - ven - ue. Bi -

- en - ven - ue, bi - en - ven - ue.   Dites - moi vot - re   nom.

Hello Everybody

Grades

1 through 3

Concepts

☐ Form: a round;   ☐ rhythm pattern.
☐ sequence;

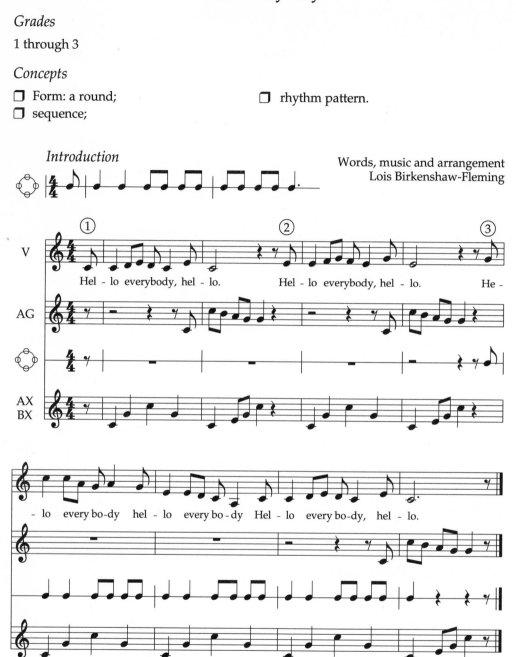

Introduction

Words, music and arrangement
Lois Birkenshaw-Fleming

Process

The song can be used in several grades depending on the complexity of the treatment.

1   Teach the song. The children discover that each phrase begins on *do, mi* or high *so*.

4

2   Teach the accompaniment patterns by patschen them first on the knees, using a speech pattern to hold the rhythm steady:

♪ | ♫ ♩ ♫ ♩ ♩ ♩ ♩ | ♩ ♩ ♩ ♩ | ♩ ♫ ♩ ♩ ♩ ♩ |
Hel- lo, hel- lo, hel- lo.   Come and play now,   It   will be fun

3   Discover the three places where ♪ | ♩ ♫ ♪ ♩ ♪ | ♩ is found. Clap this rhythm as it appears when the song is sung. Play it each time on a drum or with claves.

4   If it suits the needs of your students, sing the song as a round.

Hello, Hello

Grades

1 and 2

Concepts

☐ Names;   ☐ rondo form.

☐ vocal improvisation;

Angela Elster

Hel - lo,   hel - lo,   let's   play   the   mu - sic game.   Hel -

- lo,   hel - lo,   I   hope   you'll   sing   your   name.

Process

1   The children sit in a circle formation. Everyone sings "Hello, Hello".

2   First child to have a turn sings "My name is … " followed by four snaps.

3   The song is repeated after each child's name phrase until everyone has had a turn.

4   Once this is secure, try playing the rhythm of each name on percussion instruments then on melodic instruments using one or two notes.

5   If the group is large, try having four or five children say their names in sequence (including the snaps) before the song is repeated.

6   If children have difficulty singing their names, allow them to speak instead.

Will You Be My Friend?

Grades

2 and 3

Concepts

☐ Steady beat;
☐ word patterns;
☐ socialization.

words, music and arrangement Judy Sutton

Introduction

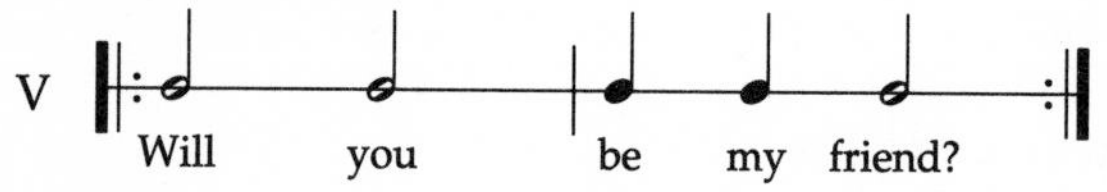

Will you be my friend?

A

1. I like sha-dows, I like sun. Come and play and we'll have some fun.
2. I like sun-shine, I like rain. 'Mem-ber me when we meet a-gain.

B

Now we will take a lit-tle walk, to meet a-no-ther part-ner. Then we'll stop.

Process

1 Teach the song.

2 Have the children find partners and together, create a body percussion part to accompany the song. Decide on one and teach it to everybody. One example might be:

Instrumental

1 Teach the parts using speech to keep the rhythm steady:

AG Will you please be my friend? I like you.

AX Can you cross your hands like this?

BX Will you be my friend?

Movement

A Begin with a random formation of partners;
chant the introduction three times;
sing the song, accompanied by body percussion and instruments.

B The partners separate and walk on the beat, taking four measures to form other pairs.

● Repeat as often as you like: the form could be ABA or ABACADA (rondo).

If I Could Sing a Song for You

Grades

4 and 5

Concepts

☐ I–V orchestration;

☐ paraphony;

☐ syncopation.

words, music and arrangement Diane Shieron

The percussion parts continue throughout the song.

V1   song for   you _   song for   you.   If   I could   sing _   a

V2   song for   you _   song for   you.   If   I could   sing _   a

SG / AG

AX / AM

BX

song for   you _   what   would you   like   to _____ hear?

song for   you _   what   would you   like   to _____ hear?

2   I'd like to hear a happy song,
Happy song, happy song,
I'd like to hear a happy song
So I can sing along.

3   Let's sing this song in harmony,
Harmony, harmony,
Let's sing this song in harmony,
It's fun for you and me.

Process

1   Teach Voice 1 part to all students by rote or note reading.

2   Have them clap the rhythmic pattern of the notes. Point out the syncopated parts and have them say the time names for these rhythms (syn-co-pa). The whole song is composed of syncopated rhythms so it is an excellent piece with which to teach or to review these.

3   Teach Voice 2 part, and sing along with Voice 1 part. The students will find that 2 is sung at a higher pitch than 1. Point out that they should sing it softer so the melody will not be obscured.

4   Teach the bass xylophone part using tonic *sol-fa*. The notes used will be *do* and *so*. Transfer these to G and D. (See chapter 24, "Tips for Teachers", for ideas on teaching changing chord accompaniments.)

5   Teach everyone the alto xylophone / metallophone part. Add this to the bass instruments.

6   Add the glockenspiel part.

7   Add the unpitched-percussion parts which also have a fairly difficult rhythm.

Extensions

●   The melodies could be played on recorders and sound quite beautiful when played together.

●   Possible form:

        A   Voice 1 only with accompaniment;

        B   Recorders: two-part with accompaniment;

        A   Voices 1 and 2 with accompaniment.

CHAPTER TWO

First Nations

The following material is as authentic as possible. Most of the accompaniments are quite simple, in keeping with traditional North American Indian and Inuit music. There are some who will object to accompanying traditional pieces with any instruments that the Native Peoples did not have, and we certainly respect that. However, we feel that these accompaniments do not overstep the bounds of good taste.

If you wish to change the instrumentation and use just drums, for instance, that is of course perfectly fine.

The Song of the Ancient People

We are the ancient people
Our father is the sun.
Our mother, the earth, where mountains tower
And rivers seaward run.

The stars are the children of the sky,
Our peoples of the plain
And ages over us both have rolled,
Before you crossed the main
For we are the ancient people
Born with the wind and the rain.

Edna Dean Proctor

Poem

O earth
for the strength
in my heart
I thank thee.
O cloud
for the blood in my body
I thank thee.

O fire
for the shine in my eyes
I thank thee.
O sun
for the life
you gave me
I thank thee.

Chief Dan George

This beautiful poem is one of many that were written by Chief Dan George, who lived on the West coast. The words to the next song were also written by him.

My Heart Soars

Grades

3 through 5

Concepts

☐ *la* tonal centre (minor key);   ☐ dance gestures.
☐ level bordun accompaniment;

words Chief Dan George
melody and arrangement Donna Otto

soars

2   The faintness of the stars,
The freshness of the morning,
The dewdrop on the flower
Speaks to me.

Process

1   Teach the song by rote or reading, focusing on the significance of the words. Discuss the beauty of the poetry of Chief Dan George.

2   Teach the body percussion pattern which will match the instrumental parts. Put this together with the song.

snap
clap
patsch
stamp

3   Look at the notation of the melody in the score. Have the recorders play this. Focus on listening to the sound and finding the tonal centre, *la*. Lead the students to understand that this is the minor tonal centre.

4   Transfer the body percussion accompaniment to the matching pitched instruments. Add the soft, muted hand-drum part.

5   Put together the vocal, recorder and instrumental parts.

6   Teach the gestures that match the poetry (see below).

7   Put everything together. The following is one suggested form:

Introduction   instrumental ostinato twice, perhaps beginning with drum part only;
          A   singing with accompaniment;
  Interlude   four measures of accompaniment;
          A   singing with accompaniment and gestures;
       Coda

Gestures

To be performed slowly and in a dignified manner.

Formation: half circle, kneeling, hands clasped in front.

Verse 1

The beauty of the trees	(*gesture half circle, palms up, waist level, left to right across body*)
The softness of the air	(*gesture half circle with right arm over head to signify sky*)
The fragrance of the grass	(*gesture half circle from left side across body, palms down – to "touch" the grass as you pass by*)
Speaks to me.	(*arms reach out waist level, move in to cross position on heart*)

Verse 2

The faintness of the stars	(*hand above eyes, look up across sky from left to right*)
The freshness of the morning	(*both hands reach up over head, palms up, look up again*)
The dewdrops on the flower	(*bring both hands down, parallel, palms up as if looking at a flower*)
Speaks to me.	(*arms reach out waist level, move in to cross position on heart, as before*)

Coda

And my heart soars.	(*slowly raise arms and body to standing position, reach and look up*)

14

Eskimo Lullaby

Grades

3 and 4

Concepts

☐ Very quiet, controlled singing;
☐ fermata;
☐ phrasing.

Still, now and hear my sing - ing:

Sleep through the night, my dar - ling.

2 We have a tiny daughter,
   Thanks be to God who sent her.

3 Though she as yet knows nothing,
   She is so sweet, I'm singing.

Process

1 Teach the song.

2 Have the students shape the phrase by singing each line in one breath, with a slight
   rise in volume toward the middle of the phrase, falling again at the end.

3 Explain the sign ⌢ – the fermata. It instructs the player to hold the note as long as is
   desired.

Extensions

● A very simple accompaniment can be added, respecting always the character of the
  piece. One example might be:

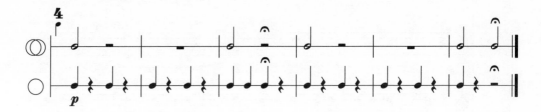

An Ojibway Melody

Grades

4 and 5

Concepts

☐ Form;

☐ canon.

1. You must not weep my small one,
    Dry your eyes now and slumber,
    Hush-a-bye, hush my dear one,
    Hear the wind blow in the pine tree.

2. Morning will bring the sunshine,
    Morning will bring the bird song,
    Hush-a-bye, hush my dear one,
    Hear the wind blow in the pine tree.

16

Ki-a-na me - a ko - nu, Ki-o-ke-na ha - tu - no,

ko - nu, Ki-a-na me - a ko - nu, Ki-o-ke-na ha -

Ki-o-ke-na ha-tu - no. _____

- tu - no, Ki-o-ke-na ha-tu - no. _____

Process

1 Many of the melodies of the First Nations of Canada are very beautiful. This haunting lullaby should have a simple accompaniment such as Keith Bissell has written.

2 The traditional instruments used were drums, rattles and notched sticks. Here the drum has been augmented by a flute or recorder and the alto glockenspiel, which do not seem to take away from the character of the piece.

3 Set the scene by discussing where the Native Peoples in Canada lived; how it was so quiet in the forest that they could actually hear the wind in the pine trees and the water running in the stream beside their tents. Discuss how the babies were wrapped snugly and laid on a cradle board that was carried on the back of the mother. Often it was secured to a tree so the wind could gently rock the baby to sleep while the mother worked nearby.

4 Describe the musical instruments most often used by the Native Peoples. Show pictures of these or visit a display in a museum.

5   Teach the song in the Ojibwa (Ojibway) language (saying it phonetically as printed) and also in English.

6   When the students know the song well, sing the song as a round.

7   Teach the timpani (bass xylophone) part by patschen it on the knees first before playing it on the instrument(s).

8   If your glockenspiel does not have a G♯, the first two measures of the glockenspiel part may be repeated instead of playing what is written.

Campfire Song to the Nighthawks

This song is part of a collection of songs and poems of the Native Peoples of the West. Alice McDougall, a Cree women from Manitoba, learned it from her mother. When the family camped out they would build a large bonfire and make bannock and tea. The fire would attract the nighthawks who would fly around and swoop down upon it. The children were taught to run after the birds and sing this song to scare them off.

Cree

Phesk phesk po ki-ten-ison, phesk, phesk, po ki-ten-ison, Phesk, phesk, po ki-ten-ison.

(Translation)
You say "pesk" to yourself or
Pesk, you'll just burn yourself.

Process

1   Use as a part of a unit on music of the First Nations.

2   Add drums, playing the beat and/or the rhythm pattern.

Ho, Ho, Wataney

Grades

3 and 4

The following is an accompaniment for the beautiful Iroquois melody "Ho, Ho, Wata-ney". It is effective when sung very simply.

trad arr Carolyn Hernandez

bourdun →

19

Sleep, sleep little one, sleep, sleep little one,
Sleep, sleep little one, now go to sleep, now go to sleep.

Dors, dors mon petit, dors, dors mon petit,
Dors, dors mon petit et bon nuit, et bon nuit.

Process

1 Echo sing to teach song and words.

2 Patsch the rhythms, then transfer them to the instruments.

3 Create a simple round dance by performing a slow, step–together dance in a circle. Combine the movement with song and accompaniment.

Extensions

● This song is also very effective accompanied only by a soft finger-cymbal sound.

Spirit of the Sun

Grades

4 through 6

Concepts

☐ *la*-pentatonic scale;
☐ ABA form.

arrangement Leslie Bricker

Warm ___ the earth and grow ___ the grain.

V Ah - ya ah - ya. ___ Ah - yah. Ah - ya - ya - ya.

AX

BM

Ah - ya ah - ya. ___ Ah - - yah.

21

2 Spirit of the water flow ,
   Spirit of the west wind blow ,
   Ahya, ahya, etc.

   B Section

   Far as man can see
   Comes the wind,
   Comes the rain with me.

   From the rain-mount
   Rain-mount far away.
   Comes the wind,
   Comes the rain with me.

   Mid the lightnings,
   Mid the lightnings flashing,
   Comes the wind,
   Comes the rain with me.

Process

1 Teach the song by rote while patschen the eighth-note pattern of the bass xylophone. Have the students identify the minor character of the piece and discover that the main note is *la*.

2 Transfer to the bass xylophone.

3 Teach the remaining parts using body percussion and speech patterns to aid memory.

4 Create a simple dance that moves in a circle formation. The steps used were basically quite simple:
   step–together, step–together.
   toe–heel (*step forward on one toe, bring heel down; repeat with other foot*)

   toe   heel

   toe–scrape (*step forward on one toe, scrape toe straight back and bring heel down; repeat with other foot*)

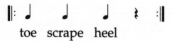
   toe   scrape   heel

5 Have the students combine these into a basic form.

6 Teach the speech section (B). A solo voice could speak the individual lines, with the rest of the group joining in on "Comes the wind, Comes the rain with me".

7 Students move freely during the above lines, representing the wind and the rain.

8 Perform the piece as an ABA form (A, song, accompaniment and dance; B, speech and free movement; A, song, accompaniment and dance).

9 Create an introduction and a coda from the accompaniment drum rhythm.

22

Lullaby

This lullaby is very old and well known among the Anishinabe. The Great Lakes Anishinabe lived on the shores of Lake Superior. Over the years, many moved West to the northern prairies where they are now called "Ojibwa" or "Saulteaux". The song was collected by Frances Densmore from Mrs. Mee in the early years of this century.

Grades

4 through 6

Concepts

☐ Phrasing;
☐ uneven metre.

trad Anishinabe

We we we we we we we we we
we we we we we we we we we we we we

Process

1 Sing very quietly and with a free rhythm, ignoring the barlines.

2 Explain to the students that the music was originally passed orally from person to person rather than written down. The shifting metres are an attempt to put the song into our conventional notation. The song should be sung in three seamless phrases.

Extensions

● The song may be accompanied by a quiet drum sound.

CHAPTER THREE

Newfoundland

Newfoundland has an incredibly rich heritage of song, most of which revolves around the sea and the dangers the fishermen experienced every time they ventured out in their boats. The small settlements that grew up over the years along the coast were accessible only by water until roads were built fifty or so years ago. This meant that during the winter months these communities were completely cut off. In these isolated outposts, singing and fiddle playing flourished and many a tale was told and set to music. Often these songs had ten to fifteen verses as they told their stories.

Other songs from Newfoundland that are popular with students are "Jack Was Every Inch a Sailor", "We'll Rant and We'll Roar", "The Ryans and the Pitmans", and "The Squid Jigging Ground".

She's Like the Swallow

This is a beautiful song from Newfoundland arranged by Keith Bissell. As the range is very wide it is best sung by fairly experienced students. It is in the Dorian mode. Have the students discover the difference between this mode and the minor scale with which they will be more familiar.

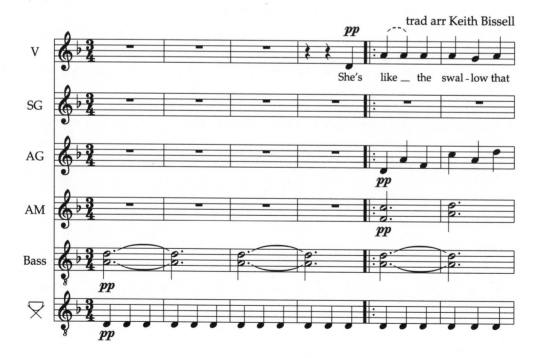

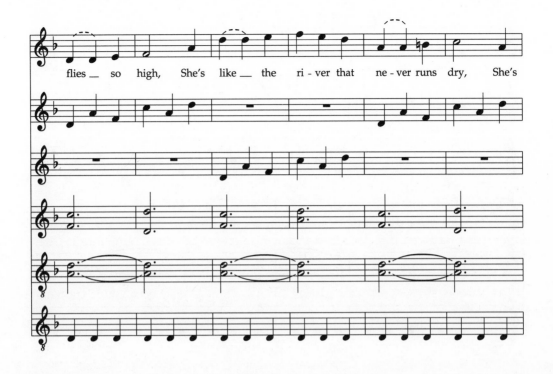

flies __ so high, She's like __ the ri - ver that ne - ver runs dry, She's

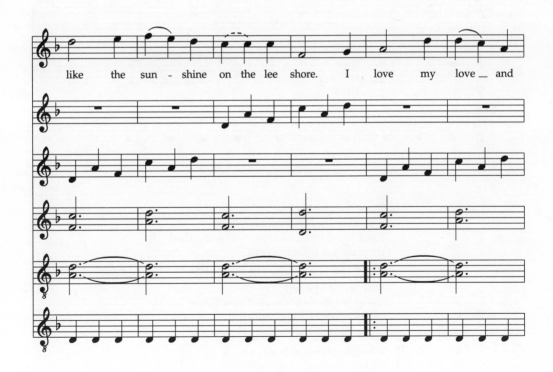

like the sun - shine on the lee shore. I love my love __ and

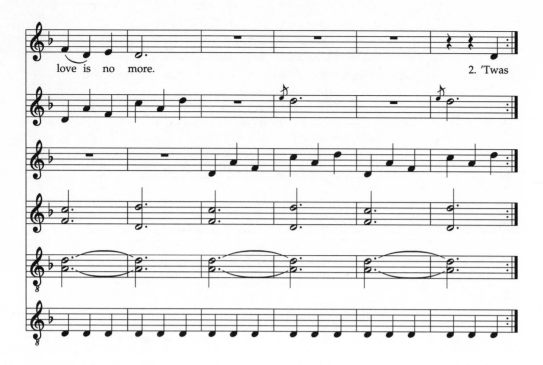

love is no more.   2. 'Twas

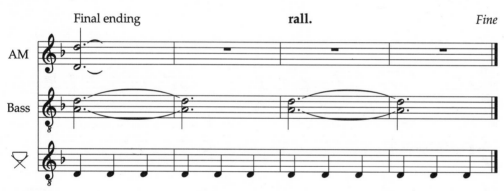

Final ending   **rall.**   *Fine*

AM

Bass

2   Out in the garden this fair maid did go,
    A-picking the beautiful primrose;
    The more she plucked the more she pulled,
    Until she got her apron full.

3   She climbed on yonder hill above
    And gave a rose unto her love,
    She gave him two, she gave him three,
    She gave her heart in company.

4   There stands a man on yonder hill,
    Who has a heart as hard as steel,
    He has two hearts instead of one,
    Oh cruel young man what have you done?

5   How foolish this young maid must be,
    To think I love no one but she,
    My heart's not made for one alone,
    I take delight in everyone.

6   Out of those roses she made a bed,
    A stony pillow for her head;
    She laid her down, no word she spoke,
    Until this fair maid's heart was broke.

Newfoundland Rondo

The names of places in Newfoundland are quite wonderful. In this contribution by Joanna Robertson some of them are used to create a rondo.

A   Newfoundland names, let's play a game,
    You find some and I'll do the same.

B   New Harbour, Heart's Delight, Cornerbrook, Cow Head,
    Musgrave Harbour, Bonavista, Little Boy, Lawn.

A   *(as before)*

C   Wreck Cove, Groates Cove, Little Seldom, Welsleyville,
    Hermitage, Pushthrough, Leading Tickle South.

A   *(as before)*

Extensions

- Find other place names on a map of Newfoundland and create additional sections.
- Add a rhythmic accompaniment to the A section, using unpitched instruments such as cabasas, claves, tambourines and drums.

The Herring

"The Herring" is an example of the very old songs that originated in the British Isles, were brought to the New World by sailors and settlers, and then were transformed during decades of singing in the small communities around the Newfoundland coast. This song is thought to have come from a late eighteenth-century broadsheet – those publications of songs that were sold in the streets of British cities for pennies. In Newfoundland it has also been known as the "Jolly Jack Herring".

Grades

4 through 6

Concepts

- ❏ Cumulative song;
- ❏ sequencing;
- ❏ uneven phrases and metre.

2   O what will we do with the old herrings' eyes?
     We'll get some puddings and sell them for pies;
     O herrings' eyes, puddings for pies
     Herrings' heads and loaves for bread, and all things like that.
     And of all the fish that's in the sea
     The herring that's the fish for me –
     Right tiddy she loo-ra, right-she loo-ra, fol-a dol dee.

3   O what will we do with the old herrings' fins?
     We'll get some needles and sell them for pins;
     Herrings' fins and needles for pins
     Herrings' eyes, puddings and pies
     Herrings' heads and loaves for bread, and all things like that.
     And of all the fish that's in the sea
     The herring that's the fish for me –
     Right tiddy she loo-ra, right-she loo-ra, fol-a dol dee.

4   O what will we do with the old herrings' backs?
     We'll get a little boy and call him Jack;
     O herrings' backs, boys named Jack
     Herrings' fins and needles for pins
     Herrings' eyes, puddings and pies
     Herrings' heads and loaves for bread, and all things like that.
     And of all the fish that's in the sea
     The herring that's the fish for me –
     Right tiddy she loo-ra, right-she loo-ra, fol-a dol dee.

28

5 O what will we do with the old herrings' bellies?
  We'll get a little girl and call her Nellie;
  O herrings' bellies and girls named Nellie
  Herrings' backs, boys named Jack
  Herrings' fins and needles for pins
  Herrings' eyes, puddings and pies
  Herrings' heads and loaves for bread, and all things like that.
  And of all the fish that's in the sea
  The herring that's the fish for me –
  Right tiddy she loo-ra, right-she loo-ra, fol-a dol dee.

6 O what will we do with the old herrings' scales?
  We'll get some canvas and sew it for sails;
  O herrings' scales, canvas for sails
  Herrings' bellies and girls called Nellie
  Herrings' backs, boys called Jack
  Herrings' fins and needles for pins
  Herrings' eyes, puddings and pies
  Herrings' heads and loaves for bread, and all things like that.
  And of all the fish that's in the sea
  The herring that's the fish for me –
  Right tiddy she loo-ra, right-she loo-ra, fol-a dol dee.

Process

1 The song should be sung with a good lilt. Instruments such as a drum could be used to play the rhythm pattern of the accumulated herring parts. One instrument (say, the tambourine) could play the rhythm pattern of the chorus: "And of all …".

2 Accompany the song with a guitar.

3 Have the students discover the uneven lengths of the phrases and the shift in the metre in the last line. These traits are very characteristic of songs from Newfoundland.

4 Can the students create other verses using different parts of the herring?

Special learners

- Some students may need visual reminders of which part of the fish comes next in the verse. It is difficult to remember the sequence. Put pictures of the parts on cards so they can be put up one at a time.

Cod Liver Oil

Grades

4 through 6

Concepts

☐ Layering vocal ostinati.

trad arr Leslie Bricker

30

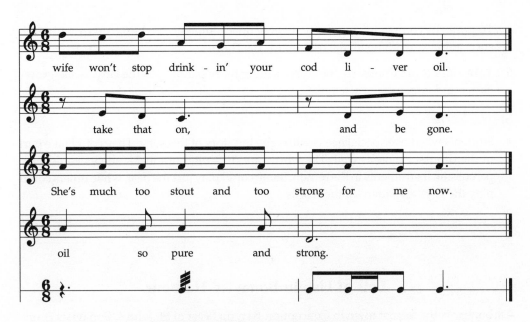

wife won't stop drink - in' your cod li – ver oil.

take that on, and be gone.

She's much too stout and too strong for me now.

oil so pure and strong.

1   I'm a young married man and I'm tired of life,
    Ten years I've been wed to a pale sickly wife.
    She has nothing to do only sit down and cry –
    Praying, oh, praying to God she would die.

2   A friend of my own come to see me one day,
    He told me my wife she was pining away.
    He afterwards told me that she would get strong
    If I'd get a bottle of dear Doctor John.

3   I bought her a bottle, just for to try,
    The way that she drank it, I thought she would die.
    I bought her another, it vanished the same.
    And then she got cod-liver oil on the brain.

4   I bought her another, she drank it no doubt,
    And then she began to get terrible stout,
    And when she got stout, well then she got strong,
    And then I got jealous of dear Doctor John.

5   My house it resembles a medicine shop,
    It's covered with bottles from bottom to top.
    But then in the morning when the kettle do boil
    O you're sure it's a-singing of cod liver oil.

Process

1   The melody for the verses is the same as for the chorus in this song.

2   Teach the melody by rote or reading.

3   Teach the ostinati, beginning with the lowest part. Layer as many as your students feel comfortable with. Combining vocal ostinati in this way gives excellent preparation for part singing.

4   To perform you might sing the first verse unaccompanied, adding a part with each succeeding verse. Sing all the ostinati for the chorus.

5   Your class could dramatize the story, adding more padding to the lady as she grows larger and larger with each verse.

Special learners

● Students who have special needs will enjoy the story of this song. They could take part in the dramatization as well. The words are difficult, but most students could play percussion instruments in the refrain. Some could play just the beat, while others could play the rhythm pattern of the words.

Lots of Fish in Bonavist' Harbour

Carbonear is the largest town in Conception Bay, just east of St. John's. Bonavista is one of the larger ports on the east coast of Newfoundland.

Grades

5 and 6

Concepts

☐ I–IV–V accompaniment;   ☐ 6/8 time;
☐ irregular phrase length;   ☐ AB form in song and movement.

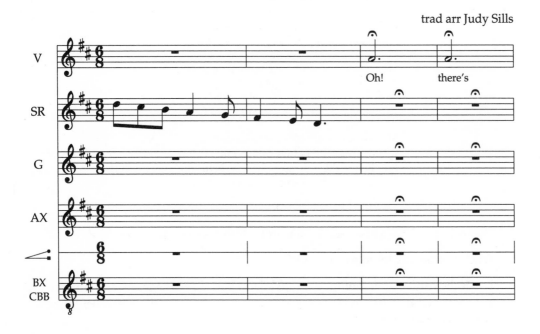

32

lots of fish in Bon-a-vist' har-bour, Lots of fish right in a-round here.

Boys and girls are fish-ing to-ge - ther, For - ty-five from

Car - bon - ear, _____ Oh! _____ Catch-a - hold this one,

Catch-a - hold this one,

catch-a-hold that one, Swing a-round this one, dance a-round she. Catch-a-hold this one,

catch-a-hold that one, Did-dle-dum this one, did-dle-dum dee. _____

2   Well now, Uncle George got up in the morning,
He got up in a heck of a tear,
Ripped the seat right out of his britches;
Now he's got ne're pair to wear.

Process

1   Teach the melody (the same for verse and chorus).

2   Teach the orchestration, one part at a time – first vocally, then on instruments. Combine the parts, adding one at a time (this might take several periods).

Movement

Formation: arrange partners in a double circle holding hands.

Verse	Measures 1 and 2	slide step to the right,
	measures 3 and 4	pat knees, clap own hands, clap partner's hands, clap own;
	measures 5 and 6	slide step to left,
	measures 7 and 8	same as 3 and 4;
	measures 9 and 10	everyone steps: right, left close, right, left close to find another partner;
Chorus	measures 1 and 2	swing partner by right elbow;
	measures 3 and 4	swing partner by left elbow;
	measures 5 to 8	promenade counterclockwise holding partner's hand;
	measure 9	turn to face partner, ready to repeat movement for verse 2.

I'se the B'y

Grades

5 and 6

Concepts

☐ I–V accompaniment;
☐ listening skills.

Introduction   trad arr Robert de Frece

I'se the b'y that builds the boat, And I'se the b'y that sails her

I'se the b'y that catch-es the fish and takes 'em home to Li - za.

2   Sods and rinds to cover yer flake,
       Cake and tea for supper,
       Codfish in the Spring of the year
       Fried in maggoty butter.

3   I don't want your maggoty fish,
       That's no good for winter;
       I can buy as good as that
       Down in Bonavista.

4   I took Liza to a dance
        And faith but she could travel!
        And every step that she did take
        Was up to her knees in gravel.

5   Susan White, she's out of sight,
        Her petticoat wants a border;
        Old Sam Oliver, in the dark,
        He kissed her in the corner.

Process

1 Teach the song by note reading using the *sol-fa* syllables.

2 Sing the song and ask the students to listen and identify the places where the harmony might change. If they have difficulty hearing this, play a bordun of G/D all the way through and have them tell you where it does not sound correct.

3 Using hand signs, sing a harmonic accompaniment using the root of the various chords. The harmonic pattern will look like:

do   so,   do   do   so,   do   so,   so'   so,   do

4 Sing the chord numbers:

I   V,   I   I   V,   I   V,   V'   V,   I

5 Sing the names of the notes:

G   D,   G   G   D,   G   D,   D'   D,   G

6 Transfer this to bass xylophones. Sing the song and play the accompaniment. The problem part will be the last two measures where the accompaniment changes to *so' so, do*.

7 If your class is ready, introduce a second part starting on the mediant. This is a good introduction to singing in harmony:

mi   re   mi   re   mi   re   re   mi
B   A   B   A   B   A   A   B

8 The introduction, played on the temple blocks (you can use a tambourine or wood-block) can also be used for interludes between verses and a coda.

9 Teach the accompaniment suggested here. Patsch the patterns on the knees first while singing the song. If the students are having problems with the alto xylophone part, devise word patterns to keep the rhythm steady:

He's   build - ing   the   boat

Extensions

- This song could be part of a unit on Newfoundland and the indispensable role fishing has had for over 300 years in the life of the island.
- Have the students find Fogo, Twillingate and Morton's Harbour on a map. They are situated around a bay in a kind of circle.

Dance

This Canadian barn dance was contributed by Joanna Robertson. It is authentic in every way except for the elbow swing which should be a two-step. The dance works well with "I'se the B'y".

Formation: arrange partners in a circle, facing counterclockwise, with inside hands joined.

Measures 1 and 2	walk forward – 2, 3, 4 (hop on 4);
measures 3 and 4	walk back – 2, 3, 4 (hop on 4);
measures 5 and 6	side step away from partner – 2, 3, clap;
measures 7 and 8	side step toward partner – 2, 3.
	Face partner and join hands on beat 4;
measures 9 and 10	four slip steps forward (counterclockwise);
measures 11 and 12	four slip steps back;
measures 13 to 16	swing with partner using right elbows.

Use the interludes to get ready for the repeat of the dance. A simple pat–clap pattern could be performed here as well.

CHAPTER FOUR

The Maritimes

There are hundreds of folk songs from the Maritimes. Most of these were collected by Helen Creighton in the 20s and 30s. Indeed, it is thought that she collected over 4,000 songs. These came mostly from the British Isles and France, but some were also influenced by the Afro-American tradition.

Besides those included here, other well-known songs students enjoy are "The Cherry Tree Carol", "Farmer Crust's Wife", "Three Crows", "Tree in a Bog", "Where Shall I Be When the First Trumpet Sounds", "The Bluenose", and "Lukey's Boat".

I'll Give My Love an Apple

"I'll Give My Love an Apple" was collected by Helen Creighton from Dennis Smith, who was more than 90 years old when he sang it for her in Chezzetcook, Nova Scotia. Of all the songs that she had collected, Creighton admitted that this was her favourite.

Grades

4 through 6

Concepts

❏ Changing-chord accompaniment;
❏ speech-rhythm improvisation.

give my love a dwel-ing with - out __ e'er a door, I'll __

give my love a pa - lace where - in she __ might __ be, That __

she might un - lock it with - out e'er __ a key.

2 How can there be an apple without e'er a core?
   How can there be a dwelling without e'er a door?
   How can there be a place wherein she might be,
   That she might unlock it without e'er a key?

3 My head is an apple without e'er a core,
   My mind is a dwelling without e'er a door,
   My heart is a palace wherein she might be,
   That she can unlock it without e'er a key.

Process

1 Teach the song by echoing phrase by phrase, from a visual of the words, and/or notation.

2 Teach the bass xylophone and bass metallophone parts by mirrored body percussion, using the speech cue:

strange   gifts   for my love

3 Add the alto metallophone part using the same rhythm, playing D and F♯.

4 Teach the alto glockenspiel and soprano metallophone parts through simultaneous imitation as the song is sung with the orchestration.

Extensions

Improvisation on riddles from Nova Scotia

- Ask the riddles and see if the students can figure out the answers.
- Say the riddles with the following rhythmic framework:

- Use the rhythm and the length of the riddles as a framework for improvisation on pitched percussion instruments.
- Set the instruments up in B minor pentatonic (remove all Gs and Cs and substitute F♯s for the Fs).
- Have the students decide which instruments will play the first half of the phrase ("question") and which the second half ("answer").
- The first half will begin on B but will not end on B. The second half may begin anywhere but must end on B. The rhythm of each half will be the rhythm of the speech pattern of one of the riddles.

42

Acadian Lullaby

This beautiful song was collected in the Acadian community of Pubnico, Nova Scotia, by Helen Creighton. This song and "Dites-Moi Donc Mademoiselle" are from the rich musical tradition of the Acadian people.

Grades

K through 3

Concepts

☐ Relaxation.

trad arr Lois Birkenshaw-Fleming

Dors, dors, le p'tit bi-bi, C'est le beau p'tit bi-bi à ma-ma.

Dors, dors, dors, dors, Dors, dors, le bi-bi à ma-ma.

De-main s'y fait beau, j'i-rons au grand-père, Dors dors, le p'tit bi-bi,

Dors, dors, dors, dors, Dors, le beau p'tit bi - bi à ma - ma.

2 Demain s'y fait beau, j'irons au grand-père,
  Dors, dors, le p'tit bibi,
  Dors, dors, dors, dors,
  Dors le p'tit bibi à mama.

1 Sleep, sleep little baby,
 You are mama's little babe,
 Sleep, sleep, sleep, sleep,
 Sleep, sleep, mama's babe.

2 Tomorrow if it's fine, we will see grandpa,
 Sleep, sleep, little babe,
 Slep, slep, slep, slep,
 Sleep, sleep, mama's babe.

Process

1 Sing the song very gently, having the children rock back and forth.

2 If desired, the children can rock dolls or their favourite soft, plush toys.

3 The older students can play the accompaniment.

Special learners

● Songs such as this have a very calming effect on children who have emotional problems or are just tense and frustrated because of their inability to succeed in school or life.

Nothing but Peace in the Land

This song was one that Helen Creighton collected from the students who attended an institution with the terrible name of "The Home For Coloured Children" in Preston, Nova Scotia. Many black people came to Canada to escape slavery in the United States and many of them settled in Nova Scotia.

The song has the feeling of a traditional spiritual.

Grades

3 through 5

Concept

☐ 3-chord accompaniment: I, IV, V.

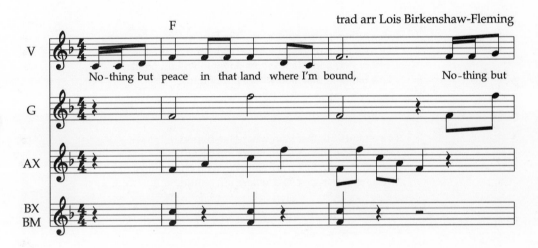

you will un-der-stand, No-thing but peace in that land where I'm bound.

2   I've a father in that land where I'm bound,
    I've a father in that land where I'm bound,
    I've a father in that land, some day you will understand,
    I've a father in that land where I'm bound.

        Chorus

3   I've a mother in that land where I'm bound,
    I've a mother in that land where I'm bound,
    I've a mother in that land, someday you will understand,
    I've a mother in that land where I'm bound.

        Chorus

Process

1   Sing the song and talk about its background. Have the students try to project the sadness of the song in the way that they sing it.

2   Teach the chord changes by having the students listen carefully as they sing the song and then decide where the harmony would require a chord change. Mark the chords needed. Have the students sing the roots of these chords as indicated and play them on a xylophone or other keyboard instrument.

3   Teach the full accompaniment.

●   The song is also effective when sung with no accompaniment.

Special learners

●   Students who have language or memory-retention problems can learn the lyrics fairly easily because there is so much repetition.

●   They could add other people such as brothers, sisters, cousins, and so on, "in that land".

46

Dites-moi donc mademoiselle

Grades

3 through 5

Concepts

☐ Language development;   ☐ AB form;

☐ rhyming words;   ☐ sequences.

trad arr Lois Birkenshaw-Fleming

Dites-moi donc ma - da - moi - sel - le, d'où __ ve - nez - vous donc?

Je viens d'Sainte - A - dè - le, et __ vous mon gar -

47

Process

1   Sing all the verses of the song.

2   Have the students invent words to replace the third line. They will have to think of a place in Canada or elsewhere and then a name that will rhyme with that place:

> Moi je viens de Montréal puis je m'appelle Henri Paul
>   de Halifax …   Jean Max …

3   Add an unpitched percussion accompaniment to the song, using different instrumental combinations for parts A and B. This will emphasize the difference between the two.

4   Sing the last two lines and have the students find the pattern that is repeated. It has the same rhythm and the same melodic line, except that it starts a note lower each time. This is called a sequence in music.

48

Nova Scotia Song

This is another song collected by Helen Creighton. Indeed it is made up of several variations she heard sung by different people. The melody originated in Scotland but the song has become almost the national anthem of Nova Scotia.

Grades

5 and 6

Concepts

❐ Major and natural minor tonalities;   ❐ I–VII accompaniment.

trad arr Linda Campbell

moun - tains dark and drea - ry ___ be for when I am far a - way on the

bri - ny o - cean tossed will you e - ver heave a sigh ___ and a wish for me?

2   I grieve to leave my native land,
I grieve to leave my comrades all,
And my aged parents whom I always held so dear,
And the bonny, bonny lass that I do adore.

3   The drums they do beat and the wars do alarm,
The captain calls, we must obey,
So farewell, farewell to Nova Scotia's charms,
For it's early in the morning, I am far, far away.

4   I have three brothers and they are at rest,
Their arms are folded on their breast,
But a poor simple sailor, just like me,
Must be tossed and driven on the dark blue sea.

50

Process

1 Teach the song, phrase by phrase. Have the students listen for the difference between phrases in the major tonality (the first and third phrases of the verses and the refrain) and the phrases in the minor (the second and fourth phrases in the verses and refrain).

2 Explain that the minor tonality is the natural minor or Aeolian mode with a flattened third and seventh.

3 Put the chord structure on the board or a chart.

I	I	VII	I
I	I	I	I
I	VII	VII	VII
I	I	I	I

4 Draw attention to the second and fourth phrases as being the same.

5 Have the students figure out where the VII chord would be (down one note with each hand).

6 Clap the "I"s and patsch the "VII"s.

7 The chord structure for the chorus is the same but the chords are broken. Patsch this on the knees, moving over to the left of each knee with the VII chord.

8 Teach the triangle and woodblock parts, snapping the first and clapping the second.

9 The alto glockenspiel part could be played by a recorder.

The Song of the Irish Moss

This piece tells about what happens on Prince Edward Island when a special weather condition dislodges seaweed (Irish Moss) from the ocean floor and deposits it on shore. Everyone rushes to gather their share of the precious harvest using anything from buckets to horses before the next tide takes it out to sea again.

Seaweed is a valuable crop and is used in the manufacture of many products including ice cream.

Grades

4 through 6

Concepts

❏ Two-part singing;
❏ advanced accompaniment of changing chords.

51

words and music Tom C. Conners
arrangement Lois Birkenshaw-Fleming

52

scoop and fork   and my wa-gon and horse, I'll be head-ing down the   shore.

2   On old Prince Edward Island, where the Irish Moss is found.
    With bags and ropes and baskets, they came from miles around.
    Thrashing through the water, being careful not to fall,
    For one good dash and a mighty splash, you could lose your overalls. *(repeat)*

3   There's horses in the water, and horses on the road,
    And here comes old Russell Aylward, and he's hauling up another big load.
    And the party lines keep ringing, and the word keeps passing on,
    You can hear them roar from the Tignish shore, "There's moss in Skinner's Pond". *(repeat)*

4   On old Prince Edward Island, there's one big hullabaloo,
    The boys and girls and old folks, they going to make a few bucks too.
    Getting wet to the neck in the ocean, where the waves all turn and toss.
    It's a free for all and they're having a ball, they're bringing in the Irish Moss. *(repeat)*

5   The moss plant boys are waiting, they pay so much a pound,
    And there goes a guy on horseback and they both look darned near drowned.
    But all those smiling faces just mean one thing to me
    For every man with a calloused hand there's a blessing from the sea. *(repeat)*

6   There's an islander somewhere lonesome, "Cause he can't be home today,"
    To have a little slip of the moonshine, and to haul another load away.
    In the land of the great potato where the lobster feasts are wild,
    We thank the Boss for the Irish Moss on Old Prince Edward Isle. *(repeat)*

Process

1   Teach the song by rote or reading.

2   Teach the second part (which lies above the melody) in the refrain if your students are at this stage in their musical development. The accompaniment is fairly difficult because of its harmonic structure and would be more suitable for the older students.

3   Work out the chord structure and have the students play the chord roots only, before moving on to learn the entire accompaniment.

CHAPTER FIVE

Québec

Québec is another province that has many, many folk songs. Most of these came originally from France but have been taken into the Québec culture.

Other songs students enjoy are: "Youpe! Youpe! sur la revière", "La poulett grise", "Marianne s'en va-t-au moulin", "Entendez-vous sur l'ormeau?" "Alouette", "A St. Malo", "C'est l'aviron", "Savez-vous plantez les choux?", "Bonhomme! Bonhomme!".

A la claire fontaine

"A la claire fontaine" has been sung in Canada from the earliest times. Champlain and his men, who were members of the Order of Good Cheer, are said to have sung it at Port Royal in 1605.

This haunting arrangement of the song gives a very special sound.

Recorders are given an important role. If you do not have tenor and bass recorder players available, have these parts played on xylophones, perhaps on both soprano and alto instruments.

Grades

4 through 6

trad arr Robert de Frece

A la clai - re fon-tai - ne, M'en al-lant pro-me-ner. J'ai trou-vé

l'eau si bel - le Que je m'y suis baig - né. Lui ya long - temps que je t'ai - me,

V

Ja - mais je ne t'oub - lie - rai.

SR

SG/AG

BM

rit.

2 J'ai trouvé l'eau si belle
   Que je m'y suis baigné;
   Sous les feuilles d'un chêne
   Je suis fait sécher.

3 Sous les feuilles d'un chêne
   Je suis fait sécher,
   Sur la plus haute branche,
   Le rossignol, chantait.

4 Sur la plus haute branche,
   Le rossignol, chantait
   Chante, rossignol, chante,
   Toi qui as le coeur gai.

5 Chante, rossignol, chante,
   Toi qui as le coeur gai,
   Tu as le coeur à rire,
   Moi je l'ai-t-a pleurer.

6 Tu as le coeur à rire,
   Moi je l'ai-t-a pleurer,
   J'ai perdu ma maîtresse,
   Sans l'avoir métité.

7 J'ai perdu ma maîtresse,
   Sans l'avoir métité,
   Pour un bouquet de roses
   Que je lui refusai.

8 Pour un bouquet de roses
   Que je lui refusai,
   Je voudrais que la rose
   Fût encore au rosier.

9 Je voudrais que la rose
   Fût encore au rosier,
   Et moi et ma maîtresse
   Dans les mêm's amitiés.

1   By the clear running fountain,
    I strayed one summer day
    The water looked so cooling,
    I bathed without delay.
            Refrain
            Many long years have I loved you,
            Ever in my heart you will stay.

2   Beneath an oak tree shady
    I dried myself that day,
    When from the topmost branch
    A bird song came my way.

3   Sing, nightingale, keep singing,
    Your heart is always gay.
    You have no cares to grieve you,
    While I could weep today.

4   You have no cares to grieve you,
    While I could weep today,,
    For I have lost my loved one
    In such a careless way.

5   She wanted some red roses
    But I did rudely say
    She could not have the roses
    That I had picked that day.

6   Now I wish those roses
    Were on the bush today,
    While I and my beloved
    Still went our old, sweet way.

Ah! si mon moine

Grades

4 through 6

Concepts

☐ Rhythm pattern;
☐ AABA form.

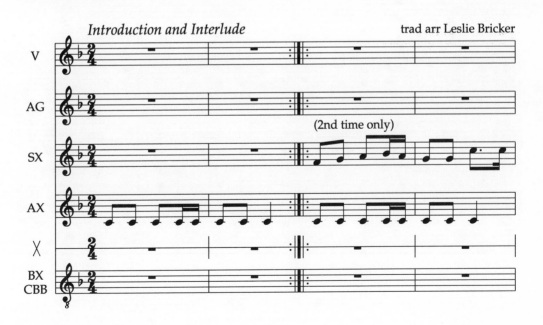

57

Ah! si mon moi-ne vou-
Un ca - pu - chon je lui
Tu n'en-tends pas le mou-

- lait dan - ser!   Ah! si mon moi-ne vou-lait dan - ser.   - lait dan - ser.
don-ne - rais,   Un ca - pu - chon je lui don-ne - rais.   don-ne - rais.
- lin lon là,   Tu n'en-tends pas le mou-lin mar - ché.   - lin mar - ché.

Fine

Dan - se mon moine dan - se! Tu n'en-tends pas la dan - se.

1   Ah! si mon moine voulait danser! (*bis*)
    Un capuchon je lui donnerais. (*bis*)

    Refrain

        Danse, mon moin' danse!
        Tu n'entends pas la danse,
        Tu n'entends pas mon moulin, lon là,
        Tu n'entends pas mon moulin marcher.

2   Ah! si mon moine voulait danser! (*bis*)
    Un ceinturon je lui donnerais. (*bis*)

3   Ah! si mon moine voulait danser! (*bis*)
    Un chapelet je lui donnerais. (*bis*)

4   Ah! si mon moine voulait danser! (*bis*)
    Un froc de bur'je lui donnerais. (*bis*)

5   Ah! si mon moine voulait danser! (*bis*)
    Un beau psautier je lui donnerais. (*bis*)

6   S'il n'avait fait voeu de pauverté (*bis*)
    Bien autres chos' je lui donnerais. (*bis*)

1   If you will come and dance with me, (*repeat*)
    A feathered cap I will give to thee. (*repeat*)

    Refrain

        Come my lass, let's trip now,
        Together let us skip now,
        Our feet will dance as we sing this song,
        Our feet will dance as we move along.

2   If you will come and dance with me, (*repeat*)
    Bright silver shoes I will give to thee. (*repeat*)

3   If you will come and dance with me, (*repeat*)
    A dress of blue I will give to thee. (*repeat*)

4   If you will come and dance with me, (*repeat*)
    A kiss or two I will give to thee. (*repeat*)

5   If you will come and dance with me, (*repeat*)
    A ring of gold I will give to thee. (*repeat*)

Process

1   Put the rhythm sequence of the two phrases of the song on the board. Ask the students to clap the rhythms and/or play them on a percussion instrument.

2   Sing the song, clapping the rhythm. How are the two patterns arranged in the song?

The students will determine that rhythm 1 is heard one time and then repeated. Rhythm 2 is heard next and then rhythm 1 again. (This might be difficult to follow as the words change.)

3   The form is AABA: can the students hear and see this clearly?

4   Teach the accompaniment by using body percussion. (For a fuller explanation of this process see chapter 24, "Tips for Teachers".)

5   Can the students create their own verses?

Dos à dos

Grades

K through 3

Concepts

❑ Rhythm pattern;
❑ ABA form.

Process

- This song can be used in Kindergarten just as a song and a dance. Children in Grade 1 may understand ABA form while those in Grades 2 and 3 can usually manage the accompaniment.

1 Teach the song, clapping the rhythm pattern.

2 Teach the dance:
   Formation: partners, facing in scatter formation.

measure 1	turn to stand back to back;
measure 2	turn again face to face;
measures 3 and 4	hold hands and change places;
measures 5 and 6	repeat 1 and 2;
measures 7 and 8	hold hands and change back to original places.

3 Perform song and dance together.

4 If the children are ready, teach the accompaniment and add to the original song and dance.

The B section could consist of standing in place and performing a little body percussion that could later be transferred to percussion instruments:

5 Put it all together in an ABA form:
   A   song plus accompaniment;
   B   body percussion with partner.

J'entends le moulin

Grades

4 through 6

Concept

❏ Rhythm patterns.

trad arr Lois Birkenshaw-Fleming

J'en-tends le mou-lin   ti-que ti-que ta-que, J'en-tends le mou-lin   ta - que.

Mon père a fait bâ - tir mai - son, J'en-tends le mou- lin ta - que;

L'a fait bâ-tir à trois pig-non, ti-que ta - que ti-que ta - que

V

SX

AX

BX

63

J'en-tends le mou-lin   ti-que ti-que ta-que, J'en-tends le mou-lin   ta - que

Coda   **rit.**

Refrain

J'entends le moulin, tique tique taque;
J'entends le moulin, taque.

2   L'a fait bâtir a trois pignons
      (J'entends le moulin, taque)
  Sont trois charpentiers qui la font,
      (Tique taque, tique taque).

3   Sont trois charpentiers qui la font
      (J'entends …)
  Le plus jeune, c'est mon mignon,
      (Tique taque …).

4   Le plus jeune, c'est mon mignon,
      (J'entends …)
  Qu'apportes-tu dans ton jupon?
      (Tique taque …).

5   Qu'apportes-tu dans ton jupon?
      (J'entends …)
  C'est un pâté de trois pigeons.
      (Tique taque …)

6   C'est un pâté de trois pigeons,
      (J'entends …)
  Asseyons-nous et le mangeons.
      (Tique taque …)

7   Asseyons-nous et le mangeons,
      (J'entends …)
  En s'asseyant il fit un bond.
      (Tique taque …)

8   En s'asseyant il fit un bond,
      (J'entends …)
  Qui fit trembler mer et poissons,
      (Tique taque …)

9   Qui fit trembler mer et poissons,
      (J'entends …)
  E les cailloux qui sont au fond.
      (Tique taque …)

Refrain

I hear the mill-wheel, tick-a tick-a tack-a;
I hear the mill-wheel, tack-a;

1   Father is building us a house,
      (I hear the mill-wheel, tack-a)
  Carpenters three work on his house,
      (Tick-a tack-a, tick-a tack-a).

2   He who is the youngest of the three,
      (I hear …)
  He is the dearest one to me,
      (Tick-a tack-a, …)

3   "What do you bring as you pass by?"
      (I hear …)
  "It is a tasty pigeon pie,"
      (Tick-a tack-a, …)

4   "Let us sit down and have a snack,"
      (I hear …)
  Sitting he made the earth to crack,
      (Tick-a tack-a, …)

5   He made the sea and the fish to shake,
      (I hear …)
  And also the pebbles in the lake,
      (Tick-a tack-a, …)

Process

1 Teach the song.

2 Clap various rhythm patterns using word patterns to keep the rhythm steady, for example:

tic - a - tic - a   ta - que,   tic - a - tic - a   ta - que,   tic   tic - a   ta - que   tic

3 Teach the instrumental parts, working out the cross-over pattern first with body percussion.

4 The story told in the verses could be dramatized.

5 As in many French songs the last two lines of one verse become the first two of the next. This leads to a very lengthy work. If you decide to sing all nine French verses, sustain interest by adding different percussion rhythms for some verses, doubling the melody on recorder for a few verses, or deleting the alto xylophone part for one verse.

65

Un Canadien errant

This next song describes the anguish felt by the singer who has been exiled because he was one of the rebels plotting against the governments of Upper and Lower Canada in the 1830s.

Grades

5 and 6

Concept

☐ Two-part harmony.

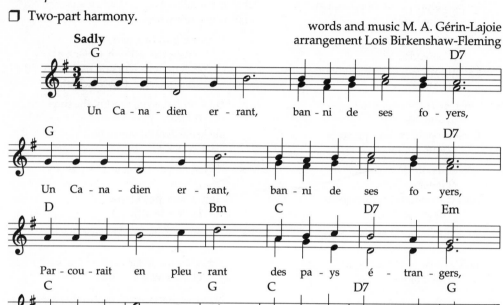

words and music M. A. Gérin-Lajoie
arrangement Lois Birkenshaw-Fleming

Un Ca - na - dien er - rant, ban - ni de ses fo - yers,

Un Ca - na - dien er - rant, ban - ni de ses fo - yers,

Par - cou - rait en pleu - rant des pa - ys é - tran - gers,

Par - cou - rait en pleu - rant des pa - ys é - tran - gers.

2 Un jour, triste et pensif,
Assis au bord des flots,
Un jour, triste et pensif,
Assis au bord des flots,
Au courant fugitif
Il adressa ces mots,
Au courant fugitif
Il adressa ces mots:

3 "Si tu vois mon pays,
Mon pays malheureux,
Si tu vois mon pays,
Mon pays malheureux,
Va, dis à mes amis
Que je me souviens d'eux,
Va, dis à mes amis
Que je me souviens d'eux.

4 "O jours si pliens d'appas
Vous êtes disparus …
O jours si pliens d'appas,
Vous êtes disparus,
Et ma patrie, hélas
Je ne verrai plus!
Et ma patrie, hélas
Je ne verrai plus!

5 "Non, mais en expirant,
O mon cher Canada!
Non, mais en expirant,
O mon cher Canada!
Mon regard languissant
Vers toi se portera,
Mon regard languissant
Vers toi se portera …"

1   Once a Canadian lad, exiled from hearth and home,
       Wandered alone and sad, through alien lands unknown,
       Down by a rushing stream, thoughtful and sad one day,
       He watched the water pass, and to it he did say:

2   "If you should reach my land, my most unhappy land,
       Please speak to all my friends so they will understand,
       Tell them how much I wish, that I could be once more
       In my beloved land, that I will see no more".

3   "My own beloved land, I'll not forget till death,
       And I will speak of her, with my last dying breath,
       My own beloved land, I'll not forget till death,
       And I will speak of her, with my last dying breath".

Process

1   Teach the song.

2   With the students, learn the second part that is written for the endings of each phrase. Sing with the song. (This is a non-threatening way to introduce two-part harmony.)

3   Learn the melody and the second part on recorders.

4   Play with the singing.

5   Add a simple finger cymbal part, for example:

The students could make up their own part.

6   Sing the five (French) verses, combining the treatments in various ways:

      verse 1   unison only;
      verse 2   add second part;
      verse 3   add finger cymbal;
   interlude   two recorders playing the melody;
      verse 4   voice sings melody, recorders play second part;
      verse 5   two voices, two recorders, plus finger cymbals.

●   If you are singing the song in English, choose from these ideas to create your own final form.

CHAPTER SIX

Ontario

Land of the Silver Birch

No one seems to know the origin of "Land of the Silver Birch". It appeared in the camp song repertoire in the 1920s and although it has a distinct Indian sound it is not thought to be authentically Indian music.

Grades

3 through 5

Concepts

❐ Experience modal sound;   ❐ canon.

where still the migh-ty moose wan-ders at will.

Blue lake and roc-ky shore, I will re-turn once more.

Boom de de boom boom, Boom de de boom boom, Boom de de boom boom,

Boo - - - - - (oo)m.

69

2 High on a rocky ledge, I'll build my wigwam (*or* campsite),
   Close by the water's edge, silent and still.
   Blue lake and rocky shore …

3 Down in the forest, deep in the woodlands,
   My heart calls out to thee, hills of the North,
   Blue lake and rocky shore …

Process

1 Learn the song including all the verses.

2 Teach the timpani part by patschen first. This requires a very steady sense of beat.

3 Teach the recorder part. To give variety it may be played with each verse or just verses 1 and 3.

4 Put it all together.

5 If desired, add a simple finger cymbal pattern played on the first beat of each measure or each second measure. This would be particularly effective if the soprano recorder were not playing.

Extensions

● The song may be sung as a round. The entry point would be after the fourth measure. This song can be sung as a partner song with "My Paddle's Keen and Bright".

John Kanaka Naka Too-la-ay

A favourite song from the lumber camp tradition.

Grades

2 through 4

Concepts

❏ AAB form;   ❏ twelve-measure song (three phrases of four measures).

trad arr Leslie Bricker

Process

1. Teach the song and have the children listen for the three phrases. Each one makes a statement for two measures and finishes with "John Kanaka Naka Too-la-ay".

2. Set the instruments up in the D, *do*-pentatonic scale (replace the Fs with F♯s and remove the Gs and Cs) and have the children improvise in 4/4 metre. Because the song is in the pentatonic scale these creations will sound well when played together (although if too many are playing at the same time, the result will be a little chaotic).

3. Work toward having one child play the first part of a phrase (the "question") and another child play the second – completing the phrase with an "answer".

4. These little creations can be used as the episodes in a rondo. The song is the A section; the first question and answer is B. The A returns and another two students perform a second question and answer as the C section. A is played again.

5. Have the students work out four-note ostinati to accompany the song.

6. Combine one or two of these with the song.

7. Teach the written accompaniment; clap or patsch the rhythms first so all can learn.

8. Create an introduction and interlude, taking rhythms from the song and playing these on a tambourine. For example:

The Banks of the Don

This song is perhaps the only known folk song that originated in Toronto. It tells of the Don Jail, a forbidding institution that still stands on the east banks of the Don river. When built it was out of town but now the city has grown up around it.

Grades

4 through 6

Concepts

☐ Triple metre.

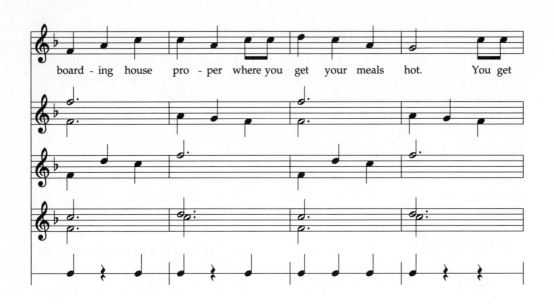

board - ing house pro – per where you get your meals hot. You get

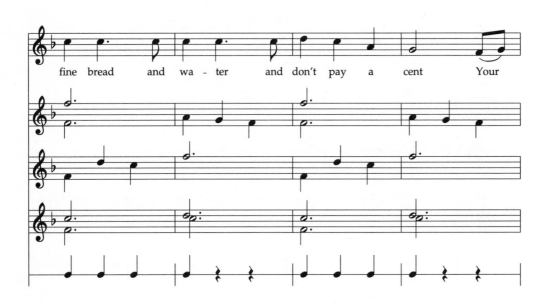

fine bread and wa – ter and don't pay a cent Your

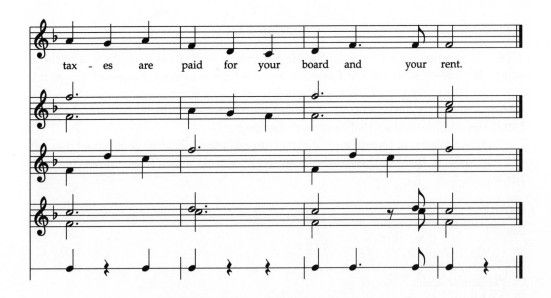

tax - es   are   paid   for   your   board   and   your   rent.

2 If you want to get into that palace so neat,
   Then cause a commotion in the middle of the street.
   You'll have a fine carriage to drive you from town
   To that grand institution just over the Don.

3 Our boarders are honest, not one of them steals,
   For they count all the knives and forks after each meal.
   Our windows are airy and barred up beside
   To keep our good boarders from falling outside.

Process

1 Sing the song and have the students discover the metre. If they have difficulty, have them count the beats or "patsch, clap, clap" to the melody.

2 Teach the instrumental parts by clapping or patschen the rhythm. To keep the rhythm steady, word patterns can be added. For example:

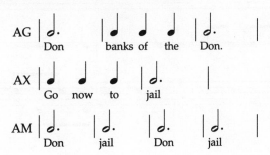

The hand drum part is more difficult. Have the students learn it from rhythmic notation or by echo clapping.

The introduction can be played between verses as interludes.

Canaday-i-o

This is an example of a song from the lumber camps in Ontario. Men flocked to these camps from everywhere to cut timber, most of which was floated down rivers in the spring, finally ending up in Montréal to be put on board ships bound for England. The men had to endure the bitter cold and rather spartan meals in the winter, and the mud, black flies and mosquitoes that came with the spring.

Cutting timber was an extremely difficult life and many songs have survived that tell of the hardships. These songs are to be found in all parts of Canada where lumbering took place.

Grades

3 and 4

Concepts

☐ Pentatonic scale;
☐ ABAB form.

all you jol - ly fel - lows, how would you like to go   And

spend the win - ter   in   the woods of   Ca - na - day - i - o?

2　　"I'm sure we'll pay good wages, we'll pay your passage out,
　　　But you must sign the papers that you will stay the route;
　　　For if you should get homesick, and say back home you'll go,
　　　We will not pay the passage out from Canaday-i-o."

3　　Our hearts were made of iron, our souls were cased with steel;
　　　The hardships of that winter could never make us yield.
　　　Our food the dogs would bark at, our beds were on the snow.
　　　We suffered worse than poison in Canaday-i-o.

4　　And now the winter's over, it's homeward we are bound,
　　　And in this cursed country we'll never more be found.
　　　Go back to your wives and sweethearts, tell others not to go
　　　To that God-forsaken country called Canaday-i-o.

Process

1　Teach the song and have the students discover that lines 1 and 3 are the same, as are 2 and 4. This gives the form *ABAB*.

2　"Canaday-i-o" is a good song with which to introduce or review the pentatonic scale. Have the students sing the version used in this song (CD FGA CD) and try to play the melody of the song on tone bars or a xylophone set up with these notes.

3　Have the students experiment with creating accompaniments to go with the song, using the same notes.

4　Teach the written accompaniment and combine it with the song.

A Mosquito in the Cabin

Grades

3 and 4

Concept

❒　Creating sound effects.

> Although you bash her,
> 　　swat her, smash her,
> and go to bed victorious,
> 　　happy and glorious
> 　　she will come winging,
> 　　and zinging,
> 　　wickedly singing
> 　　over your bed.

You slap the air
    but she's in your hair
    cackling with laughter.
You smack your head,
    but she isn't dead –
    she's on the rafter,
She's out for blood –
    yours, my friend,
and she will get it, in the end.
She brings it first to boiling point,
    then lets it steam.
With a fee, fi, fo and contented fum
    she sips it
    while you dream.

Myra Stilborn

Process

1   Say the poem aloud, pointing out the sound words.

2   Explore with the students various sound effects that could be made by body percussion, instruments and voice that would enhance the effect of the poem.

3   Choose some of these and put them together with the poem.

The Black Fly

Winter in the swamp, c'est pas le paradis, hein? It's better than summer in the swamp. Imagine-vous donc – there's one hundred thousand mosquitoes sleeping beneath the snow, right under your feet!

from Axeman's speech in Cold Comfort, *a play by "Tanglefoot"*

The black flies are the scourge of the north woods of Canada. The early survey crews and the road and rail builders were often literally driven mad before the days of bug repellent. Balsam gum and grease might seem to be poor substitutes for the preparations that are on the market today, but the smell was probably so bad that they were of some use.

Grades

4 and 5

Concepts

❐ Verses in major key, chorus in minor;
❐ form.

words and music Wade Hemsworth
arrangement Lois Birkenshaw-Fleming

'Twas ear-ly in the spring when I de-cide to go, For to

work up in the woods in North On - ta - ri - - o, And the

un - em - ploy - ment of - fice said they'd send me through to the

Chorus

Lit - tle A - bi - ti - bi with the sur - vey crew, And the

80

81

2   Now the man called Toby was the captain of the crew
And he said, "I'm going to tell you boys what we're going to do,
They want to build a power dam and we must find a way
For to make the Little Ab flow around the other way."

3   It was black fly, black fly everywhere,
A-crawling in your whiskers, and a-crawling in your hair;
A-swimming in the soup and a-swimming in the tea;
Oh the devil take the black fly and let me be.

4   Now the bull cook's name was Blind River Joe;
If it hadn't been for him – we'd have never pulled through
For he bound up our bruises, and he kidded us for fun
And he lathered us with bacon grease and balsam gum.

5   At last the job was over; Old Toby said: "We're through
With the little Abitibi and the survey crew."
'Twas a wonderful experience and this I know
I'll never go again to North Ontar-i-o.

Process

1   Analyse the form of the song, which is very unusual. The verse is fairly straight-forward – ABAB – but the chorus is CDEFG, five phrases, each one different.

2   Ask the students to listen to the tonality of the verse (major) and the chorus (modal).

3   Try the accompaniment. Melodic instruments are used for the verses only, as the chords in the chorus change too many times.

4   Play the tambourine part to accompany the chorus.

5   Can the students find the Abitibi river (the "Little Ab") on a map of northern Ontario?

CHAPTER SEVEN

The Prairies

Other songs from the Prairies that students enjoy are "Flunky Jim", "The Alberta Homesteader", "The Little Old Sod Chanty", and "Saskatchewan".

Old Grandma

This arrangement by Keith Bissell works well with older students who have an Orff background. It was written specially for the Scarborough Schools Orff Ensemble, directed by Joan Sumberland. The song talks of times long past and the language cannot be said to be politically correct, but it certainly is an accurate representation of pioneer history.

Canadian folk song
arrangement Keith Bissell

Old Grand-ma when the west was   new ___

___ She   wore hoop-skirtsand bus-tles   too. _____   When

85

2   She worked hard seven days a week
     To keep Grandad well-fed and sleek.
     Twenty-one children came to bless
     Their happy home in the wilderness.

3   Twenty-one boys, oh, how they grew!
     Big and strong on bacon too.
     They slept on the floor with the sheep and goats,
     And they hunted in the woods in their oil-skin coats.

4   Twenty-one necks Grandma would scrub,
     Twenty-one shirts in the old wash tub,
     Twenty-one meals three times a day:
     It's no wonder Grandma's hair turned gray!

5   Great Grandad was a busy man;
     He washed his face in the frying pan.
     He shaved his beard with a hunting knife,
     And he wore the one suit all his life.

Process

1   Because the song is so long, play the recorder interlude after verses 2 and 4 only.

2   Play the ending after verse 5.

The Horsemen in the Cloud

In this song the singer dreams about thunder, and describes it as the sounds made by the hooves of horses. These dreams were very important to the Teton Sioux. The song was collected by Paul Glass.

Grades

4 through 6

Concept

☐ Creating a drum rhythm.

Horse - men are com - ing from North and the West. They fly through the air and in - to the clouds. With gal - lop - ing hooves and thun - der - ing sounds, They came to me, They came to me.

Process

1 Sing the song with a simple drum accompaniment such as the following:

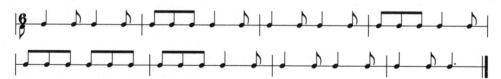

2 Create an ABA form. Sing the song with the drum accompaniment (A); then accompany the drum pattern with another of eight measures (B); finally, repeat the song with its original accompaniment (A). The following is one suggestion for a drum pattern for the B section:

Riel's Farewell

Louis Riel was the leader of the Métis rebellion in the Red River Valley, Manitoba, in the 1870s and 1880s. The land that the Métis owned was being taken from them to be given to the new settlers who were flocking in. Riel was outlawed to the United States for a time and was later captured in Canada, tried and sentenced to death. He was hanged at Regina in 1885 for his part in the rebellion. It is thought that he wrote this song to his mother from jail just before his death.

Grades

5 and 6 (over several classes)

Concepts

❐ I–V harmony;
❐ improvising an accompaniment.

words and music Louis Riel

I send this let-ter to __ you, To tell my grief and pain __ And as I lie im-pri-soned, I long to see you a-gain. __ Oh my be-lo-ved mo-ther, And all my com-rades dear, __ I write these words in my heart's blood No ink or pen __ is here. __

2   My friends in arms and children,
Please weep and pray for me.
I fought hard for our country
So that we might be free.
When you receive this letter
Please weep for me and pray
That I may die with bravery
Upon that fearful day.

1   C'est au champ de bataille,
        J'ai fait crier mes douleurs,
        Où tout 'cun doute se passe
        Ça fait frémir les coeurs.
        Or je r'çois-t-une lettre
        De ma chère maman.
        J'avais ni plume' ni encre.
        Pour pouvoir lui écrire.

2   Or je pris mon canif,
        Je le tempai dans mon sang,
        Pour écrir'-t-une lettre
        A ma chère maman.
        Quand ell' r'çevra cett' lettre
        Toute écrit'de sang,
        Ses yeux baignant de larmes,
        Son coeur s'allant mourant.

3   S'y jette à genoux par terre
        En appelant ses enfants:
        Priez pour votr' p'tit frère
        Qui est au régiment.
        Mourir, c'est pour mourir,
        Chacun meurt à son tour;
        J'aim' mieux mourir en brave,
        Faut tous mourir un jour.

Process

1   Learn the song in French or English, or a combination as appropriate for your group.

2   Have the students listen while you play the song on a chording instrument. When they hear the I chord, tap one finger on the other hand: when they hear the V, pat knee with five fingers. (At this point simplify measure 11 by staying on I.)

3   Work out the chord pattern for the whole song. It is:

        ‖: I   V   I   I
           I   V   I   I :‖ *Fine*
           I   V   I   V
           I   I   V   V   *D.C. al fine*

4   Have the students sing in parts to *sol-fa* syllables either the chord roots or the chord changes:

5   Divide the students into two groups with instruments. On instruments have them find and play first the roots then the triads. Have one group play chord I and the other, chord V:

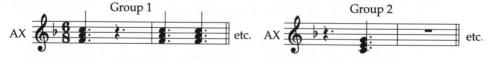

Continue until both groups are able to play both chords on one instrument.

6   Have the students play the triad in broken form instead of as a chord:

Find places where the triad could be played descending instead of ascending.

7   As the students become more comfortable they can devise improvisations on chord notes which may include passing notes and more elaborate rhythms; for example:

Students waiting to have a turn should sing.

The bass xylophone (or a cello) could play the chord roots. This might suit the needs of certain students better, although everyone should have a chance to improvise.

8   Decide on a final form, which may include an improvised introduction, interludes, a coda, and/or a broken chord accompaniment.

● Use a recorder to double the melody.

(Lesson plan by Catherine West)

Adieu de la mariée à ses parents

This is a Saskatchewan Métis song that has been arranged for recorder and Orff instruments. It would be suitable for older students.

Saskatchewan Métis song
arrangement Robert de France

92

93

CHAPTER EIGHT

British Columbia

Kettle Valley Line

When the West was being settled, just after the train lines were put through to British Columbia, the Kettle Valley Line was built from Hope, B.C., to Lethbridge, Alberta. In spring-seeding and harvest time, workers would hitch-hike on top of the train from Hope to Lethbridge, and make the return journey to the lumber camps of British Columbia in the fall.

Because none of these men paid the fare, it became necessary to have "railway bulls" or police officers to patrol the trains.

Grades

3 through 5

Concepts

❏ Moving tonic accompaniment;   ❏ minor key.

music Stanley Triggs words Ean Hay
arrangement Donna Otto

Line!   I al - ways ride up on the roof, I could

ride in - side but what's the use? So I al - ways ride up

on   the roof   on the Ket-tle   Val - ley   Line!

2   I buy a sandwich from the cook, on the Kettle Valley Line   (*repeat*)
     I buy a sandwich from the cook,
     And he pockets my money, the dirty crook,
     When I buy a sandwich from the cook, on the Kettle Valley Line.

3   The railway bulls are gentlemen, on the Kettle Valley Line   (*repeat*)
     The railway bulls are gentlemen,
     We'll never see their like again,
     Yes, the railway bulls are gentleman, on the Kettle Valley Line.

4   They tip their hats and they call you "Sir", on the Kettle Valley Line   (*repeat*)
     They tip their hats and they call you "Sir",
     Then chuck you in the local stir,
     But they tip their hats and call you "Sir", on the Kettle Valley Line.

Process

1   Teach the song by reading or by rote.

2   Discuss the form of the melody (AABA) – a very common folk-song form.

3   Teach the movement.

4   Sing the song in the character of a railroader and include movement.

5   Teach the instrumental parts.

Movement

Formation: scatter and "freeze" into different positions.

Introduction	as the hand drum is played, move heads in place and then assume starting position;
measures 1–2	hands on hips, step right with right foot, left foot close (*repeat*);
measures 3–4	step right, clap, slap inside right foot with left hand; step left, clap, slap inside left foot with right hand; step right, step left;
measures 5–8	repeat measures 1–4;
measures 9–12	heel right while "pulling whistle" with left hand (for two counts); heel left while "pulling whistle" with right hand;
measures 13–16	repeat measures 1–4.

Instruments

1   Teach bass xylophone part through patschen.

2   Teach alto/soprano xylophone part through patschen.

3   Combine these parts with the singing.

4   Teach the soprano/alto glockenspiel and soprano metallophone parts by dividing them up and calling them "bottom" and "top":

top	play F and D; move to D and A;
bottom	play D and A; move to A and F.

5   Combine all parts with the singing.

6   The introduction could be a cumulative entry of unpitched percussion, sounding like a train gradually gathering speed:

cabasa, playing eighth notes;
hand drums, played with fingertips in circular motion;
wooden train whistle or mouth sound, occasionally.

7   Once these instruments have all begun, sing the song with the melodic accompaniment.

8   The four measures of the introduction, with all instruments playing, could be used as interludes as well.

9   For an ending gradually stop the unpitched percussion until only the drum is playing, then slow down.

Vancouver

Grades

2 through 4

Concepts

☐ Creating sound effects.

> In Spring it sprinkles,
>> In Summer too,
> In Fall it pours
>> Buckets on you.
> In Winter it rains
>> Cats and dogs
> From heavy clouds
>> Through heavy clouds
>> Through soupy fogs.
> All year long
>> Rain drops and drops
> In Vancouver
>> It never stops.

Robert Heidbreder

This is not a particularly flattering picture of Vancouver's weather but it does seem to rain there a great deal. Of course, when the rest of Canada is still hidden under a blanket of snow, Vancouver has crocuses blooming!

Process

1   Create the sound effects of different kinds of rain with mouth, body percussion or instruments. Try, for example:

    ♦ soft, quick notes on a drum;
    ♦ lightly played claves;
    ♦ quiet, occasional finger cymbal sounds;
    ♦ gently rolled maracas.

2   Carpets of sound to underlie the reading of the poem can be created using metallophones, glockenspiels and xylophones.

Special learners

● Students who have special needs will be able to participate in these sound-making activities and gain confidence by having their creations accepted by the group.

To Work Upon the Railway

The building of railroads in Canada was vitally important to its development as a nation. They were the primary means of transportation and communication in olden days. Indeed, in many places in Canada today the most important means of transport is still the railway.

Grades

4 through 6

Concepts

❑ Practising the cross-over pattern;
❑ rhythm.

trad arr Lois Birkenshaw-Fleming

Chorus
Billy me-oo re-eye re-aye, Billy me-oo re-eye re-aye,
Billy me-oo re-eye re-aye, To work upon the railway.

2   In eighteen hundred and forty-two,
   I left the old world for the new,
   'Twas my bad luck that brought me through
   To work upon the railway.

3   It's "Pat do this", and "Pat do that",
   Without a stocking or cravat,
   Nothing but an old straw hat,
   To work upon the railway.

Process

1 Teach the song, explaining the background.

2 Sing the bottom note of the chords of the accompaniment, first to *sol-fa* syllables, then to letter names:

la	la	so	do	do	la	la	so	la
A	A	G	C	C	A	A	G	A

3 Practise the hand-over-hand accompaniment by patschen on the knees, saying the names of the chord roots at the same time. Transfer this to the alto xylophone.

4 Work out the accompaniment for the metallophone also by patschen on the knees.

5 Point out that the music for the chorus is the same as for the verse.

6 Clap the tambourine part, say the names of the note lengths, and then play them on the tambourine during the chorus.

7 Add a little rhythmic introduction created by the students on the claves. Use it as the interlude between verses and as a coda at the end.

Movement

Formation: groups of four partners, in lines, facing each other.

1 The head couple holds hands and skips eight times to the foot of the line and eight back. They then drop hands and each skips down the outside to the foot of his/her line where they join hands again and swing for eight counts.

2 The next couple takes its turn.

3 Sing the first verse again at the end to give everyone a turn.

Drill Ye Tarriers

The tarriers were the men who helped to build the Canadian Pacific Railway across Canada. It was hard and dangerous work, and the bosses of the men could be brutal. When the line was finished in 1885, people came from all over the world to settle the West.

Grades

4 through 6

Concepts

☐ I–VII accompaniment;   ☐ sixteenth notes in three different patterns.

trad arr Judy Sills

come down hea-vy on the cast - iron drill"; and drill ye Tar - ri - ers

drill!   Drill ye Tar-ri-ers drill.   O we work all day for

su-gar in our tay,   On the C. P. rail-way, so drill ye Tar-ri-ers drill!

V

SM

AX
AM

BX
BM

102

2   Our new foreman is Dan McCan,
I tell you sure he's a mighty mean man!
Last week a premature blast went off
And a mile in the air went big Jim Goff,

        So drill ye tarriers drill …

3   Well next time pay day comes around,
Jim Goff was short one buck he found.
"What for?" says he, came this reply:
"You were docked for the time you were up in the sky!"

        So drill ye tarriers drill …

Process

1   Teach the melody by rote. The song has a very wide range and many students may have difficulty with the high notes. Work on extending the range of the students by performing sequentials and other voice drills before teaching the song.

2   Add the instrumentation.

Movement

Formation: in a circle, dancing individually.

Verse

Measures 1–2	step right, left behind, right, "pound hammer"
measures 3–4	step left, right behind, left, pound hammer;
measures 5–8	repeat measures 1 to 4;
measures 9–10	in place, step right, pound; step left, pound.

Refrain

Measures 11–12	step right, left in front, making a half turn to face out of the circle; step right and pound hammer;
measures 13–14	step left, right in front, making a half turn to face into the circle again; step left and pound hammer;
measures 15–16	step right, left, right, left into circle;
measures 17–18	step left, right, left, right out of circle; back to place, clapping on beats 2 and 3.

CHAPTER NINE

Yukon and North-West Territories

The Spell of the Yukon (excerpt)

I wanted the gold and I sought it;
I scrabbled and mucked like a slave.
Was it famine or scurvy – I fought it;
I hurled my youth in a grave.
I wanted the gold and I got it –
Came out with a fortune last fall, –
Yet somehow life's not what I thought it,
And somehow the gold isn't all.

No! There's the land (Have you seen it?),
It's the cussedest land that I know,
From the big, dizzy mountains that screen it,
To the deep, deathlike valleys below.
Some say God was tired when He made it;
Some say it's a fine land to shun;
Maybe; but there's some that would trade it
For no land on earth – and I'm one.

Robert W. Service

This poem describes the hardships and heartaches of the gold rush and how in spite of all that, some men were caught for life by the rugged beauty of the Canadian North.

The poem could be used in conjunction with the song "The Klondike".

Northern Lights

This song and activity tell of the wondrous sight of the northern lights. They are a common occurrence in Canada, but still bring a feeling of awe to those who see them.

Grades

K and 1

Concepts

❏ Creative movement;
❏ colours.

104

Judy McAlpine

The moon is out, the stars are bright, it's qui - et
on ___ this win - ter night And in the sky so
cold and clear, the north - ern lights start to ap -
- pear. Red lights, spar - kle, green lights spar - kle,
blue lights, spar - kle, yel - low lights spar - kle

improvise on glockenspiel, finger cymbals and with movement

But when the sun pokes out her
head, It's time for the lights to go to bed.

Process

1 The children sit on the floor, curled up with transparent coloured scarves draped over their heads. The colours used should correspond to the colours mentioned in the song.

2 Everyone sings, and when each individual's colour is sung s/he rises and imitates the movement of the lights, "sparkling" for the duration of the improvisation.

3 At the end of the song, each sits down again with scarves still over his/her head.

4 For the improvisation, set glockenspiels up in the F pentatonic scale and have children play "sparkle" music. Triangles and finger cymbals could also be used.

The Rain

This song was inspired by the life-giving properties of rain and was created by a group of teachers in Whitehorse who call themselves "Sundog". It has a quiet, modal feeling almost like Native American music.

Grades

3 through 5

Concepts

❑ Creating sound effects;
❑ creativity.

Narrator:

This is a song about the rain,
And how water in the form of rain
Nourishes and replenishes all of creation,
And of how this water is millions of years old,
And how it falls from the sky,
And how this cycle has continued
Since the beginning of time.
This is a song about … the rain.

Process

1   Three long, slow, descending whistles.

2   Start the rain stick and continue throughout.

3   Play the following melody twice on a recorder with rain stick sound.

4   Add hand drums and shakers to the rain stick sound playing two measures of the interlude.

5   Play the recorder melody again with this accompaniment.

6   Play two measures of the accompaniment as an interlude.

7   Introduce the voice. The melody is performed twice more with accompaniment.

8   End the piece by stopping the instruments one by one, with the rain stick last. End with one long, low, slow whistle.

●   Create other combinations and solos of different instruments and voice.

106

Special learners

● This activity would be very suitable for students with special needs. There would be a place for everyone, whatever their disability, in the accompaniment. The creative portion, planning just what instruments will be played and what sounds made, would allow everyone to contribute in a meaningful way.

Composed and created by the group Sundog
Phil Gatensby
Douglas Smarch Jr.
Nedra McKay
Ken Bloor

The Klondike

One of the largest gold strikes in history was made near the Klondike River in 1896. During the short time that it lasted, 25,000 men poured into the Yukon in search of the gold that in the beginning could be seen poking out of the mud and between rocks. Many made fortunes and many lost everything they had, but it was an unbelievably exciting time.

The words to the song are thought to have come from a prospector who told them to Charles Cates, the mayor of Vancouver. The song might have been written in British Columbia, as Moodyville was a suburb of Vancouver in those days, but the subject matter is certainly the Yukon, which is why it has been included in this chapter.

arr Lois Birkenshaw-Fleming

five - pound note   And a   clod on your heel   is a   quid _____

_____   Klon - dike _____   Klon - dike _____

La - bel your lug - gage for   Klon - - dike,   for there ain't   no

luck in the town to - day, there ain't no work __ down Moo - dy - ville way, Pack up your traps and be off I say off and a - way to the Klon - - dike.

2   Oh they scratches the earth and it tumbles out,
More than your hands can hold,
For the hills above and the plains beneath
Are cracking and busting with gold.

CHAPTER TEN

Weather and Seasons

Nature Canon

Grades

4 through 6

Concepts

☐ Form;

☐ canon.

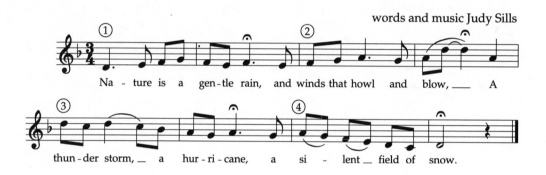

words and music Judy Sills

Na - ture is a gen-tle rain, and winds that howl and blow, ___ A

thun - der storm, ___ a hur - ri - cane, a si - lent ___ field of snow.

Process

1   Teach the melody line by line on a neutral syllable ("lai", "lo", "no", etc.).

2   Add the words when the melody is secure. First say the words in rhythm, then sing them with the melody.

3   Sing in a two-part, then a four-part, canon.

The Weather Song

Grades

1 through 3

Concepts

☐ Beat;

☐ half-note pattern;

☐ language development.

trad adapted and arr Lois Birkenshaw-Fleming

Hey Mis - ter wea - ther - man, wea - ther - man, wea - ther - man,

What will the wea - ther be to - day? It's go - ing to be sun - ny,

sun - ny, sun - ny, sun - ny, It's go - ing to be sun - ny to - day.

Process

1 Learn the song.

2 What other kind of weather might the weatherman predict? snowy/rainy/blowy/ sleeting/freezing/very hot (change the rhythm)/cloudy.

3 The song can be sung in "question and answer" format (AB) with one group asking the question and the other group singing the answer.

4 Practise the instrumental parts with speech and body percussion first.

patschen: sun - ny sun - ny   clap: hot   hot

5 Transfer these to instruments.

6 Add percussion instruments for each verse that would describe the "sound" of the weather. Let the children choose those they would think best. Some ideas might be:
   ♦ a cymbal for the sun;
   ♦ "pitter patter" sounds on a drum or claves (played very lightly);
   ♦ hands rubbed across a drumhead for the wind.

Special learners

● Students with language difficulties and/or developmental delays often need some extra "aids" to foster their creative language. Show pictures of different kinds of weather – blowy, snowy, rainy – to help promote discussion.

La Météo

Clientèle

1re et 2e cycles du primaire

Concepts

☐ Sens de la phrase;   ☐ créativité;
☐ co-ordination motrice;   ☐ expression corporelle et musicale.

paroles et musique Marcelle Corneille

É - cou - te la chan - son du vent ___   Improvisation _____

Re - gar - de la chan - son de la nei - ge   Improvisation _____

112

2	Ecoute la chanson de la pluie …	Regarde la chanson de la neige.
3	Ecoute la chanson du tonnerre …	Regarde la chanson de la neige.
4	Ecoute la chanson de l'orage …	Regarde la chanson de la neige.
5	Ecoute la chanson de tempête …	Regarde la chanson de la neige.

Démarche pédagogique

1 Chanter chaque couplet en le faisant suivre d'une improvisation:

a) instrumentale:
    vent   métallophone
    pluie   carillons
    tonnerre   timbale/grosse cymbale
    orage   tous les instruments
    neige   carillon tubulaire/crotales;

b) de mouvements corporels adaptés aux couplets;

c) de sonorités vocales ou corporelles adaptées aux couplets.

2 Illustrer chacun des couplets:

le professeur pointe l'illustration, les élèves chantent le couplet approprié;

le professeur pointe deux ou plusieurs illustrations, par exemple, vent et tonnerre pour marquer la tempête.

3 Accompagner le chant de chaque couplet avec l'improvisation instrumentale et réaliser la section "improvisation" corporellement.

4 Demander à quelques étudiants de pointer les illustrations de leur choix pendant que les autres chantent les couplets appropriés.

5 Suggérer aux élèves de créer de nouveaux couplets en associant la température qui convient à certaines saisons de l'année:

Ecoute la chanson du vent …	Regarde la chanson du printemps
Ecoute la chanson de la pluie …	Regarde la chanson du printemps

Fall Is Fun

Grades

K through 4

Concept

☐ *do–re–mi* song (folkloric).

words and music Carolyn Hernandez

Process

1 Sing the song. Teach it by rote or by using hand signs and *sol-fa* syllables if you are working with children in Grades 1 or 2.

2 Teach the actions. Perform the song and actions together.

114

Fall is fun	right hand, palm facing forward, makes a circle (a "cool wave");
Fall is fun	repeat with left hand;
Children run	make running motions with hands;
Catch the sun	reach out as if catching a large ball;
Leaves fall down	hands flutter high to low;
On the ground	both hands, palms down, make large circles near the ground;
In the fall	both hands repeat the "cool wave".

3 Prepare the instrumental parts with patschen and/or clapping first then transfer them to instruments.

4 If your students have begun learning the recorder, teach them the melody by echoing.

5 Play the first four measures of the alto and bass xylophone parts for an introduction and an ending.

6 The final form could be:
   A song with accompaniment;
   B recorder plus accompaniment;
   A song plus accompaniment plus actions.

7 Create other verses:

> … cold winds blow, bringing snow …
> … leaves turn red, overhead …

Special learners

- This is a very easy song to sing because of the limited number of notes and the small range of the melody.

November Round

Grades

2 and 3

Concept

❐ Form: canon.

music traditional
words and arrangement Gaynor Low

On a cold No - vem - ber day   Clouds fly by   all   black and grey.

Leaves have fal - len   to the ground.   And the wind blows   them a - round.

2   On a cold November day,
Clouds fly by all black and gray,
Snow flakes falling to the ground
Twirling, swirling all around.

Process

1   This would be a good song to teach by *sol-fa* syllables.

2   Teach the accompaniment using speech patterns and body percussion. Transfer it to instruments:

clap
patsch   AX

○   clap

X   snap

3   When the song has been learned well, sing it as a two- or four-part canon.

4   Change the month to October or December if desired.

116

Winter

The Snowstorm

Grades

2 and 3

Concepts

❏ Speech ostinati;
❏ movement levels;
❏ canon form.

> Heave, ho, Buckets of snow,
> The giant is combing his beard,
> The snow is as high, as the top of the sky
> And the world has disappeared.
>
> *Dennis Lee*

Process

1 Have the children create speech ostinati based on the words of the poem or on the whole idea of snow and winter. Two examples might be:

Fee   fi   fo,   fum   More snow,   more snow

Go-ing,   go-ing,   gone,   Oh no!   Go-ing,   go-ing,   gone,   Oh no!

2 Divide into three groups. Have one group say the poem while the other two say the ostinati.

3 Start ostinato 1; then add ostinato 2; then the poem.

4 Say the poem with the spoken accompaniment in a two-part canon. Parts enter at the beginning of each line.

Movement

Line 1	pretend to shovel snow;
Line 2	comb a "beard";
Line 3	show how high the snow is with arms over head;
Line 4	crouch down, hiding head in arms.

(Contributed by Angela Elster and Alison Kenny-Gardhouse)

117

Because every part of Canada is affected to some extent by winter, weather is a very important concern for all Canadians. In many parts of Canada knowledge of what the weather will be is a matter of life and death.

The following Inuit poem expresses the joy of seeing the sun return to the world in spring because in the farthest north there is no sun at all for many months.

Eskimo Chant

There is joy in
Feeling the warmth
Come to the great world
And seeing the sun
Follow its old footprints
In the summer night.

There is fear in
Feeling the cold
Come to the great world
And seeing the moon
– Now new moon, now full moon –
Follow its old footsteps
In the winter night.

translated by Knud Rasmussen

Process

1 Say the poem freely, trying to create the mood, first of the warmth and then of the cold, by voice colour.

2 A simple drum accompaniment could be played, alternating the dynamics slightly by playing a little more loudly for the first verse and very softly for the second.

3 Small, ringing sounds could contribute to the cold feeling in the second verse. Experiment with finger cymbals, keys suspended from a string and jingled together, or notes played in a free tempo, very softly, on a glockenspiel.

Nose, Nose, Jolly Red Nose

"Nose, Nose, Jolly Red Nose" is a setting by Doreen Hall of a very old verse.

Grades

2 and 3

Concepts

❏ Language development;
❏ playing different note values in each hand.

118

words traditional
music and arrangement Doreen Hall

119

Process

1 Learn the song by rote or by using *sol-fa* syllables.

2 Explain that all the spices mentioned are part of a warm drink that helps to chase away the cold. (Some teachers often change the words to "I've been out where the cold wind blows".)

3 Practise each instrumental part on the knees first.

4 The glockenspiel part can be divided between two players but it is really easier than it looks – the notes follow one another in both hands because the note B has been removed to give the pentatonic scale.

5 Before playing the alto xylophone part, practise patting quarter notes with one hand and half notes with the other.

6 Try walking quarter notes and clapping half notes.

7 Walk half notes and play quarter notes on a drum.

8 Patsch the entire alto xylophone part on the knees before transferring it to the instrument. If it is still too difficult, divide it between two students.

● The above four steps are valid if the song is sung at a tempo that allows walking the quarter-note beat. If it is sung faster and the half note is a good tempo for children to walk to, the quarter-note pattern will become a running movement.)

Movement

● The students themselves can create a movement pattern. The following would be one very simple idea.
  Formation: a circle with one person inside (two or three if the circle is huge).
  Measures 1–4   Students in outside circle join hands and walk 16 steps to the left (stopping on the word "nose"), then 16 steps to the right, back to their original places. The person in the centre claps and marks time.
  measures 5–6   The outside circle does a patsch or clap to the beat while the inside student points in time (for two counts) to each person, in turn, round the circle, stopping when the song ends. The centre person changes places with the last student that he or she pointed to, and the game is repeated.

● *An alternative movement pattern*
  Formation: a circle as before, with the children holding hands.
  Measures 1–2   Walk four steps into the circle, starting with the right foot;
  measures 3–4   walk four steps out of circle, again, starting with the right foot;
  measures 5–8   walk eight steps to the right.
  (This pattern also presupposes that the song is sung fast enough for the children to walk comfortably on the half notes.)

Sleigh Bells

Grades

2 through 4

Concepts

❏ Rhythm pattern and notation.

trad arr Ada Vermeulen

Galloping across the plains Racing in the moonlight

Hoof-beats pounding on the snow and all the sleigh bells ringing
Hoof-beats pounding on the snow oh listen to the bells Hey!

Process

1   Teach the song, asking the children to play the half-note pattern on their knees. Show the notation for this and have them sing the song, playing the half-note pattern and saying "ta-ta" or a word pattern taken from the song, such as "bells, bells".

2   Transfer this to the metallophone and play it with the song.

3   Teach the hand-over-hand xylophone pattern by patschen. Say "ta-ta" or "sleigh bells ringing" to keep the rhythm steady. Combine it with singing.

4   Transfer this to the xylophone.

5   Teach the glissando part and play it with the song. (Remember to have the B♭ on the instrument.)

6   Add sleigh bells ad lib.

7   Combine them all with the song.

8   A little movement pattern could be created.

Movement

Formation: a circle, holding hands, standing beside partner.

Measures 1–4	six slide steps to the right, turning and stamping on 7 and 8;
measures 5–8	repeat to the left, turning to partner on 7 and 8;
measures 9–12	link right arms with partner and swing vigorously, stopping to stamp on "ringing";
measures 13–16	link left arms and repeat, stamping on "bells Hey!" throwing hands into the air.

9   Create an interlude of eight measures to be played on drum or tambourine.

Bonhomme de neige

Clientèle

1re à 3e année

Concept

❐ Improvisation.

paroles et musique Guylaine Myre

Bon - homm' de nei - ge blan - che, sais - tu à quoi je pen - se, tu

s'rais bien plus co - quet a - vec ce pe - tit bé - ret!

2   ... tu s'rais bien mignon, avec ce petit nez rond! (*improvisation*)
3   ... tu s'rais plus beau encore, avec ce petit foulard! (*improvisation*)
4   ... tu s'rais plus rigolo, avec ces petits grelots! (*improvisation*)
5   ... tu es si réussi, où je te veux comme ami! (*reprise*)

Démarche pédagogique

Ajout du jeu dansé

1   Les enfants sont disposés en cercle autour d'un enfant jouant le rôle du bonhomme de neige.

2   Tout en respectant la pulsation de ♩, les enfants se passent le béret, d'un à l'autre jusqu'à la fin du refrain.

3   L'enfant qui reçoit le béret va coiffer le bonhomme de neige et les autres font une ronde pendant l'improvisation instrumentale.

4   Le jeu reprend mais les enfants doivent faire circuler le nez rouge, le foulard, les grelots, correspondant aux paroles des couplets.

Signs of Spring

Grades

2 through 4

Concepts

- Speech rhythms;
- voice colour;
- speech ostinati.

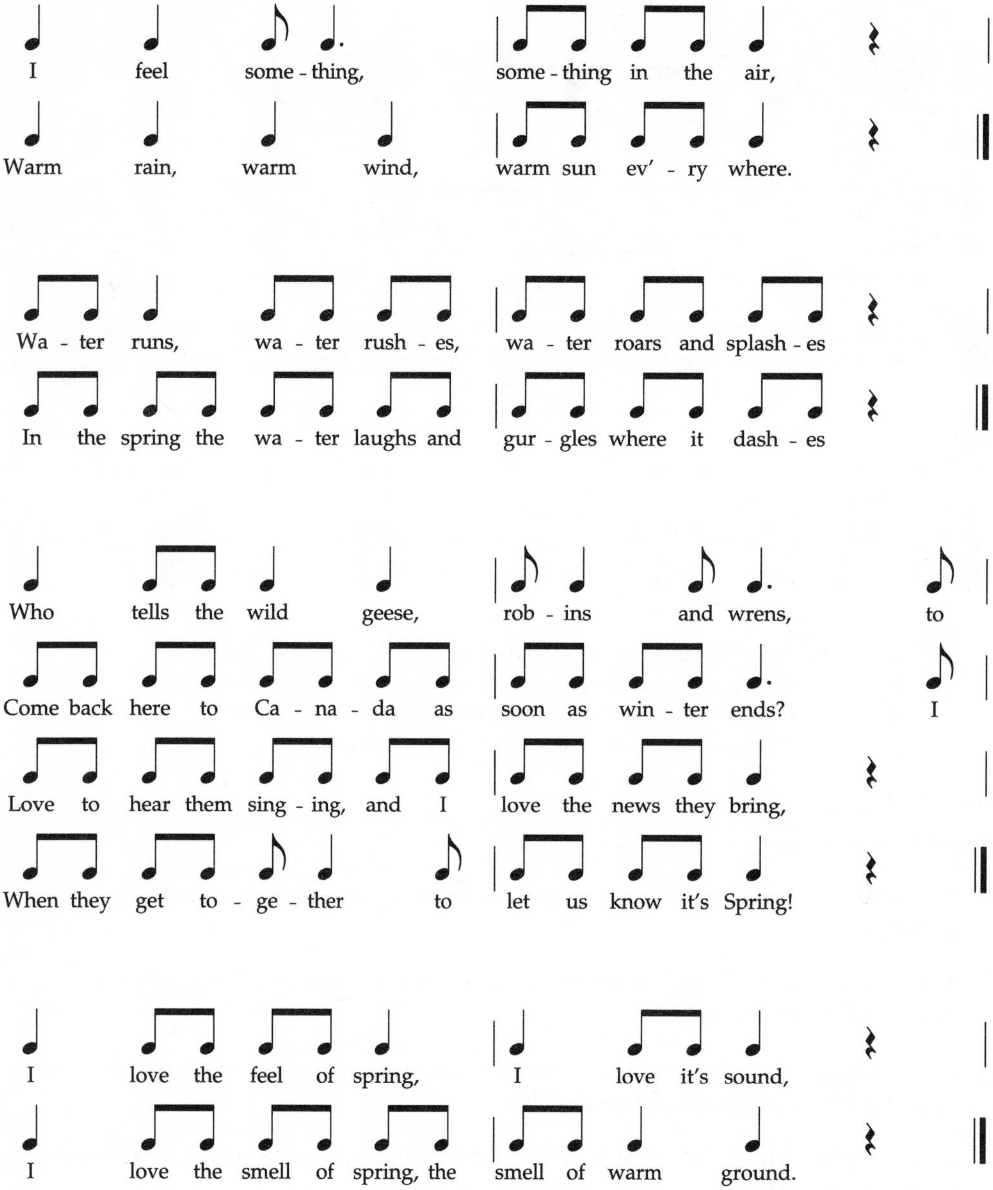

I feel some-thing, some-thing in the air,

Warm rain, warm wind, warm sun ev' - ry where.

Wa - ter runs, wa - ter rush - es, wa - ter roars and splash - es

In the spring the wa - ter laughs and gur - gles where it dash - es

Who tells the wild geese, rob - ins and wrens, to

Come back here to Ca - na - da as soon as win - ter ends? I

Love to hear them sing - ing, and I love the news they bring,

When they get to - ge - ther to let us know it's Spring!

I love the feel of spring, I love it's sound,

I love the smell of spring, the smell of warm ground.

Process

1 Choose a chant and say it with good voice colour and inflection.

2 Clap the rhythm pattern and play it on a drum.

3 Say the rhythmic time names and write these on chart paper or on the board.

● Some of the chants, particularly "Who tells the wild geese", can be accompanied by speech ostinati, for example:

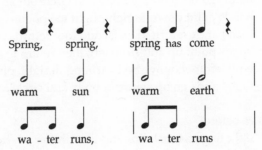

(Contributed by Ross Brock)

Springtime Is Coming!

This song is very popular in Japanese schools. It was taught to Carolyn Hernandez by the mother of a child at her school.

Grades

2 and 3

Concepts

☐ Putting appropriate motions to a song;
☐ creating an accompaniment.

traditional Japanese

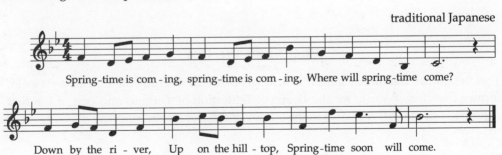

2   Springtime is coming, springtime is coming,
     See how springtime comes,
     Birds will be singing, flowers will be blooming,
     My heart sings a song.

Process

1 Learn the song by phrases; learn the motions then join the two together.

Movement

Verse 1

Measure 1	Hands point out to right side, then return to waist;
measure 2	hands point out to left side, then return to waist;
measures 3–4	hands go up centre of body and circle out and back to waist.
measure 5	hands point down to right, right toe points out to right, then hands return to waist and foot returns to place;
measure 6	hands point up and front left, then return to waist;
measures 7–8	with left foot, move body around to right, pivoting on right foot, hands go up centre of body and circle out and back.

Verse 2

Measures 1–4	as before;
measure 5	right fingers touch lips and then flutter overhead;
measure 6	bend over, "pick" a flower and bring it to the nose to smell;
measures 7–8	pivot again in place, hands go up centre of body and circle out, coming back to cross over the heart.

2 Set the instruments up in the B♭ pentatonic scale (B♭–C–D–F–G) and have the students improvise a simple accompaniment using a bordun and a very simple four-note ostinato. Alto xylophones and metallophones would sound well. Add a finger cymbal, perhaps playing only on the first note of every other measure.

Extensions

- For performance, children can secretly have flower petals in their hands and these can scatter about during the performance.
- Students can play the melody on recorders as a B section while the rest perform the motions without singing. The form will be ABA.

What Shall We Do?

This delightful, traditional song was arranged for Orff instruments by Harvey Perrin, former Director of Music for the Board of Education of Toronto and one of the first supporters of the Orff approach in the school systems of North America.

Grades

1 and 2

Concepts

❑ Glissando;
❑ language development.

trad arr Harvey Perrin

What shall we do when we all go out,
all go out, all go out? What shall we do when we
all go out, When we all go out to play?

Process

1 Teach the song by rote.

2 Each child has a chance to suggest what he or she would do playing outside. Incorporate these suggestions into the song.

3 To make this part of a spring unit, confine the answers to what they would do at this time of the year by ending the song with "In the springtime of the year".

> We'll plant some flowers when we all go out …
> We'll dig in the garden when we all go out …
> We'll play catch …
> We'll ride our bikes …
> We'll play soccer …

4 Imitate the actions of the suggested activities.

Instrumental

1 Patsch the basic alternating hand pattern on the knees.

2 Discuss glissando. Show the students how it is played (replace the B with a B♭ on the xylophone). Tell the children that we play the glissando on the word "out" the first three times it is heard in the song (when "out" is followed by a rest).

3 This accompaniment would be best used with late Grade 1 and Grade 2 children. It is too difficult for Kindergarten age but they would be capable of singing the song unaccompanied.

Extensions

● Change the ending to "In the autumn (winter, summer) of the year" and talk about things you can do all year long.

● A little unit can be constructed by performing "Springtime is Coming," several of the little chants, and "What Shall We Do?" one after the other.

Doux printemps

Clientèle

1re et 2e années

Concepts

❒ Mimer l'action du printemps;
❒ creativité.

trad arr Claire Rousseau

Doux prin - temps, quand re - vien - dras - tu? Faire pous - ser de

Démarche pédagogique

1 Cette chanson traditionnelle est très appréciée des plus petits.

2 Les xylophones alto et basse jouent en "noires" pour aider les enfants à sentir la pulsation.

3 Chanter la chanson en faisant une ronde.

4 A la fin, rester sur place et mimer une action qu'on aime faire au printemps: imiter un bonhomme de neige qui fond au soleil; jouer à la corde à danser; jouer à la marelle; faire de la bicyclette; planter des fleurs ou des légumes; montrer un bougeon qui ouvre; montrer une fleur qui pousse.

5   L'enseignant joue huit pulsations ou improvise pendant que les enfants miment l'action choisie.

6   Entre les actions improvisées, reprendre la chanson comme un refrain.

Plique, ploque la pluie

Clientèle

1re et 2e années

Concepts

☐ La phrase musicale;   ☐ le rythme régulier;
☐ entendre et produire des tons différents avec les effects sonores;
☐ explorer les onomatopées en imitant les sons de la pluie.

> Plique, ploque la pluie
> Goutte et dégouline
> Belles bottes, grosses bottes,
> Flic-flac-floc.

Démarche pédagogique

1   Montrer à réciter la comptine comme un perroquet, lentement, rapidement, etc.

2   Choisir un endroit du corps pour scander le rythme de la comptine en utilisant un son corporel différent pour chaque phrase.

3   Choiser les instruments de la petite percussion, comme les claves, les grelots, ou les triangles pour imiter la pluie.

(Contribution de Leslie Bricker)

Le jeu de l'orage

Clientèle

1re et 2e années

Concepts

☐ Les crescendo et diminuendo;   ☐ développer le contrôle moteur fin.

Démarche pédagogique

1   Les enfants et le professeur s'assoient en cercle.

2   Le professeur imite une pluie légère avec le bout des doigts.

3   Tour à tour, chacun des enfants s'y joint, alimentant l'effet sonore.

130

4 Le professeur change de mouvement, employant deux, trois, quatre puis cinq doigts, faisant gronder l'orage. Les enfants suivent l'un après l'autre.

5 La procédure inverse est adoptée pour créer un diminuendo.

(Contribution de Leslie Bricker)

Clouds

James Reaney is one of the best-known poets and playwrights in Canada. One of his recent works is an adaptation for the stage of *Alice Through the Looking-Glass*.

Grades

5 through 7

Concept

☐ Creating sound effects to heighten the meaning of the poem.

> These clouds are soft, fat horses
> That draw Weather in his wagon
> Who bears in his old hands
> Streaked whips and strokes of lightning.
> The hooves of his cattle are made
> Of limp water, that stamp
> Upon the roof during a storm
> And fall from dripping eaves;
> Yet these hooves have worn away mountains
> In their trotting over the Earth.
> And for manes these clouds
> Have the soft and various winds
> That can still push
> A ship into the sea
> And for neighs, the sable thunder.

James Reaney

Process

1 Read the poem several times with the students and talk about the meaning of the many images and metaphors.

2 Have the group decide on various sound effects that would describe and enhance the meaning of these images.

● An exercise such as this cannot be rushed. At first the tendency is to put in a sound effect for everything – the whips, the dripping eaves, the lightning; but gradually as the process evolves, the students themselves take out more and more until often what is left is just a carpet of sound that serves as a rich, aural background for the poem.

131

The Little Brown Tulip Bulb

Grades

K and 1

Concepts

❏ Creating sound effects with voice sounds and instruments;
❏ dramatizing a story using free movement.

Story Teller (leader)

Out in my garden there's a little brown tulip bulb sound asleep under all the ice and snow.

> Ask one or several children to be tulip bulbs. They curl up on the centre of the floor and go to sleep. The other children stand on the side ready to be the **wind**, the **rain** or the **sun**. Some children are seated in front of instruments, ready to play.

One day the wind comes from the sky and blows all over the garden.

> The wind children move their arms around to imitate wind and walk or run around the garden making wind sounds.

> (Music: four measures of wind-like sounds (glissandos) improvised on xylophone, drum (by rubbing the drum head), or piano.)

The wind goes to the tulip bulb's door, knocks [woodblock], and says "Wake up tulip bulb. It's Spring!" But the tulip bulb says in a slow, sleepy voice, "I'm too tired," and goes back to sleep. The wind goes back to its home in the sky.
Another day the rain comes from the sky, and rains all over the garden.

> The rain children imitate the rain falling and dripping while they walk or run around the garden making rain-like sounds.

> (Music: four measures of "drip-drop" sounds improvised on a xylophone, glockenspiel, woodblock, piano, or other instrument of the children's choice.)

The rain goes to the tulip bulb's door, knocks and says, "Wake up tulip bulb. It's Spring!" But the tulip bulb says in a slow, sleepy voice, "I'm too tired," and goes back to sleep.
The rain goes back to its home in the sky.
Another day, the sun comes from the sky, and shines all over the garden.

> The sun children make a big sun with their arms, and walk slowly around the garden, making no sound.

> (Music: four measures of a soft repeated note on glockenspiel, xylophone or piano, or perhaps a soft note played on a gong. Let the children experiment.)

The sun goes to the tulip bulb's door, knocks and says, "Wake up tulip bulb. It's Spring!" But the tulip bulb says in a slow, sleepy voice, "I'm too tired," and goes back to sleep.
The sun goes back to its home in the sky.
How can we wake up the sleepy tulip bulb???

One day the wind, and the rain, and the sun all come to the garden together.

> The wind, rain and sun children move around the garden.

132

(Music: a short, improvised sequence of the former wind, sun and rain music played together.)

They all go to the tulip bulb's door, knock and say, "Wake up tulip bulb. It's Spring!" They make so much noise that the tulip bulb cannot stay asleep any longer.

The wind, rain and sun children sit on the floor and watch as the tulip bulb slowly grows taller and taller.

(Music: a melody starting low and growing higher and higher on pitched instruments.)

And the tulip bulb slowly grows into a beautiful tulip flower.

Out in my garden there is a beautiful tulip flower.

Process

1   Read and discuss the story.

2   Talk about the various sounds and choose suitable vocal or instrumental sounds to describe the rain, the wind, and the sun and the knocking. Choose different students to play these. Some additional ideas might be:

wind improvisation	vocal sounds; drums rubbed; sandblocks;
rain improvisation	light fingers on drums; maracas played softly; claves played softly;
sun improvisation	have the children create sounds that would describe the sun; a large cymbal, played softly, is a good sound.

3   Choose a person to be the flower. He or she can crouch on the floor, covered by a colourful piece of light cloth – silk would be wonderful.

4   Choose others to be the rain, the wind and the sun.

5   Act out the story, bringing in the sound effects where needed.

6   Put everything together. It might take several lessons to work through everything.

7   Make sure that all children have a chance to take part doing the sound effects, singing, playing the instruments and the acting.

● The story can be told equally well substituting a plant, a tree or a bush for the tulip.

Special learners

● Children who have special needs respond to this story. There are parts that are simple enough for everyone to participate. It takes a lot of courage for some children to take the part of the flower, but when they do it gives a boost to their self-esteem.

(Story and ideas by Donna Wood)

CHAPTER ELEVEN

Animals

The Frog Game

Grades

K through 2

Concepts

☐ Minor key;   ☐ ball-throwing co-ordination.
☐ taking turns;

words traditional
music Angela Elster

Process

1 Sing the song and teach it by echoing.

2 Give each child a turn with a bean bag. (A green one, shaped like a frog, would be wonderful.) Have them pass the bag back and forth from one hand to the other on the strong beat, ♩ ♩. Stop when the music stops and just say the three "ribbitts".

3 To play the game, the children sit cross-legged on the floor in a circle. Place a drum upside down in the centre. Every time the song is sung through, each child in turn has a chance to throw his or her bean bag into the drum. Everybody keeps trying until they manage to get their bean bag into the drum.

4 Hand back the bean bags and repeat the song and the actions.

5 Can the children think of instruments that might sound like the frog? – guiro, cabasa. Play the instruments when the "ribbitt" comes in.

Special learners

- Language-delayed children can join in just on the frog sound.
- The act of passing the bean bag back and forth develops co-ordination, and listening while the act of throwing it into the drum gives practice in throwing co-ordination. Structure the game for success by choosing the large basket instead of the smaller drum and by moving the child closer to the basket for his or her throw.
- Playing the game develops the art of taking turns.

Jolie Annabelle Marie

Clientèle

Maternelle et 1re année

Concepts

☐ La précision de la pulsation;   ☐ les rimes.
☐ le schéma corporel;

Jo - lie An - na - belle Ma - rie, At - trape une pe - tite che - nille

Elle a grim - pé sur sa mère. Aus - si sur son pe - tit frère,

Tous ont dit, "An - na - belle Ma - rie, en - léve ta vi - laine che - nille."

Démarche pédagogique

1   Les enfants chantent la chanson en mimant les gestes:
        tenir "la chenille" dans les mains en coupe;
        montrer "la chenille";
        faire marcher les doigts sur un bras, puis l'autre;
        repousser "la chenille".

(Contribution de Leslie Bricker)

Bear Comes Knockin'

Grades

K through 2

Concepts

☐ Rhythm pattern;   ☐ social skills.

words and music Diane Shieron

Moderato

Bear comes knock-in'   at   my door   Bear comes knock-in'   at   my door

Bear comes knock-in'   at   my   door   knock-in' come a knock-in'   at   my   door.

Knock knock knock   knock-in' come-a knock-in'   Bear comes knock-in'   at   my door!

136

Process

1 Teach the song.

2 Teach and play the game. This much might be difficult enough for the youngest children.

3 Teach the instrumental parts, starting with the bass xylophone. If the eighth notes are too difficult in this part and in the parts for percussion instruments, substitute quarter notes instead.

Game 1 (easiest)

Small circle formation with a "bear" in the middle. Bear walks around the circle while everyone sings the song. Every time the words "at my door" appear in the song, the bear claps his/her hands twice and then claps both hands once of the person he or she is facing at the time. When the song is finished, the last person the bear has clapped hands with becomes the new bear and the game repeats.

Game 2 (substitution game – more difficult)

Formation: circle, facing in as above.

1 Sing song – no actions.

2 Sing song;

take away the words "at my door" and substitute clap, clap, snap;

substitute woodblock for clap and finger cymbal for snap.

3 Sing song;

take away "knockin'" and substitute two stamps (big drum).

4 Sing song;

take away "bear comes" and substitute "bottom slaps" (hand drum).

5 Sing song;

take away the last words "knockin' come a" and substitute patschen (claves).

● Non-pitched instruments can be substituted for the body percussion. See the suggestions above or incorporate your own ideas.

Special learners

● It will be difficult for children who have special needs and those who are very young to remember all these body percussion patterns. Include as many as possible or just clap the rhythm pattern each time.

Dinosaurs

Grades

K and 1

Concepts

☐ Moving slowly to half-note tempo;   ☐ ♩ and ♩ notes.

words and music Lois Birkenshaw-Fleming

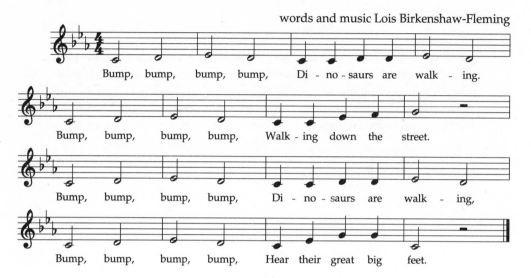

Bump, bump, bump, bump, Di - no - saurs are walk - ing.

Bump, bump, bump, bump, Walk - ing down the street.

Bump, bump, bump, bump, Di - no - saurs are walk - ing,

Bump, bump, bump, bump, Hear their great big feet.

Process

1   Clap the rhythm pattern of the words.

2   Play this on a drum – the larger the better.

3   Have the children show you how large dinosaurs would move.

4   Sing the song and add the movement.

5   If the children are ready, have them play a steady quarter-note bordun of C and G as an accompaniment on the bass xylophone.

6   Use this song as a part of a unit on dinosaurs.

Dans mon jardin

Clientèle

3e et 4e années

Concepts

☐ Mode dorien (*ré*) l'expérience;   ☐ forme: AB (couplet–refrain).

138

musique et paroles Claire Rousseau

139

- saure, un trach - o - don, un sté-go-saure, un ul-tra-saure, un dip-lo-do - cus.

2   En creusant plus profondément
       Ont surgi de la terre
       Deux longs crocs et puis des ossements
       Recouverts de poussière.

Démarche pédagogique

1   Parler des dinosaures – sujet favori des enfants – les identifier – les imiter: imiter leurs cris, leur démarche et …

2   Ajouter des percussions: par exemple, bloc chinois pour "les ossements".

3   Entre les deux couplets, ajouter un couplet à la flûte-à-bec.

4   Ajouter des nuances dans le refrain, ⊂=====⊃

Forme finale

Introduction (parlée):

         Dans mon jardin je suis allé(e)
         Planter un marronier
         J'étais en train de creuser
         Et voici ce que j'ai trouvé

Couplet 1 et refrain;
Couplet instrumental et refrain;
Couplet 2 et refrain.

Bees

Grades

K through 3

Concepts

☐ Rhythmic speech; ☐ notation;
☐ speech ostinati; ☐ ABA form.

Process

1 Teach the speech, clap the rhythm and perhaps play it on an unpitched percussion instrument.

2 Older children can notate the rhythm patterns and read them using the time names.

3 The youngest children (and those who have special needs) might use just the A section. Say it clapping the rhythm pattern of the first measure, turn around on the second measure.

ABA form

1 (easiest) Play some "bee flying" music on a piano, recorder or xylophone and for the B section have everyone fly around the room during the interlude, coming to a stop when the music ends. Then perform the A section again. The form will be ABA.

2 Say the A section all together. One person (or a small group) says the first chant (B). All say the A section again. This is more difficult.

Extensions

● The four patterns can be played as a round, each entering after the previous one has played the first line.

(Contributed by Ruth Berger)

Five Fat Fleas

Grades

2 through 4

Concepts

☐ Counting backwards;

☐ inner hearing.

words Dennis Lee
music and arrangement Judy Sills

142

flea flew, a flea flew, a flea flew and then there were none.

2   Four fat frogs on tumble-down logs
     Did somersaults one by one.
     A frog flew, a frog flew, a frog flew, a frog flew,
     A frog flew and then there were none.

3   Three fat cats on tumble-down mats …

4   Two fat ants in dancing pants …

5   One fat bee on a billy goat's knee …

6   No fat gnomes on dinosaur's bones …

Process

1   Teach melody by rote.

2   Teach first verse and actions, following the suggestions of the words, then add the
     succeeding verses.

3   Teach the accompaniment as body percussion, then transfer to instruments.

4   Put it all together, perhaps adding two measures of accompaniment as an introduction
     and as interludes.

Extensions

● Can the children create other verses using the original form as a pattern?
● Try keeping the fleas as the subject for each verse. Sing the last "a flea flew" silently
  and clap the rhythm pattern. Each verse, add another silent "a flea flew" until by the
  end these are all just clapped.
● The rhythm pattern of each could be played on a drum.

Special learners

● Singing songs such as this will help develop inner hearing – so necessary for fluent
  reading.
● It will be helpful to have pictures of the animals to be sung about as a visual aid.

143

Little Green Bug

The traditional tune of "Skip to My Loo" has been used as the melody for this song.

Grades

1 through 4

Concepts

☐ Speech;
☐ rhyming words;
☐ creativity;

☐ language development;
☐ changing chord accompaniment.

music traditional
words Joe Berarducci

Process

1 Teach the words first, by saying them in different ways (high voices, low voices, quickly, slowly, sweetly, angrily, and so on).

144

2   Create body percussion patterns. The degree of difficulty will depend on age and experience level. It might be that the pattern will be as simple as: pat, clap, pat, clap. If possible try something a little more challenging, such as the following:

    Formation: scatter, in partners.

    Pat, clap (own hands), clap right hand of partner, clap own;

    pat, clap (own), clap left hand of partner, clap own;

    pat, clap both partner's hands, pat, clap both partner's hands;

    pat, clap (own), clap both partner's hands, three times quickly.

3   Try leaving out key words, taking away one each time the song is sung. Replace them by clapping the rhythm pattern, for example:

    Ottawa, mother-in-law, silk, straw, Ottawa.

4   Replace the claps with percussion instruments.

5   Sing with all the words except those replaced by instruments, or sing entirely in head and have only the instruments play on "their" words.

6   Teach the accompaniments by rote or, if the students are able to understand changing chord accompaniments, work through chord changes. (See chapter 24, "Tips for Teachers", for an explanation of one teaching method to use.)

Extensions

● Have the students create their own verses using other place names. The following are some examples:

> Little purple cow from Lake St. Clair,
> Went to the movies and got a scare,
> This is how she lost her hair,
> Little purple cow from Lake St. Clair.
>
> Grandpa John from Edmonton,
> Jumped up high and sang a song,
> It was very loud and very long,
> Grandpa John from Edmonton.
>
> A dog named Max from Halifax,
> Was very smart and played the sax,
> He could use a phone and send a fax,
> That dog named Max from Halifax.
>
> A cat named Maude from Montreal,
> Went to a very fancy ball,
> She danced a jig right out to the hall,
> That cat named Maude from Montreal.

Special learners

● Children who have speech difficulties will be helped by the speech work. Saying lyrics in this way helps the learning process and also serves to focus attention.

● Creating other verses will extend vocabulary and give practice in rhyming words. Most children will be able to play the accompaniment if a shape- or colour-coded chart is made to show the changes visually (see chapter 24, "Tips for Teachers").

CHAPTER TWELVE

Transportation

Up Like a Rocket

Age

Babies to K

Concepts

☐ Rhythmic movement;
☐ body percussion;
☐ instrumental.

Process

1 Hold the baby or young child on your knees as you sit in a chair or on the floor. Lift him/her up over your head for the first two measures, lower for the next two, and lean way out from side to side for the last four measures.

2 Older children can learn the body percussion and later transfer this to instruments.

3 Simplify the accompaniment if necessary.

146

The Transportation System

Grades

2 through 4

Concept

☐ Language development.

David E. Walden and Lois Birkenshaw-Fleming
arrangement Lois Birkenshaw-Fleming

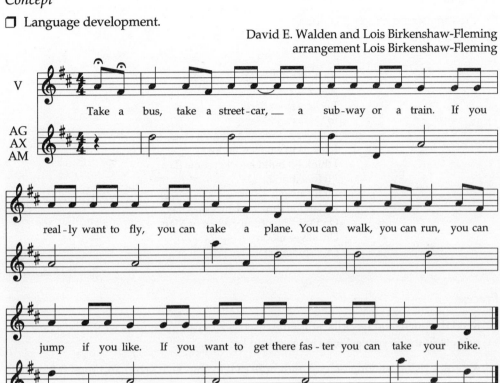

Take a bus, take a street-car, __ a sub-way or a train. If you real-ly want to fly, you can take a plane. You can walk, you can run, you can jump if you like. If you want to get there fas-ter you can take your bike.

2   There's a two-wheel, a three-wheel, a five-speed or ten,
    There are bicycles for ladies and bikes for men.
    There are motorcycles, racing cars and all kinds of boats,
    If it's water you are crossing, you can swim or float.

3   You can glide on a glider, you can crawl on your knees,
    You can drive, you can fly, you can do what you please.
    There are many ways of traveling from here to there.
    With the transportation system you can go anywhere.

Process

1   This song covers many forms of transportation. Make a list of these. Can the children think of others? It might be possible to write a new verse incorporating the new suggestions.

2   Use the accompaniment if it suits the needs of your children. Teach it by rote.

3   Add unpitched percussion as colour/sound instruments if you wish.

147

Rockets

Grades

2 and 3

Concepts

☐ Creating sound effects to a poem;
☐ rondo form.

> Rockets are flying out in space,
> Rockets are flying every place,
> Rockets from Earth
> to Venus and Mars,
> to silver moons and shining stars,
> Rockets to galaxies far away,
> I think I'll build a rocket some day,
> I'll fuel it first,
> I'll fly away,
> I'll land in time for Christmas day,
> On Pluto, Neptune, Saturn or Mars,
> On silver moon
> Or a shining star.

Robert Heidelbreder

Process

1   Read the poem and have the students discuss what sound effects would best describe rockets flying in space. Some ideas might be:

♦ voice rising, staying on one high note (while ship is in orbit) and then falling as the ship comes back to earth;
♦ play the same sounds as above on a piano, xylophone or slide whistle;
♦ create the sounds of the engine.

2   Have everyone say, "10, 9, 8, 7, 6, 5, 4, 3, 2, 1, BLAST OFF!!" as an introduction.

Rondo form

● Have everyone learn the first five lines (to the end of "stars") and make them the A section of a rondo (ABACADA). Create speech patterns about space for the episodes. Here are some ideas:

B   Past Pluto and Jupiter and out into space,
We'll travel so fast we'll be first in the race.

C   We'll roar off to Saturn and one of its moons,
Then to Uranus through darkness we'll zoom.

D   We may see a comet as we speed in our ship
All through the galaxy, then homeward we'll zip.

- Have the children create a body percussion accompaniment that could be transferred to unpitched percussion instruments for the A section:

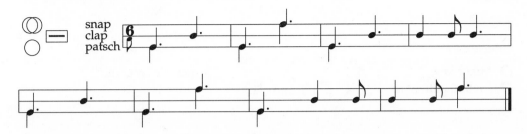

B, C, D   Children create their own body percussion accompaniment.

Roll that Big Truck

Ages

2 through 5

Concepts

☐ Body awareness;
☐ vocabulary.

Ruth Berger

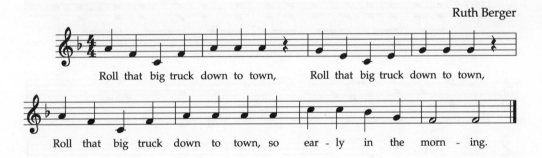

Process

1   Roll hands quickly over one another; one way for the first two measures, then the other way for the next two. Clap the rhythm pattern of the words for the last two measures.

2   Encourage the children to create other verses:
      Fill that big truck up with sand …
      Fill that big truck up with snow …

3   Dramatize the extra verses.

149

Train Ride

Grades

1 and 2

Concepts

❏ Minor key;   ❏ melodic contour.

❏ rhythm pattern of ♩ ♩ ♩ 𝄽, ♫ ♩ and ♫♫ ;

trad arr Leslie Bricker

150

Process

1   Teach the song. Let the children hear the difference between major and minor tonality by singing or playing the song using a F♯ instead of the F♮.

2   Play ♩ ♩ ♩ 𝄽 , ♫ ♩ and ♬ ♩ patterns on a woodblock or drum. Can the children discover that the patterns are the same except that ♫ ♩ is twice as fast as ♩ ♩ ♩ 𝄽 , and ♬ ♩ is twice as fast as ♫ ♩ ? Have them clap the patterns.

3   Have the children make a "map" in the air or on the chalkboard or chart paper of the melodic contour of the melody, i.e. the rises and falls.

4   Make lists with the children of the cities and towns the train might go to. Group eight of these to form a B section. These can be said by individuals or groups.

> Halifax, Charlottetown, Montréal, Toronto, Winnipeg, Regina, Edmonton, Kamloops
>
> or   Whitehorse, Vancouver, Calgary, Saskatoon, Brandon, Trois Rivières, Fredricton, St. Johns

ABA form

A   song plus accompaniment;
B   speech patterns of cities – could be accompanied by the rhythms played on a cabasa or sand blocks;
A   song as above.

Rondo form

As above but add a second or third speech pattern and one more repetition of the A section.

Subways, Buses and Streetcars

Grades

2 through 4

Concepts

☐ Tonic *sol-fa*: *do, mi, so;*   ☐ speech;
☐ canon;   ☐ language.

words and music Lois Birkenshaw-Fleming and David Walden
arrangement Lois Birkenshaw-Fleming

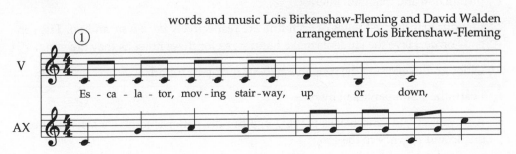

Es - ca - la - tor, mov - ing stair - way, up or down,

2   Buy a ticket at the wicket, put it in the box,
    Through the turnstile you may go with tokens in the slots,
    Down the staircase to the platform, waiting for the train,
    Make sure you know where you're going, to get back again.

3   Hold on tight, the train is moving, going very fast,
    When we reach our destination, we are here at last,
    Transfer to a bus or streetcar, everyone must run,
    People hurry, pushing, shoving, journey's nearly done.

Process

1   The song has many words and should be sung fairly quickly. It is probably more suited to older children who can pronounce the words distinctly. Teach the speech one line at a time varying the tempi, the pitch and the timbre of the words to assist speech production and maintain interest.

2   Identify that the first notes of each line are respectively *do, mi, so,* and *mi.* The song ends on *do.* Have the students make hand signs for these notes as they are sung.

3   Older grades can sing the song in a two- or four-part round.

4   Learn the accompaniment by rote.

5   Add cabasa and sand blocks playing eighth-note patterns to give a sense of hurry, bustle and urgency to the song.

CHAPTER THIRTEEN

Our World

The Diver

Grades

4 through 6

Concept

☐ Sound effects to heighten the meaning of the poem.

> I would like to dive
> Down
> Into this still pool
> Where the rocks at the bottom are safely deep,
>
> Into the green
> Of the water seen from within,
> A strange light
> Streaming past my eyes –
>
> Things hostile;
> You cannot stay here, they seem to say;
> The rocks, slime-covered, the undulating
> Fronds of weeds –
>
> And drift slowly
> Among the cooler zones;
> Then, upward turning,
> Break from the green glimmer
>
> Into the light,
> White an ordinary of the day,
> And the mild air,
> With the breeze and the comfortable shore.

W. W. Ross

Process

1 Have the students explore sounds that would conjure up impressions of cool water, green light, waving weeds, and so on. Some ideas might be: tremolos on metallophones, the soft sounds of finger cymbals, glissandos on glockenspiels, plucking piano strings. The group will doubtless think of many more.

2 Decide where to use these ideas and say the poem with them as an underlying carpet of sound.

Neighbourhood Noises

Age

3 through 5

Concepts

☐ Creativity;   ☐ sound awareness.

☐ vocabulary development;

music traditional
words Marianne Kennedy

The police-man blows a whis - tle, a whis - tle, a whis - tle, The

police - man blows a whis - tle, ...   (*make three whistle noises*)

2	The carpenter uses a saw ...	(*make sawing sounds*)
3	The plumber bangs the pipes ...	(*sounds of banging on metal*)
4	The firetruck has a siren ...	(*siren!*)
5	The doctor uses a stethoscope ...	(*make heartbeat sounds*)
6	The dentist cleans your teeth ...	(*brush teeth with sound effects*)
7	The ice-cream truck plays some music ...	(*play on a glockenspiel*)
8	The knife-sharpener rings a bell ...	(*bell sounds*)

Process

1   Introduce the lesson by asking the children what noises they might hear in their neighbourhood and what noises they might associate with various community helpers. (Do not be surprised at some of the answers!)

2   Teach the song, one verse at a time.

3   Add the sound effects.

4   Create new verses using some of the children's suggestions above

5   Create actions for each verse.

Special learners

● This song develops vocabulary in a totally painless way. Have pictures of various noise-makers and community helpers to make the experience more meaningful.

● Everyone can take part in making the sound effects. If you have students who are hearing impaired in your classroom, give them a sound effect that has a low pitch so there is a better chance of their hearing it.

● Making the sound effect when it is time in the song will give children who have special needs a feeling of achievement and self-worth.

154

Skyscraper

Grades

3 and 4

Concepts

☐ Creative movement;   ☐ co-operative team effort.

poem Dennis Lee
music and arrangement Judith Sills

Sky - scra - per, sky - scra - per, scrape me some sky,

Tic - kle the sun as the stars go by, Tic - kle the stars while the

sun's climb-ing high, then sky-scra-per, scrape me some sky.

Process

1 Teach the song and the accompaniment.

2 Experiment with creating movements in groups that would reflect the building of a tall skyscraper. What sounds could you use to accompany this activity?

Final form

Introduction

A group of eight people "builds" a skyscraper accompanied by an improvised rhythm pattern, eight measures long, played on instruments (such as claves and drums) that would imitate building sounds. Number 1 makes a shape on the strong beat of the first measure, and holds it. The second person joins the shape with his/her own shape, on the first beat of measure 2, and holds it. Carry on in this way for eight measures (for eight people).

A Sing the song with the orchestration. The skyscraper remains motionless.

B The skyscraper moves (very carefully), scraping the sky. The children can improvise an accompaniment during this part on unpitched percussion instruments, and melodic instruments set up in the key of F pentatonic.

A Sing song with orchestration while the skyscraper is still.

Special learners

● Children who have special needs can take part in creating movement and in improvising the accompaniment to the introduction and the B section.

156

Parcours!

Clientèle

6e année du primaire

Concepts

☐ Accompagnement des percussions;
☐ rap (parler-rythmé).

Démarche pédagogique

Forme: AB (couplets–refrain)

couplet 1	rap avec accompagnement des percussions non mélodiques;
refrain 1	chant accompagné des percussions mélodiques et non mélodiques;
couplet 2	rap … ;
refrain 2	chant accompagné … ;
couplet 3	rap … ;
refrain 1 et 2	superposés avec accompagnements.

× = main ouverte ♩ = poing droite ♩ = poing gauche

Refrain

paroles et musique Claire Rousseau

157

V1 — Je trouv' la vie "su - per", je trouv' que "c'est l'en - fer".

V2 — Sou - vent l'a - ve - nir me pa - rait fra - gi - le.

Je rêve de li - ber - té, je rêve de m'en - vo - ler!

Et bâ - tir sa vie n'est pas si fa - ci - le!

Rap

1er couplet

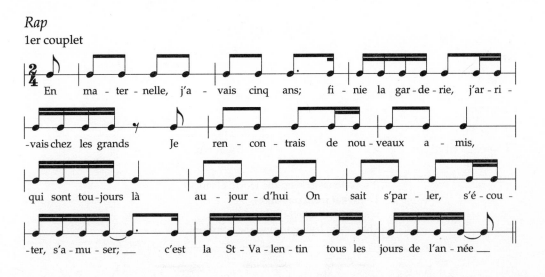

En ma-ter-nelle, j'a-vais cinq ans; fi-nie la gar-de-rie, j'ar-ri--vais chez les grands Je ren-con-trais de nou-veaux a-mis, qui sont tou-jours là au-jour-d'hui On sait s'par-ler, s'é-cou--ter, s'a-mu-ser; ___ c'est la St-Va-len-tin tous les jours de l'an-née ___

2e couplet

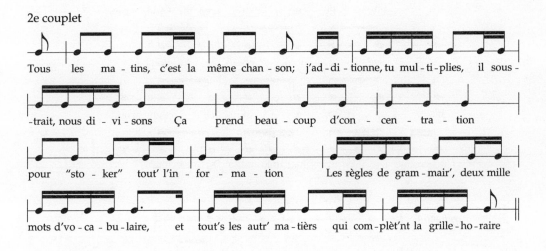

Tous les ma-tins, c'est la même chan-son; j'ad-di-tionne, tu mul-ti-plies, il sous--trait, nous di-vi-sons Ça prend beau-coup d'con-cen-tra-tion pour "sto-ker" tout l'in-for-ma-tion Les règles de gram-mair', deux mille mots d'vo-ca-bu-laire, et tout's les autr' ma-tièrs qui com-plèt'nt la grille-ho-raire

3e couplet

Et puis le se-cond-air', c'est dé-jà l'an pro-chain! Des fois, ça fait peur d'y pen--ser c'est cer-tain! ___ Ça prend beau-coup d'cou-rage pour ne pas dé-cro-cher; ___ il faut aus-si du flair pour choi-sir un mé-tier ___ Se-cré-taire, ex-plo-ra-teur, femme d'af--faire ou bien doc-teur; c'est une af-faire de tête, c'est une af-faire de coeur!

It's Up to Us

Grades

3 and 4

Concepts

- ☐ Verbal ostinati;
- ☐ speech rhythm;
- ☐ listening skills;
- ☐ ABA form.

It's up to us to keep the world clean,
To save it from pollution,
It's up to us to tell the world
That we're trying to find the solution.

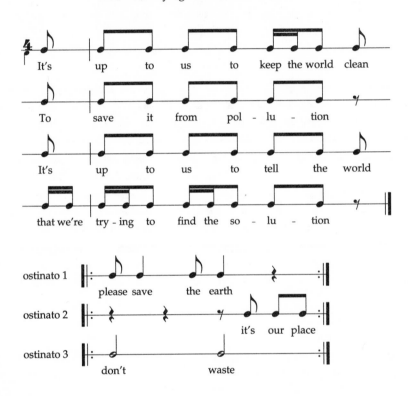

Process

1 Read the words of the chant from a chart.

2 Clap the rhythm of the chant.

3 Say rhythmic time names while clapping if this suits the need of your students.

4 Alternate between clapping the rhythm and saying the words of the chant. The leader can give the signal to change from one to the other by playing a triangle or finger cymbals.

5   Repeat the above procedure to learn the three ostinati.

6   Once secure, add one ostinato at a time to the chant until all the parts are secure.

7   Transfer the parts to small percussion instruments; for example, a woodblock for the chant, a tambourine for ostinato 1, a drum for ostinato 2, and a triangle for ostinato 3.

8   Perform in ABA form. Section A is the chant with all parts added, and B is the rhythm played on small percussion instruments.

(Contributed by Angela Elster)

The Elders Are Watching

Grades

5 through 7

Concepts

☐ Creating a sound carpet for a poem;
☐ minor melody with bordun accompaniment.

Chorus

words Dave Bouchard
music and arrangement Judy Sills

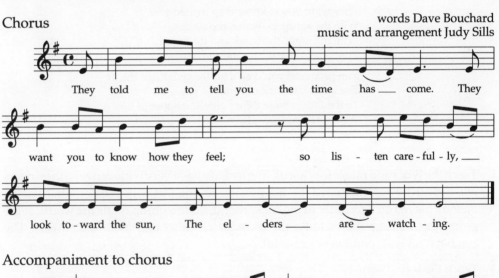

Accompaniment to chorus

161

Sound carpet, accompaniment to spoken verses

1   They told me to tell you they believed you
    When you said you would take a stand.
    They thought that you knew the ways of nature.
    They thought you respected the land.

2   They want you to know they trusted you
    With the earth, the water, the air,
    With the eagle, the hawk and the raven,
    The salmon, the whale and the bear.

3   You promised you'd care for the cedar and the fir
    The mountains, the sea and the sky.
    To the Elders these things are the essence of life.
    Without them a people will die!

Process

1   Teach the lyrics and music for chorus. The melody has a very wide range so the singers
    will have to be experienced. If it is not possible to sing this with your group, have the
    melody played on a recorder in the background while a group reads the words. If the
    group can manage the melody, the recorder can also play with the singers. The
    combination will sound very beautiful.

2   Teach the sound carpet.

3   Have the students practise reading the poem with feeling. Choose some to read each
    verse.

Movement for chorus

They told me	*point to self (right hand);*
to tell you	*point in front of self (right hand);*
the time has come	*make circle with both hands;*
They want you	*point to audience (right hand);*

162

to know	*point to head (right hand);*
how they feel	*place both hands on heart;*
So listen carefully	*lean forward with right hand cupped behind ear;*
look toward the sun	*point with left hand to corner;*
The elders are	*shade eyes with right hand while looking left;*
watching	*shade eyes with left hand while looking right.*

Final form

Introduction

chorus	with or without recorder;
verse 1	read, with sound carpet accompaniment;
chorus	
verse 2	read, with the sound carpet;
chorus	
verse 3	read, with the sound carpet;
chorus	
coda	three repetitions of last two measures with a ritard. the last time.

- The performance will be very effective if the readers are placed in different areas of the room.

Special learners

- Students who have special needs could take part in creating the sound carpet.

Picketty Land

Grades

2 and 3

Concepts

❐ Rhythm;   ❐ co-ordination.

❐ language development;

words, music and arrangement Joan Linklater

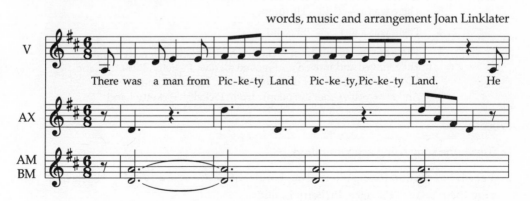

marched and marched and marched all day   Pic - ke - ty, Pic - ke - ty   Land.   A

nic - er man you   ne - ver did see,   Pic - ke - ty, Pic - ke - ty   Land,   And

now you've met   the   man ___   from Pic - ke - ty, Pic - ke - ty   Land.

2   There was a lady …   She skipped …

3   There was a boy …   He jumped …

4   There was a girl …   She slid …

5   These are the people from Picketty Land, Picketty, Picketty Land,
    They moved and moved and moved all day, Picketty, Picketty Land,
    Nicer people you never did see, Picketty, Picketty Land,
    And now you've met the people from, Picketty, Picketty Land.

Process

1   Teach the song using echo imitation.

2   Patsch the rhythm (using alternating hands) of ♩♩ ♩ ♩♩ ♩ |♩. ♪ |each time you
    sing the passage "Picketty, Picketty Land".

164

3 Explore various gross motor movements including walking, skipping, jumping and sliding. These can be done to a drum playing the appropriate rhythms.

4 Sing the song while doing the actions indicated in the various verses.

5 Sing and perform the actions again, but this time stop on each "Picketty, Picketty Land", and patsch the rhythm of the words.

6 Learn the instrumental parts. (Be sure to keep singing while practising these parts on the knees, in the air or on the instruments.)

7 Add percussion instruments:

on the words
"Picketty, Picketty Land"
or all through the piece   temple blocks to ♩ ♫ ♩ ♫ ♩ | ♩. 𝄾· |;
verse 1   timpani on D–A–D–A;
verse 2   woodblock;
verse 3   tambourine on the rest at the end of each phrase;
verse 4   sand blocks.

Dance

Formation: couples in two lines, facing inwards (could be done individually).

Verse 1   head couple marches down "alley" between the two lines and takes its place at the bottom of each line;
verse 2   the second couple skips down the alley;
verse 3   the third couple jumps down the alley;
verse 4   the fourth couple slides down the alley.

8 Combine song, movement and instruments.

9 Create an introduction, interludes and ending using the distinctive rhythms of the song. Play these on drums or claves:

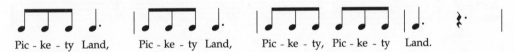

Pic - ke - ty Land,   Pic - ke - ty Land,   Pic - ke - ty, Pic - ke - ty Land.

Special learners

- Those children who have speech difficulties can join in on the repeated part "Picketty, Picketty Land". It could be a "special" part because "we need more voices to make these words important".
- The movement pattern is simple enough for almost everyone. Visually impaired children would have no difficulty, and children in wheelchairs could wheel these down the "alley" as well.

Monsieur Bordeleau

Clientèle

3e et 4e années

Concepts

☐ Forme ABA.

Partie A

paroles et musique Guylaine Myre

Vo - gue, vo - gue Mon - sieur Bor - de - leau, c'est ton nom pe - tit ca - not._____ Vo - gue, vo - gue Mon - sieur Bor - de - leau, ra - mer sur l'eau c'est si beau._____

Accompagnement

CS
CA

XA

glissando

MS
MA

XB
MB

Partie B

Mais pour-quoi voit-on flot - ter des bou-teil-les de co - la?

Des dé - chets, des pa - piers, je - tés ça et là!

Mais pour-quoi voit-on flot - ter des bou-teil-les de co - la?

Mon - sieur Bor - de - leau et moi, on ne com - prend vrai - ment pas!

Accompagnement (partie B)

Démarche pédagogique

Forme

Intro	accompagnement instrumental (huit mesures);
A	chant accompagné;
B	parler-rythmé accompagné des percussions non-mélodiques seulement;
A	chant accompagné;
coda	répéter la dernière phrase "ramer sur l'eau c'est si beau" en decrescendo.

Round and Round

Grades

4 through 6

Concepts

☐ Dorian mode;   ☐ continuity and predictability of life on Earth.
☐ a round;

Process

1   This beautiful round is in the Dorian mode. Have the students listen carefully to the tonality. Have them play the scale of C major on the piano or xylophone but start on low D and end on high D. This is the Dorian mode.

2   Could they improvise other melodies in this mode? Perhaps they could sing these or play them on a recorder.

3   Sing in a three-part round.

CHAPTER FOURTEEN

The Canadian Mosaic

Bienvenue au Carnaval!

Clientèle

3e et 4e années

Fine

Aie! Aie! Aie! C'est in-fer-nal, Mo-nu-men-tal mais o-ri-gi-nal!

Couplets

Thé-â-tral, A-ni-mal, Ar-se-nal tout à fait gé-nial!

169

De Mon-tré-al jus - qu'à La-val, Du Por-tu-gal jus-qu'au Sé - né-gal!

D.C. al Fine

2   Régional, Provincial
     National, International
     Tropical, Occidental
     Oriental, c'est phénoménal.

Down by the Banks

"Down by the Banks" and "African Children's Clapping Song" were collected by Carolyn Hernandez from children in her school in St. Albert, Alberta. They reflect the cultural mosaic of Canada and the variety of music that is naturally part of the child's world.

Grade

3

Concepts

❏ Beat;   ❏ syncopation.
❏ movement;

170

Down by the banks of the han - ky - pan - ky where the

bull frog jumped from bank to ban - ky with a

Eeep! Iip! Oop! Op!

Hey Bob - ba re - ba with a ker - plop!

Process

1   This is a song the children sing for fun. Any learning should be pretty much incidental. If too much conscious attention is paid to the learning outcomes, the children will lose interest in the song.

    ♦ Singing with the body percussion will emphasize beat.
    ♦ Teach the song by rote; children learn the syncopation by echoing you.
    ♦ Children experience the "sound" of a beat during a "rest".

2   The melody is quite difficult by our developmental standards with its semi-tones, but children seem to pick it up very quickly.

Movement (done on the beat)

Formation: partners facing each other in a double circle.

Measure 1	clap own hands, clap partner's right hand;
measure 2	clap own hands, clap partner's left hand;
measure 3	clap own hands, clap both partner's hands;
measure 4	clap own hands, snap;
measures 5–8	repeat measures 1–4;
measures 9–12	hands on hips, each jump four times to left to find a new partner;
measure 13–14	make a circle in place, clapping on first note;
measure 15	snap, pat knees.

● The movement can also be done with one partner. Just jump four times in place and do not change partners.
● Repeat as often as you wish.

Instrumental

Unpitched percussion instruments can be added such as a drum and cabasa or tambourine. Play a swinging beat such as swish, play, swish, play... Try two drum beats in measure 16 to make a strong ending for the song.

(Contributed by Carolyn Hernandez)

171

African Children's Clapping Song

Grades

2 through 4

Concepts

☐ Co-ordination;
☐ uneven rhythm.

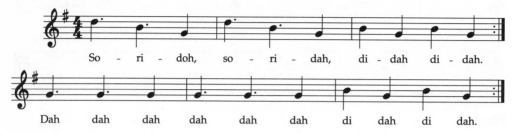

Process

● This is another song that is learned by rote because the rhythm pattern is quite advanced, though children seem to learn it in a play setting almost by osmosis.

1 Teach the song using the echo technique.

2 Demonstrate the actions while singing.

Actions

Formation: partners, facing each other, in random formation.

Measure 1

	So	one person brings hands down on palms of partner's hands which are coming up in a brush action – they connect on "ri";
	dah	clap own hands;

repeat
measure 3

	di	hit back of partner's right hand;
	dah	clap own hands;
		repeat;

repeat the actions of first three measures
measure 4

	Dah	clap partner's right hand;
	dah	clap partner's left hand;
	dah	clap own hands;
measure 5		repeat measure 4;
measure 6		same as measure 3.

Add a hip swing to the beat.

This action looks very complicated when written out in this fashion but when performed it will be easier to see the pattern.

- Find a tape of African drumming with a suitable tempo and use it as an accompaniment for the children's game. The children will experience an authentic rhythmic accompaniment.

(Contributed by Carolyn Hernandez)

The next two accompaniments were written by Harvey Perrin who was the Director of Music for the Toronto Board of Education and a very early supporter of the Orff approach in Canadian music education.

Silver Moon Boat

Grades

3 through 5

Concepts

☐ Songs ending on a note other than the tonic.

Process

1 Teach the song either by rote or by tonic *sol-fa*. It uses only the five notes of the pentatonic scale but many students might find it difficult to learn because of the unfamiliar sound.

2 Discuss what kind of mood is created when the song ends on *mi*.

3 Sing through the two verses very softly with phrasing and expression.

4 Teach the accompaniment.

5 Create an introduction, perhaps playing just two measures of the accompaniment. Do the students have any ideas of something else to do for an introduction?

6 Teach the students to play the melody on the recorder.

Possible form

Introduction;
    verse 1   singing with accompaniment;
    recorder plays melody with accompaniment;
    verse 2   sing with accompaniment and recorder playing melody.

Cantonese folk song
English words and arrangement Harvey Perrin

Lit - tle sil - ver moon rides the

sky like a boat, Past the twink-ling stars it will float, light-ly float.

Sail lit - tle moon boat, to the West. Sail lit - tle moon boat,

while I rest.

2 Little silver moon carry me past the stars,
Carry me aloft in the sky up to Mars,
Sail little moon boat to the West,
Sail little moon boat while I rest.

174

Philippine Lullaby

Grades

3 and 4

Concepts

☐ First-beat rest;

☐ alternating instrumental parts.

Apayao* folk song
accompaniment and adaptation Harvey Perrin

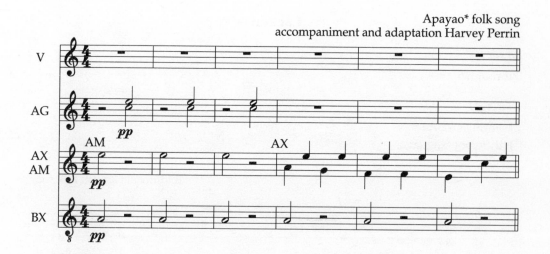

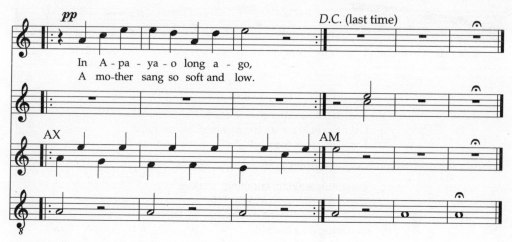

In A - pa - ya - o long a - go,
A mo-ther sang so soft and low.

D.C. (last time)

* pronounced "A-pie-ay-o"

2   My tiny blossom do not weep,
My little baby go to sleep.

175

Process

1   Most lullabies are written in 3/4 or 6/8 time. This one is in 4/4. It is a challenge to sing it softly and with a kind of swinging motion so that it sounds like a lullaby.

2   Work on having the students begin exactly on the second beat when the voices enter. It might help to have them clap very softly or brush one hand against the other on the rest at first.

Lachen

Grades

3 through 5

Concepts

☐ Form: a round;
☐ different language.

traditional German folk song

La - chen, la - chen, la - chen, la - chen, kommt der Som - mer ü - ber das Feld,

ü - ber das Feld kommt der Som - mer, ha ha ha, la - chen ü - ber das Feld.

> Laughing, laughing, laughing, laughing,
> Comes the summer over the field,
> Over the field comes the summer, ha, ha, ha,
> Laughing over the field.

Another version which is very popular goes:

> Laughing, singing, laughing, singing,
> Come the children over the hill,
> Ha, ha, ha, ha, ha, ha, ha, ha, ha, ha, ha, ha,
> Laughing over the hill.

Process

1   Sing the song in unison, then in a two-part or four-part round, depending on the numbers in your group and the abilities of your students.

2   Sing in German if possible.

Mama Paquita

Grades

3 through 5

Concepts

- ❒ Syncopation;
- ❒ vocabulary development;
- ❒ changing chord accompaniment.

Brazilian folk song
arrangement Vera Flaig-Schultz

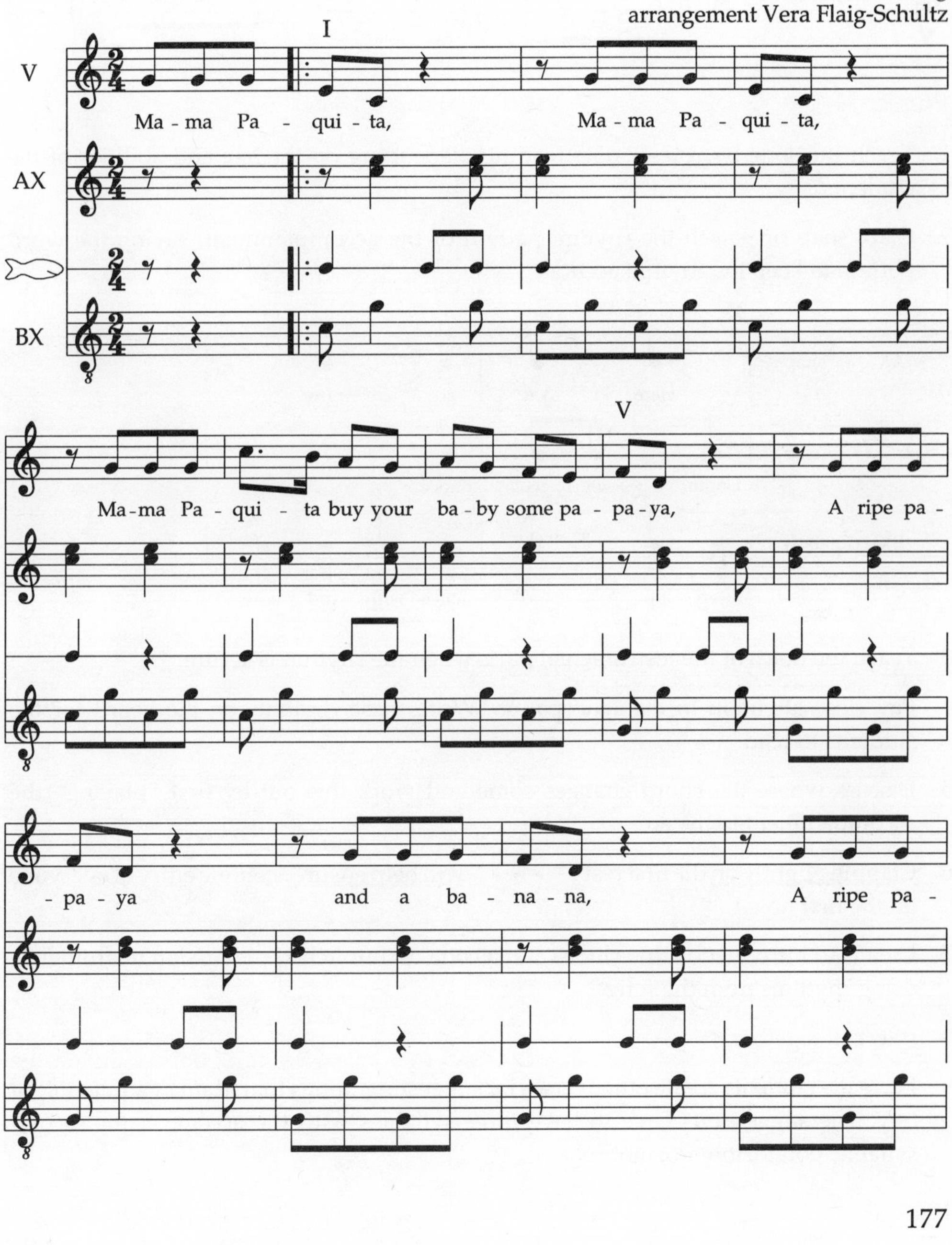
I
V
V
AX
BX
Ma - ma Pa - qui - ta, Ma - ma Pa - qui - ta,
Ma - ma Pa - qui - ta buy your ba - by some pa - pa - ya, A ripe pa -
- pa - ya and a ba - na - na, A ripe pa -

- pa - ya that your ba - by will en - joy, ma - ma - ma - ma, Ma - ma Pa- -joy.

Process

1 Teach the song by rote or note reading, depending on the age and abilities of the students.

2 Clap, snap or patsch the rhythm pattern of the accompaniment, saying the word pattern to keep the rhythm accurate.

3 Teach the notes of the instrumental parts when the rhythm is secure.

4 Pay close attention to the syncopation. Write these rhythms on the board for the students to read.

5 Discuss where the chord changes come and work this out by first "playing" the accompaniment in the air.

6 Clapping lightly on the first rest ♪♫♩ will help ensure accurate entry of everyone on the first note.

7 Create an introduction, interludes and a coda on unpitched percussion instruments, using rhythms from the song.

8 Put it all together.

9 Have the students create other verses by suggesting things that Mama Paquita might buy. The suggestions have to have three syllables with the accent on the second syllable: potato, tomato, umbrella …

- Younger children will enjoy just singing this song. The changing chord accompaniment might be too difficult for them.

Special learners

- All will enjoy this song. The words may be difficult, but children who have special needs could perhaps join in on "Ma-ma, Ma-ma, Ma-ma" and play this rhythm on a tambourine or a cabasa.

Kagome

This well-known song is a favourite with Japanese children, and has also become a favourite with children who have sung it in Canada.

Grades

2 and 3

Concepts

☐ Sound awareness;   ☐ socialization.

English words Keith Bissell
arrangement Lois Birkenshaw-Fleming

Ka - go - me, Ka - go - me, In the cage you have to stay

You can ne - ver fly a - way, We shall guard you night and day,

slowly

Duck and swal - low, all fall down! Who's be - hind you? Can you say?

Process

Movement game

Formation: children in a circle, holding hands, with one in the middle, eyes tightly shut.

1 All sing, walking slowly in a circle around the middle child.

2 At "Duck and swallow all fall down," everyone in the circle squats down in place and sings the last line: "Who's behind you? Can you say?"

3 During the last line the teacher gives a silent signal to one child who goes quietly to stand behind the child in the middle. He or she sings on one or two notes: "Who am I?" or "Guess who I am?" or "Who do you think I am?"

4 If the first child has trouble guessing, have the other child "sing" clues such as: "I have red hair" or "I have a blue shirt on" until the correct name is guessed.

5 The children change places and the game is repeated with a new person in the centre.

6 Try the very simple accompaniment if this suits the needs of your group.

Obwisana

Grades

K through 3

Concepts

☐ Beat;   ☐ cross rhythms
☐ eye–hand co-ordination;

children's song and game

Ob – wi – sa – na   sa   na – na,   Ob – wi – sa – na   sa.

Ob – wi – sa – na   sa   na – na,   Ob – wi – sa – na   sa.

Process

This little passing game can be played on several levels of difficulty. Sticks or small stones can be used equally well as objects to pass.

1 The children kneel or sit cross-legged in a circle. Each child has one stick (or stone) on the floor in front of him or her. On beat one, the children pick up their sticks. On beat two they put them down in front of the child on their right. Beats three and four repeat the actions of beats one and two.

2　Repeat to the end of the song.

3　Start slowly, gradually increasing the tempo as the children gain confidence.

4　For a more difficult variation, the children are in the circle formation as before but this time they have two sticks (or small stones) in front of them. On beat one both sticks are picked up. On beat two, they are tapped together. On beat three they are passed to the right as before and placed in front of the child seated on the right. On the fourth beat the pattern is repeated.

5　This gives an action in three beats done with a song in 4/4 time but most children can master the task without too many problems!

Special learners

● The first game would probably be possible for most students if it were played at a slow tempo. The more challenging one might prove impossible. Have the child with difficulties play a steady beat on a drum to accompany the rest or devise a different passing pattern that has four beats (pick up, tap, tap, put down).

Early in the Morning (Kum Bahur)

Grades

4 through 6

Concepts

☐ Form: a round;　　　　　　　　　　☐ changing chord accompaniment.

Process

1   Sing the song in unison, playing the root of the chords on a melodic instrument. Have the students discover that the accompaniment changes in the third measure of each line: C–C–G–C. Discover that the change goes to the fifth of the scale so the chord symbols would be: I–I–V–I.

2   Sing the song starting on different notes, for example D, E♭, B, B♭, or F. Let the students find out which notes would be the first and fifth of each scale. Play the roots of the chords in the different keys.

3   When the song is known well, teach the written accompaniment.

4   Sing the song as a three-part round.

Hill and Gully Rider

Grades

3 through 5

Concepts

- ☐ Syncopation;
- ☐ form;
- ☐ phrasing;

- ☐ extracting rhythms from melody;
- ☐ creativity.

traditional Jamaican folk song
arrangement Helen Neufeld

Hill and gul - ly ri - der hill and __ gul - ly,

Hill and gul - ly ri - der hill and __ gul - ly, Took my

horse and come down, hill and _ gul -ly, But my horse done stum-ble down

hill and _ gul -ly, And the night -time come and tum-ble down, hill and _ gul -ly.

unpitched percussion

coconut shells

BB   (F bar)

2   Oh, the moon shine bright down,
     Hill and gully
     Ain't no place to hide in town,
     Hill and gully.
     And a zombie come a-riding down,
     Hill and gully.

3   Oh my knees they shake down, ...
    And my heart starts quaking down, ...
    Ain't nobody going to get me down, ...

4   That's the last I set down, ...
    Pray the lord don't let me down, ...
    And I run 'till daylight breaking down, ...

Process

1   Introduce the song.

2   Write out the rhythmic notation and clap this, identifying the syncopation.

3   Teach the melody of the song either by rote or by reading.

4   Identify phrases and find repeated measures.

5   Isolate rhythmic motifs and clap these, especially "hill and gully" and "hill and gully rider".

6   Teach the bass bar and tone bar parts, then the rest of the accompaniment. (If you do not have bass bars, substitute a bass xylophone or bass drum.)

7   Practise singing with accompaniment. Decide on the form.

8   Layer the percussion accompaniment parts according to the decided plan.

9   Have those students in the class who are not playing clap the rhythm of the song. Transfer this rhythm to temple blocks.

10 Teach the movement.

11 Put it all together. Perform all verses with singing and percussion interludes.

Movement

Measure 1	right foot steps right, left foot joins, bend knees, come up;
measure 2	left foot steps left, right foot joins, bend knees, come up;
measures 3–4	repeat the first two measures;
measure 5	sway to right, sway to left;
measure 6	right foot steps right, left foot joins, bend knees, come up;
measure 7	sway to left, sway to right;
measure 8	left foot steps left, right joins, bend knees, come up;
measure 9	turn around in four counts;
measure 10	bend knees, come up, jump ¼ turn to left, snap.

● Repeat for each verse, facing the four different directions.

Final form

Introduction	percussion;
verse 1	singing, movement and tone bar;
interlude	
verse 2	accompaniment, movement, plus some unpitched percussion;

interlude
    verse 3   accompaniment, movement, plus other percussion;
interlude
    verse 4   same as verse 3;
      coda

- For the introduction, layer the percussion, perhaps beginning with bass bar (or large bass drum), then bongo, coconut shells (or woodblock), maracas and cowbell, each entering after one measure. When all have entered, continue percussion, adding the temple blocks playing the rhythm of the song over the other instruments.
- Some combination of these instruments can play eight or ten measures for interludes and a coda. Have the students decide which to use.
- Have the students create other verses. This is a simple task because they have to think of three statements that tell a story. The "Hill and gully" is repeated after each line.

Special learners

- Students with language and speech difficulties can just sung the words "Hill and gully" on the one note each time they appear. This rhythm could be played on a drum very easily.

Rise Up, O Flame

A wonderful round that has been sung around campfires for generations, it evokes the element of fire which from ancient times has symbolized the energy of life.

Grades

3, 4 and up

Holidays

Gobble, Gobble

Grades

K through 2

Concepts

❑ Solo singing;   ❑ ABA form.

❑ language development;

anonymous arr Alison Kenny-Gardhouse

Gob - ble, gob - ble, gob - ble, gob - ble says the tur - key big and fat

Gob - ble, gob - ble, gob - ble, gob - ble I want food and that's that!

What do you want lit - tle tur - key? I would like some _____

Process

1 Introduce the piece first as a poem. Children learn by echoing one line at a time. Be expressive!

2 Use the poem as an A section and a hand drum improvisation (played by the leader or perhaps a skilled student) as B. The children stand still during the A section and "mime" turkeys during the B section.

3 Introduce the melody. The children can continue to be turkeys while the leader alone sings the song several times.

4 The children skip as the leader sings the song. (The song could be accompanied with a hand drum.) When the song ends, the leader sings to one child the question "What do you want little turkey?" The chosen child responds by singing, "I would like some spaghetti" (or hay, pizza, marshmallows, etc.). The leader pretends to produce the food from the hand drum and the child "gobbles it up".

5 Continue until everyone has had a turn.

Special learners

● This song is excellent for slow learners. They might not be able to answer in complete sentences, but they could ask for things that they would "like".

Turkey in the Pan

Grades

1 and 2

Concepts

☐ Beat;
☐ rondo form;
☐ listening;

☐ memory retention;
☐ language development.

> Turkey in the pan,
> Turkey in the pan,
> Turkey with ————
> Eat it if you can.

Process

1 Sit in a circle formation.

2 Talk about the different items of food that you might eat with turkey, either at Thanksgiving, Christmas, or any other time of the year.

3 Teach the poem through echo imitation.

4 Demonstrate substituting names of food in the blank part of the poem.

5 Once this concept is secure, begin the game.

6 Recite the speech pattern, patsching the beat.

7 Each child around the circle has a chance to substitute the name of a food as the game is repeated.

8 The word must be one that hasn't been used before, and it must be spoken on the beat.

9 Try different categories, such as vegetables, traditional holiday fare, purple food, junk food, and so on.

Extensions

● Try composing your own food speech-pattern with the group, for example:

> Eggs in a pan,
> Eggs in a pan,
> Eggs with ————
> Eat them if you can.

> Monster Mash in the pan,
> Monster Mash in the pan,
> Monster Mash with ————
> Eat it if you can.

(Contributed by Angela Elster)

188

Here We Go Trick or Treat

Grades

1 through 4

Concepts

☐ Rhythm;   ☐ *so–mi* practice.

Part A

words Joe Berarducci

Part B

189

Process

1 Teach the children the song, without the accompaniment if the group is young. They will recognize the melody as "Looby-loo", so the learning process will be easy.

2 Have the group stand in a circle holding hands with one child outside.

3 Depending on the age and ability of the children, have the circle hold hands and skip eight times sideways to the right, two skips to each measure, then eight times to the left, while the child outside the circle skips round in one direction for the eight measures.

4 The person nearest the outside child then turns to face him or her. Everyone recites part B while the two who are facing perform this body percussion part:

clap partner's
clap
patsch

5 At the end the outside child sings on two notes (*so*, *mi*) or says:

> Trick or treat,
> Trick or treat,
> Change with me
> And keep the beat.

6 The two facing partners change places and the game is repeated with the new person on the outside of the circle.

7 One person can play the rhythm pattern of part B on claves or a woodblock.

8 If you are working with an older group, add the accompaniment.

L'Halloween s'improvise

Clientèle

4e à 6e années

Démarche pédagogique

1 Sur des musiques inspirées des thèmes de l'Halloween, l'enseignant fait circuler les enfants derrière un drap éclairé par l'arrière (principe des ombres chinoises), en leur demandant d'exprimer corporellement ce que suggèrent les musiques.

2 Chaque enfant, avec l'instrument de son choix, improvise au sein du groupe selon les thèmes ou les sentiments reliés à la fête de l'Halloween. L'enseignant tient le rôle d'animateur et de chef d'orchestre.

3 L'enseignant propose un sentiment et contrôle l'ensemble dans son jeu instrumental.

4 Faire prendre conscience des effets intéressants en terme de: crescendo, diminuendo, tensions mélodiques, effets de surprise, accelerando, etc.

5 Les enfants sont regroupés en équipe de cinq ou six. Chaque équipe pige un thème relié à l'Halloween. Avant la présentation, chaque groupe a droit à une minute de préparation pour planifier son scénario et la participation de chaque membre de l'équipe. La présentation derrière l'écran (ombres chinoises) sera accompagnée par une trame sonore vocale et / ou instrumentale improvisée par l'équipe.

6 Après la présentation de chaque équipe, la classe relève les meilleurs éléments des improvisations afin de créer collectivement une histoire qui sera mimée derrière l'écran et sonorisée.

● Thèmes suggérés pour l'activité (étape no 5 dans la démarche): la tempête dans la nuit; la maison hantée; les fantômes en concert; la parade des costumes; la danse des sorcières; le sac de bonbons; le réveil des squelettes; la ballade des chats noirs.

(Contribution de Sylvie Guertin et Chantale Parent)

Hallowe'en Night

Grades

2 and 3

Concept

☐ Creating sound effects.

> I saw a ghost on Hallowe'en night.
> I saw a ghost, all spooky white.
>
> But ...
>
> > I wasn't scared.
> > I knew what to do.
> > I stared at that ghost,
> > And I yelled "BOO!"
>
> Up flew that ghost. It cried in fright.
> It screamed and ran right out of sight.
> I scared that ghost with all my might.
> I scared that ghost on Hallowe'en night.

Robert Heidbreder

Process

1 Have the children learn the poem and say it dramatically with different voice inflections. The first two lines could be said in a rather scared voice and the last part of the poem with growing confidence. The "BOO!", of course, is the climax of the piece.

Sound effects

● Have the children create ghostly sound effects. Here are some ideas: playing slow, very quiet notes on metallophones or gongs; rubbing hands lightly over drum heads;

scrunching Styrofoam cups together; saying "Ooooooooo" very quietly in ghostly voices; rattling claves together to imitate skeletons rattling.

● The poem could be acted out.

Special learners

● Be very careful not to upset children with sounds and actions that are too scary. Saying the poem dramatically with sound effects in a darkened room, for instance, could lead to serious upsets.

La danse des squelettes

Clientèle

1e à 3e années

Concept

❐ Le mode dorien (*ré*).

paroles Dominique Chauveau
musique Claire Rousseau

Démarche pédagogique

1 Improviser huit pulsations avec des bruits de bouche, des onomatopées pour créer l'ambience d'Halloween.

2 Reprendre la chanson en changeant deux mots: par exemple, "Sorcières" à la place de "squelettes"; "chaumière" à la place de "cachette". Une nouvelle série de bruits de bouche peut être improvisé sur huit pulsations pour imiter les sorcières.

3 On peut aussi ajouter des mouvements.

Shell Out, Shell Out

Grades

K and 1

Concepts

❑ Self-confidence;   ❑ language development.

> Here we go dancing through the town,
>   Shell out, shell out we say!
> We wander up the street and down,
>   Shell out, shell out we say!
> John is a goblin, Jessie's a ghost,
>   Shell out, shell out we say!
> We're out to scare you, that is our boast,
>   Shell out, shell out we say!
> Mary's a princess, Ned a black cat,
>   Shell out, shell out we say!
> Nina's a witch with a big black hat,
>   Shell out, shell out we say!
> Here we go dancing through the town,
>   Shell out, shell out we say
> We wander up the street and down,
>   Shell out, shell out we say!

Marianne Kennedy

Process

1 Substitute actual children's names and the characters they portray. Give everyone a turn, even though this may take several repeats of the poem. Singling the children out like this gives them a sense of importance and self-worth.

2 It may be difficult to include the names of all the characters in the rhyming pattern (Ninja Turtles and similar names do make difficulties). The poem can be said using numbers instead of names:

> One is a goblin, one is a ghost,
> Two are princesses and one a black cat …

3 Point to the various children in turn.

4   One child could play the drum for the rhythm pattern of the chorus.

Shell   out,   shell out   I   say!

Special learners

● This is an excellent activity because each child is made to feel important.
● If some children have difficulty saying all the words, have them learn and say only "Shell out, shell out we say!"

Hanukkah

Grades

1 through 4

Concepts

☐ Beat;
☐ rhythm;
☐ creativity;
☐ vocabulary development.

Process

This activity tells the story of Hanukkah. You will need a Menorah, some candles, a dreydl, Hanukkah gelt and a picture of an oil lamp.

All sing

Spin   lit - tle   drey - dl   Ha - nuk - kah   will   come,

Spin   lit - tle   drey - dl   Soon   your   spin - ning's   done.

Narrator

Hanukkah is an important Jewish holiday which is celebrated in December. It is a joyous time for children and adults.

All sing (using the above melody) and patsch to the beat

Light the Menorah, Hanukkah is here,
Light the Menorah, Hanukkah is here.

Narrator

Hanukkah lasts for eight days. Each night a candle in the Menorah is lit at sundown. By the eighth night all candles are lit. An extra candle, or "shammash", is used to light the other candles. The shammash stays lit every night. (Demonstrate all this.)

194

All sing (melody as before)

> Burn little shammash, Hanukkah is here …

Narrator

Long ago the Jewish people won a great victory over their enemies, but when they took back their temple they found that there was just enough sacred oil for the holy lamp to last for one night. Then a great miracle happened – the lamp burned for eight days and nights. Hanukkah is a time to remember and celebrate this miracle.

All sing

> A miracle, a miracle, Hanukkah is here …

Narrator

Children are given presents which sometimes take the form of chocolate money called "gelt". Families celebrate with special food such as apple sauce and latkes. Latkes are potato pancakes.

All sing

> Apple sauce and latkes, Hanukkah is here …

Narrator

Children play a game with dreydls. A dreydl is a spinning top with four sides. There is a Hebrew letter on each side. These are the first letters of the four words "Nes", "Gadol", "Hayah" and "Sham", which mean "A great miracle happened here".

All sing

> Spin little dreydl, Hanukkah is here …

The leader asks questions; the children answer, clapping the rhythm:

How long does Hanukkah last?
    eight days
What are some special Hanukkah foods?
    apple sauce, latkes
What special presents are children given?
    gelt
What is a spinning top called?
    a dreydl
What happened on Hanukkah?
    a miracle

These activities tell the story of Hanukkah in terms that young children can understand. Adapt them to suit the needs of the children you are teaching.

- A simple bordun pattern of D and A can be played on the beat on a xylophone to accompany the song.

(Contributed by Dawn Davis)

The following are two Hanukkah songs and a poem that could be sung with young children at this time of the year.

Count the Candles

words and music Lois Birkenshaw-Fleming

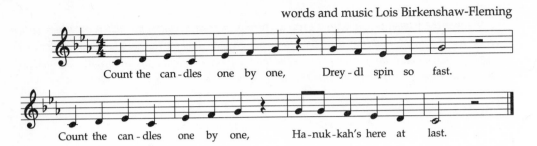

Count the can-dles one by one, Drey-dl spin so fast.

Count the can-dles one by one, Ha-nuk-kah's here at last.

Process

1 Sing this song. Count the candles on the Menorah and sing the song again.

2 It could be accompanied by a simple bordun of C and G, played on a xylophone.

Hanukkah Song

traditional

One lit-tle can-dle burn, burn, burn, Ha-nuk-kah is here.

One lit-tle can-dle burn, burn, burn, Ha-nuk-kah is here.

2 Two little candles burn, burn, burn,
   Hanukkah is here,
   Two little candles burn, burn, burn,
   Hanukkah is here.

3 Three little candles …

4 Four little candles …

5 Five little candles …

6 Six little candles …

7 Seven little candles …

8 Eight little candles …

Process

1 The song can be sung each night as a lighted candle is added. It can also be sung in a group as the whole activity of lighting the eight candles is worked out.

196

2   When all the candles are lit, sing the last verse:

> 9   Dance little candles, dance, dance, dance,
>   Hanukkah is here,
>   Dance little candles, dance, dance, dance,
>   Hanukkah is here.

Poem for Hanukkah

Grades

1 through 3

Concepts

☐ Vocabulary development.

> Hanukkah, Hanukkah
> We can hardly wait,
> Hanukkah, Hanukkah,
> Hurry don't be late!
>
> Apple sauce and latkes,
> Fill up your plate,
> Hanukkah is here now,
> Hurry, don't be late!
>
> Spin little dreydl,
> Whirring sound you make,
> Hanukkah is here now,
> Hurry don't be late!

Dawn Davis

Process

1   Create a body percussion accompaniment to go with the poem.

2   Use the poem with one or two of the Hanukkah songs to make a little unit.

● There are many other well known Hanukkah songs such as "I Have a Little Dreydl" and "Hanukkah is Here at Last". These could be included in the unit as well.

Special learners

● All the Hanukkah material in this book would be useful for slow learners. There is a lot of repetition in the words and music. The music is easy to sing and there are many opportunities for everyone to contribute ideas for sound effects and dramatization.

Bethlehem Lay Sleeping

Grades

3 and 4

Concepts

☐ Melody with *fa*;
☐ cross-over bordun.

Polish carol
arrangement Diane Shieron

lit - tle Je - sus was his name, so Long, long a - go (long, long a - go).

2 Kings came to adore Him, Long, so long ago,
   They knelt down before Him, Long, so long ago,
   Wand'ring shepherds left their sheep
   To see their little Lord asleep, Long, long ago (echo).

3 Angels sweetly singing, Long, so long ago,
   Sent His praises ringing, Long, so long ago,
   Children, too, their love may bring
   To Him who came to be our King, Long, long ago (echo).

Process

1 Teach the song with all three verses.

2 Teach the cross-over pattern on the knees, then transfer it to the bass xylophone.

3 Teach the alto xylophone part by telling the children that they play after they hear "ago".

4 Teach the glockenspiel part by first clapping it and "playing" a glissando in the air.

5 The percussion part may be played by finger cymbals or a triangle, or you might alternate these.

Special learners

● The repeated phrases "Long, so long ago" and "Long, long ago" can be learned and sung by students who would have difficulty learning the rest of the words.

Il est né

Grades

Upper elementary choir and Orff withdrawal groups

Concepts

☐ I–V accompaniment;

☐ harmony;

☐ *ré* mineur pentatonique authentique.

traditional French carol
arrangement Helen Neufeld

2   Qu'il est beau, comme il est charmant!
     Que ses grâces sont donc parfaites.
     Qu'il est beau, comme il est charmant!
     Qu'il est doux, qu'il paraît aimant.

3   Une étable est son logement,
     Un peu de paille est sa couchette.
     Une étable est son logement,
     Pour un Dieu quel abaissement!

4   Partez, ô rois de l'Orient,
     Venez vous unir à nos fêtes.
     Partez, ô rois de l'Orient,
     Venez adorer cet Enfant.

5   O Jésus! ô Roi tout puissant,
     Tout petit enfant que vous êtes.
     O Jésus! ô Roi tout puissant,
     Régnez sur nous entièrement.

1   He is born, the holy Child,
     Play the oboe and bagpipes merrily,
     He is born the holy Child,
     Sing we all of the Saviour now.

2   O how lovely, O how pure,
     Is this perfect Child of Heaven;
     O how lovely, O how pure,
     Gracious gift of God to man!

3   Jesus, Lord of all the world,
     Coming as a Child among us,
     Jesus, Lord of all the world,
     Grant to us Thy heav'nly peace.

Process

1   Teach the melodies of the refrain and couplets as note-reading exercises, the refrain for recorder and the verses in thirds for glockenspiels or voices.

2   There are several verses. In performance, these could be divided among different class groups with all joining in on the chorus.

3   Play the melody and harmony of the third verse on recorders, sometimes with singing and sometimes alone with the instrumental accompaniment.

4   As a listening lesson let the students discover the changes of harmony and indicate them in movement. Clap the bass xylophone part on the left side for the Gs and the right side for Ds. Identify which phrases need a V(D) harmony and which need a I(G), and on which words the changes occur. Do this for the first verse only.

5   Teach the instrumental accompaniments and combine them with the singing.

Christmas Polka

Grades

4 and 5

Concepts

❏ I–V accompaniment.

Slovakian folk song
arr Gaynor Low

Process

1   Teach the song and the accompaniment. This is an excellent song for reviewing I–V chording.

2   The introduction and ostinato for the first part imitates the great joyous sound of church- and clock-tower bells.

3   Add drums and tambourines at the refrain. They could play some variation of the polka rhythm ♩. ♪| ♩ ♩

4   Create a dance using the polka step – right, left, right; left, right, left – to the polka rhythm.

204

Wind Through the Olive Trees

Grades

4 and 5

Concepts

- ❏ Triple metre;
- ❏ I–V accompaniments;
- ❏ AABA form.

words and music anonymous
arrangement Diane Shieron

Winds through the o - live trees soft - ly did blow. _____

'round lit - tle Beth - le - hem long, long a - go.

Sheep on the hill - side lay white as the snow _____

Shep - herds were watch - ing them long, long a - go.

Process

1 Teach the song, having the students perform a body percussion part that will show the triple metre. Pat–clap–clap would be one, pat–clap–snap another. Ask the students to create their own.

2 Teach the bass xylophone part, singing it in tonic *sol-fa* using the hand signs. Sing the part using the note names. The students will quickly hear that the third phrase has a different harmonic progression while the fourth phrase is the same as the first two.

3 Play the accompaniment on the bass xylophone.

4 Teach the alto xylophone part and add it to the bass to accompany the song.

5   The glockenspiel part is difficult. Coming in on the second beat takes practice. Start by gently patting the knees on the first beat and then clapping the instrumental part. Then play on the glockenspiel, playing "in the air" on the first beat and on the instrumental on the second.

6   Add the tambourine. Note the change in measures 9–12.

7   Put it all together and add the singing.

8   Recorders could play the melody as it is fairly straightforward.

Final form

Sing the entire song with accompaniment.

Play the melody on recorders with accompaniment for the first eight measures, then add the singing for the remainder of the song.

An introduction and an interlude could be created by playing two or four measures of the accompaniment.

New Year's Song

Grades

3 through 5

Concepts

❑ Integration of chant, song and body percussion.

words and music Gaynor Low

A brand new year has star-ted, so, come sing with me. We'll

sing and play to-ge-ther, and hap-py we will be.

Process

Movement game

1   The students form a circle, holding hands and standing beside their partners.

2   They sing the song and skip to the right seven times, changing direction on the eighth beat.

3   Then the students skip to the left seven times, turning to face their partners on the eighth beat.

4　They say the chant once, performing these actions:

clap partner's hands
clap
patsch

5　The students repeat the chant, but on the last two measures pass right shoulder to right shoulder with their partners and walk four steps to meet a new partner coming the other way. Patsch during the walking and perform the last measure (clap, clap, clap partner's hands with new partner).

6　Create a little two-measure rhythmic introduction to be played on a percussion instrument such as a drum. This will give time for the children to get ready to begin again.

7　Repeat whole sequence, starting with the song.

Chant

> New Year's Day, New Year's Day
> We'll make our resolutions on
> New Year's Day.

Instruments

A simple accompaniment might be:

Extensions

- Change "year" to "month", "day", "week", and so on.
- The chant will also have to be changed:

> A brand new day, A brand new day,
> We'll sing and play together on this brand new day!

Purim's Here

Purim is a Jewish festival of celebration. The events connected with it are as joyous as the music.

Grades

4 through 6

Concepts

☐ AB form;　　　　　　　　　☐ recorder.
☐ dance;

208

Process

Dance

Formation: small circles of five to six chidren, placed around the room, standing tall and proud.

A section

1 Place hands on your neighbour's shoulders (but not around their neck);
2 step to the right with the right foot, close with the left; repeat;
3 step to the left with the left foot, close with the right; repeat;
4 when moving to the right, face right, when moving left, face left;
5 repeat the whole pattern.

B section

1 Take your hands from shoulders and join them with your neighbour's, then walk into the circle in the rhythm

             right,   left,   right left right

the last three are stamps: raise your arms;

2 repeat the walk-and-stamp pattern back out of the circle; lower your arms;
3 repeat the whole pattern.

At the end of the B section, quickly return your hands to your neighbour's shoulders – as in the A section – so the dance can be repeated without any break.

Instrumental

1 Play the melody on recorders (or sing it to a neutral syllable: "lah" or "lai").

2 Add tambourines and drums for interest. The drums could play a simple rhythm throughout, with the tambourine joining on the B section. Here are some suggestions:

(Contributed by Carolyn Hernandez)

209

As I Went Out to Play

Grades

K through 2

Concepts

☐ Pitch;

☐ movement;

☐ dramatization;

☐ language development;

☐ creativity.

words and music Birthe Kulich

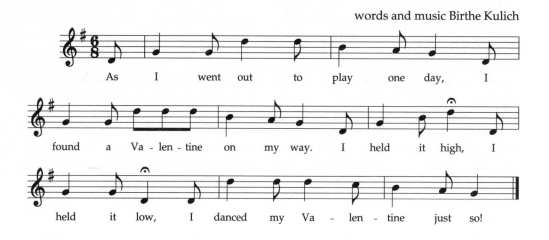

Process

1 Sing the song with the children sitting in a circle.

2 Put four or five Valentines on the floor in the middle.

3 Have four or five children (the number depends on the size of the group and the space available) skip around for the first four measures, pick up a Valentine, hold it up high and then hold it low. Finish the song by dancing with the Valentine.

4 Put the Valentines back on the floor and repeat with different children.

Extensions

● Ask the children where else they might go out to play and what they might find there. The rhythm of the song might have to be changed. Indeed, some rests might have to be substituted for notes, depending on the rhythm of the new words and the number of syllables.

> As I went to the woods one day, I found an acorn on my way,
> I held it high, I held it low, I held my acorn – just so.
>
> As I went to the beach … seashell …

Le messager des baisers

Clientèle

1e à 3e années

Partie A

paroles et musique Guylaine Myre

Je suis le p'tit mes - sa - ger de ton va - len - tin gê - né,

pour toi il a com - po - sé la me - lo - die des bai - sers

Partie B

la, la, la, la, la *(baisers)* la, la, la, la, la

la, la, la la, la, la, la, la

Accompagnement

CS
CA

XA

XB
MB

Démarche pédagogique

Danse

1 Pendant la partie A, les enfants font une ronde en chantant.

2 À la partie B, ils s'arrêtent et font avec leur voisin ce jeu de mains:

baisers
mains avec
partenaire
mains
cuisses

Valentine Poems and Sayings

Here is a collection of Valentine poems and sayings. Some of these have been written in Valentine cards and autograph books of children (mostly girls) for generations.

> Remember me on the river,
> Remember me on the lake,
> Remember me on your wedding day
> And save me a piece of your cake.
>
> When you are washing in the tub,
> Think of me before you scrub.
> If the water is too hot,
> Cool it but forget-me-not.
>
> When you are old and cannot see,
> Put on your specs and think of me.
>
> May your life be like a piano,
> Straight, upright and grand.

These rhymes are fun to say and can be used with songs to form a Valentine unit.

Some of these poems lend themselves to a body percussion accompaniment.

arrangement Carolyn McMillan

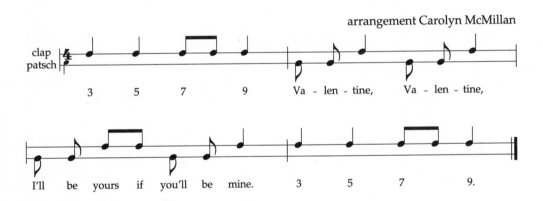

Ukranian Lullaby

This beautiful melody would be suitable for use with older students who have had some Orff experience. The arrangement is fairly challenging.

traditional
English translation and arrangement Marcelline Moody

In the man - ger bare. _____ See the Christ _ Child _ there. _____

Si - lent - ly, An - gels their watch now are keep - ing,
Soft - ly, your mo - ther will sing while you're sleep - ing

Lul - ly, Lul - ly, Sleep lit - tle Ba - by sleep.

Accompany throughout with the following:

* (can be two players)

Recorder interlude:

* (or SR written an octave lower)

213

Continue the accompaniment above, and add the following SG and AX parts or play entirely unaccompanied.

Repeat the song with the original accompaniment plus the SG and AX parts, and add the following parts for AG and bass bars:

End with three measures of accompaniment played very quietly and coming to rest on D, F♯ and A on the first beat of measure 4.

214

CHAPTER SIXTEEN

Basics

This section contains songs, poems and activities that help to develop knowledge of concepts such as months of the year, days of the week, counting, colours, and so on. While the children are enjoying singing and playing, they are learning these concepts almost subliminally and at the same time developing their musical skills.

Many of the songs and poems have words that can be changed to include more vocabulary.

Breakfast Song

Grades

K through 2

Concepts

❏ Beat;   ❏ language development.
❏ rhythm pattern;

words and music Ruth Berger

The things I eat for break-fast are ea - sy to des - cribe.

Hot things and cold things, All feel good in - side.

Process

1 Sing the song and have the children clap and/or pat the steady beat (on their knees, heads, toes, …).

2 Play the beat on an unpitched percussion instrument such as a drum or the claves.

3 Set up two instruments in F pentatonic and have two children at a time play any note (on the beat) to accompany the song.

4   Try a steady bordun of F/C together or with alternate hands (a broken bordun).

5   Talk about what the children have had for breakfast. Have everyone choose one food that is their favourite.

6   Have four children stand at the front of the room, each holding a drum, tambourine, claves or tic-toc block.

7   Sing the song with accompaniment. At the end the children at the front say their favourite food and play the rhythm pattern on their instruments, one at a time. They each might repeat it several times.

8   Choose four more to come up and repeat the song and activity.

9   For extra interest, have a child play a glissando on a glockenspiel in between each food (replace the B with a B♭).

Pizza

Gonna make a pizza
Gonna make it fast

Gonna eat it slowly
Gonna make it last

Gonna add tomatoes
Pepperoni too

Gonna make a pizza
And share it, with you.

Sonja Dunn

● Use this delightful little poem when working with the subject of food.

A Lemon and a Pickle

Grades

3 and 4

Concepts

☐ Reinforcement of tic-a ti, ti tic-a and tic-a-tac-a rhythm patterns;
☐ rhythmic independence;
☐ rondo form;
☐ creativity.

Process

1 Teach the verse rhythmically, with attention to dynamics and inflection.

2 Keep the beat while saying the verse (by clapping, stamping, patschen, and so on).

3 Notate the rhythm pattern of the body percussion ostinato

4 Say the rhythm names of this ostinato.

5 Divide the class into two groups: one group says the verse and the other group says the rhythm names of the ostinato. The rhythm of the ostinato can be changed to suit the abilities and experience of the children and to focus on your objectives.

6 Perform the rhythm of the ostinato on one level of body percussion (for example, clapping), and say the verse at the same time.

7 Perform the ostinato as written using the three levels of body percussion and say the verse at the same time.

8 Have the children think of favourite foods that go together and create a two-measure pattern:

Rondo form

A Lemon and pickle verse with body percussion ostinato;
B first favourite food pattern, done four times:
    1 saying words,
    2 clapping rhythm,
    3 saying rhythm names,
    4 clapping rhythm;
A as before;
C second favourite food pattern, same treatment as section B;
A as before;
D third favourite food pattern, same treatment as section B;
A as before.

(Contributed by Carolyn McMillan)

Diddle Diddle Dumpling

This poem is from the Mother Goose heritage which forms the basis of the folklore of English-speaking children the world over.

Grades

2 and 3

Concepts

☐ Use familiar verse in challenging way;   ☐ listening.
☐ verbal ostinato;

218

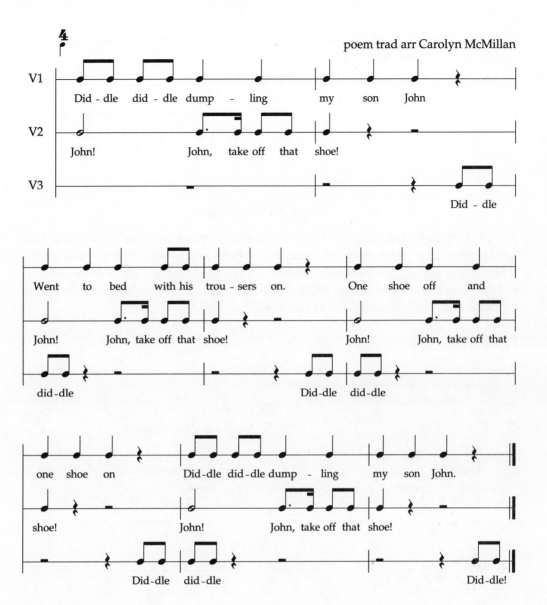

poem trad arr Carolyn McMillan

Process

1 Teach the text ensuring that the rhythm is secure. Note the rests. (The text could be used to review the basic rhythm names.)

2 Teach the second ostinato. Find the clue in the text for the entry of this ostinato (the rest).

3 Divide the group in two: one says the poem, the other the ostinato.

4 Teach ostinato number 1. Note the length of "John", the rhythm and the rests.

5 Divide into two groups: one says the poem, the other the ostinato.

6   Divide the class into three groups: one says the poem, the second, ostinato number 1, and the third, ostinato number 2.

7   Play the rhythms of the ostinati on unpitched percussion instruments and use them as an additional accompaniment for the text.

(Contributed by Carolyn McMillan)

Davey Dumpling

Advertising jingles are written to be remembered (by children as well as adults). This arrangement uses one of the most successful of these jingles and combines this with a creative variation of "Diddle Diddle Dumpling". The basic rhythm pattern of the ostinato can be found in many beloved children's songs. The company that used the jingle capitalized on this familiarity and its elemental nature.

Grades

K and 1

Concepts

❑ Beat;   ❑ creativity;
❑ AB or ABA form;   ❑ language development.

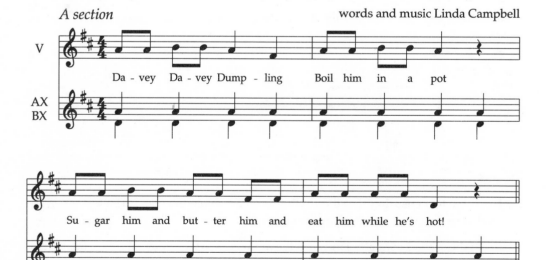

Bass and alto xylophones keep the beat as in section A while the above is said.

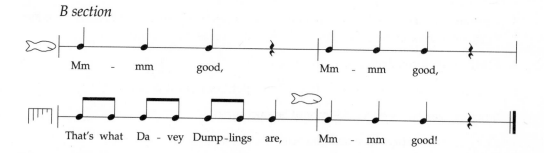

Mm - mm good, Mm - mm good,

That's what Da - vey Dump-lings are, Mm - mm good!

Extensions

- Can the children use this basic pattern and change the words to create new songs?

Donny, Donny donut,
Cook him in the pot.
Sugar him and eat him,
Yum! that hits the spot.

Special learners

- Using a pattern or form such as this makes it easier for children to create new words and poems. These activities can lead to improved reading skills if the creations are written down and used for reading practice. Because they are the children's own creations, they will generate great interest.

I Love to Read

Grades

2 through 4

Concepts

☐ Beat;
☐ rondo form;
☐ creativity;

☐ vocabulary development;
☐ memory retention.

I read in the morning,
I read at night,
I read, read, read
Every book in sight

Angela Elster

Process

1 Teach the chant by rote.

2 In a seated circle formation recite the chant while patching the beat.

221

3   Once secure, discuss the various things we read, such as the titles and types of books, magazines, newspapers, billboards, the backs of cereal boxes, and so on.

4   Have the children decide on one or two ideas.

5   The children say their idea(s) between the repetitions of the chant.

6   Once an idea has been used it cannot be said again.

7   Complete the entire circle and end with the chant.

8   For an even greater challenge try repeating all the ideas backwards as they accumulate.

On the Ball

Grades

2 through 4

Concepts

☐ Beat;
☐ numerical awareness;
☐ practice of multiples;

☐ listening;
☐ development of the ability to think ahead.

Process

1   In a circle formation a ball is passed from child to child. Everyone counts out loud as the ball is passed.

2   When this is secure, repeat the pattern, but this time on the number "five" – or any multiple of "five" – the ball is tapped on the floor instead of being passed, and the number is not said out loud. The trick is to keep the steady beat and pass to the next person on the next number.

3   If a child says a multiple of "five", or incorrectly says a different number, to keep everyone in the game, correct the problem and continue. If your group of children is comfortable with the elimination technique, the child who has made the mistake goes into the centre of the circle and tries to detect the next error. He/she changes places with the child who has committed that error and the game continues.

Extensions

●   Try using more difficult multiples – 3, 6, 9, ... or 4, 8, 12, ...
●   Try reversing the format, saying only the multiples out loud and internalizing the other numbers.
●   Change the direction of the ball at the sound of a selected instrument such as a triangle.

(Contributed by Angela Elster)

Where Are You Going?

Grades

2 and 3

Concepts

☐ Triple metre;   ☐ creativity.

☐ vocabulary development;

trad arr Keith Bissell

Where are __ you __ go - ing, go - ing, go - ing,
I'm go-ing to __ mar - ket, mar - ket, mar - ket,

Where are __ you __ go - ing this morn - ing so fair?
I'm go-ing to __ mar - ket, this morn - ing so fair.

223

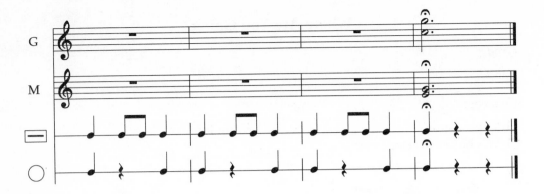

Process

1 Teach the song by rote.

2 Sing and add the body percussion accompaniment of patsch, clap, clap.

3 Have the children count the body percussion, saying "1" on the patsch. They will quickly discover that there are three beats to each measure: triple metre.

4 Teach the accompaniment, working it out first in body percussion.

5 Clap the hand drum and woodblock parts while singing the song. These can also be written on the board or on chart paper, and the time names may be said by the children as they clap.

6 Create other answers to the question "Where are you going?" The rhythm of the melody might have to be changed slightly.

> I'm going to the meat store …
> I'm going to school now …
> I'm going to walk my dog …
> I'm going to the park now …

New Shoes

Ages

2 through 5

Concepts

☐ Beat;   ☐ vocabulary development (colours).
☐ tone matching;

words and music Ruth Berger

New   shoes,   new   shoes,   which   co - lour   do   you   choose?

224

Process

1   Children sit in a circle. Place paper "shoes" of different colours on the floor in the middle. One child is chosen, the song is sung and if the child is

      age 2–3   s/he goes into the middle, chooses a shoe and perhaps names its colour;

      age 4   the chosen child walks into the middle, picks up a shoe and answers the question in the song by singing the colour (on *so–mi* if possible);

      age 5   the child chooses and sings a complete sentence – for example, "I choose yellow" – on two pitches (*so–mi*) or three (*so–mi–la–so–mi*).

2   The words could be changed to other items of clothing – hats, scarves, socks, and so on. This will develop the children's vocabulary even further.

Special learners

●   This is an excellent song for special learners. It develops vocabulary and it gives individual children ability-related tasks thereby ensuring success and building self-confidence.

●   The activities can be adapted for children in wheelchairs, and the colours can be signed for deaf children who are in a signing program.

Loose Tooth

Grades

2 and 3

Concepts

❐   Development of the ability to express rhythmic elements of a text using internal rhythmic sense;

❐   timbre of instruments.

> I had a loose tooth, a wiggly, jiggly loose tooth.
>
> I had a loose tooth, hanging by a thread.
>
> So I pulled my loose tooth, this wiggly, jiggly loose tooth.
>
> And put it 'neath my pillow and then I went to bed.
>
> The fairy took my loose tooth, my wiggly, jiggly loose tooth,
>
> So now I have a quarter and a hole in my head!

anonymous

Process

1   Copy the verse on to a chart or chalk board, complete with circles and underlining, perhaps using different colours.

2 Teach the verse with inflection and dynamics and a strong rhythmic sense.

3 Clap the rhythm of the verse.

4 Say the entire verse and replace the words that are underlined with a clap.

5 Follow the above procedure, replacing the words that have wavy underlining with patschen.

6 Replace the circled words with a snap.

7 Replace the boxed word with a tongue click.

8 Say the whole poem this way several times.

9 Have each individual in the group select an unpitched percussion instrument and then join others whose instruments have the same timbre. Form three groups, for example: woods (claves, woodblocks, etc.), skin (drums), metals (cymbals, gongs, triangles, etc.).

10 Replace the clap with the skins, the patschen with woods, and the snap with metals. The one tongue click should be given to one appropriate instrument.

11 To perform you could have the entire poem said first with no substitutions. On the second time, replace the underlined words; the third time, the wavy-lined words; the fourth time, the circles and the tongue click.

Extensions

● Try the same activity with other poems, for example:

> You don't drink milk 'cause it's cold as ice.
>
> You don't drink milk 'cause it goes down nice.
>
> You don't drink milk 'cause you're (running) (late.)
>
> You drink milk 'cause it (tastes) (so) (great.)

anonymous

Special learners

● This is an appropriate activity for children who have special needs. It helps to develop their listening awareness as well as their reading skills.
● The exercise would be more successful if the underlining and circling were done in different colours so they would be easier to distinguish.

(Contributed by Carolyn McMillan)

Counting's Easy

Grades

K and 1

Concepts

☐ Numbers;

☐ contrast between a "metric" poem and free rhythm.

> Counting's easy – 1 2 3
> I'll count bees and chimpanzees.
>
> Counting's easy – 4 5 6
> I'll count pucks and hockey sticks.
>
> Counting's easy – 7 8 9
> I'll count pigs and porcupines.
>
> Counting's easy – 10 10 10
> I'll count tigers in their dens –
>
> If …
> They're sleeping very tight
> and have no teeth so they can't bite
> and have no claws so they can't maul
> and if like kittens they are small.
>
> Then …
> I'll count tigers, count them all
> 10 10 10
> If they're small.

Robert Heidbreder

Process

1 Say the poem in strict rhythm until the fourth verse. Say the part after "If" freely, a little fearfully, and rather quickly and breathlessly.

2 Resume the metric speech for the next line, pausing before saying, in a "little" voice, "if they're small".

3 Clap the rhythm of the numbers or play it on a drum.

Special learners

● It would help to have ten pictures of tigers to put out in front of the children, one at a time as they are added in the poem.

Pink

Grades

K through 2

Concepts

❏ Colours;
❏ creativity;

❏ language.

> What's my favourite colour?
> Well, what do you think?
> That's an easy question
> My passion is pink
> I don't care a bit for yellow or brown
> Red, green and orange
> Just make me frown
> Magenta and turquoise
> Put 'em on file
> Chartreuse and purple
> They aren't my style.
> So it's …
> Pink on the walls
> Pink on the chairs
> Pink on the porch
> Pink on the stairs
> Pink in the kitchen
> Pink on the floors
> Pink in the basement
> Pink on the doors
> Pink on the ceiling
> Pink on the roof
> Come to my house
> if you want the proof

Sonja Dunn

Process

1 Teach the children the poem and have them say it with a good rhythm.

2 Unpitched percussion instruments such as drums, tambourines and claves could be added, either playing the rhythm pattern or the beat.

3 Change the colour and say the poem, talking about a new colour. The first part will have to be re-written to rhyme, but the last half of the poem works well just by substituting the new word.

> What's my favourite colour?
> Well, I'll tell you true,
> That's an easy question,
> My passion is blue …

> What's my favourite colour?
> Well, I hope you don't frown,
> That's an easy question,
> My passion is brown …

Special learners

● This may be a difficult poem for children with language-learning difficulties. It would

228

help them (and the rest of the class) to remember the words better if you had a picture of the inside of a house and pointed to each part in turn (the wall, chairs, porch, and so on) as the poem is being said.

Monday, Monday

Grades

K through 2

Concepts

☐ Beat;   ☐ alliteration.

☐ ♩, 𝅗𝅥, 𝅝;

words, music and arrangement Lois Fallis

2   Tuesday, Tuesday, Tilly Ty Tuesday, Tilly Ty Tuesday, Till Ty Too.
3   Wednesday, Wednesday, Willy Wy Wednesday, Willy Wy Wednesday, Willy Wy Woo.
4   Thursday, Thursday, Thilly Thy Thursday, Thilly Thy Thursday, Thilly Thy Thoo.
5   Friday, Friday, Filly Fy Friday, Filly Fy Friday, Filly Fy Foo.
6   Saturday, Saturday, Silly Sy Saturday, Silly Sy Saturday, Silly Sy Soo.
7   Sunday, Sunday, Silly Sy Sunday, Silly Sy Sunday, Silly Sy Soo.

Process

1   Learn the song with all the verses.

2   Learn the accompaniment using body percussion and speech patterns to prepare for steady playing:

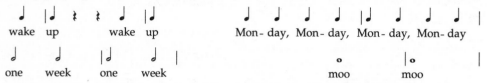

Learn the speech pattern. This changes, of course, as each day is sung.

Dance (Kindergarten)

Formation: a circle, one child in the middle.

1   For the verse the child in the middle walks round the circle one way, the others walk in the opposite direction.

2   At the end of the verse, everyone chants the speech. The child in the middle points to the other children in turn, on the beat if possible, starting with the child nearest to where he / she stopped at the end of the verse. The child pointed to on the word "next" is the next person in the middle. Repeat to the end of the week, subtracting one day each time until there are "no days left".

Dance (grades 1 and 2)

Formation: two circles, each child of the inner circle facing a partner on the outer circle.
For the singing
    Clap your own hands, clap your partner's right hand with your right;
    clap your own, hands, clap your partner's left hand with your left.
    Do this a total of four times.
For the speech
    Everyone turns to face counter-clockwise and the partners join hands. They walk to the beat around the circle for twelve paces.
    On "six days left" the inner circle stands still while the outer circle continues for four more paces to join up with a new partner.
Repeat the dance.

Special learners

●   Children who have developmental delays will find this an easy activity, especially the first dance. Children in wheelchairs can also take part in the song and the activity.

CHAPTER SEVENTEEN

Stories, Fables, Music and Drama

Story Theatre

Stories from the oral tradition, such as myths, legends and folktales, are dramatized through symbolic, suggestive action. Perfomers perform their own narration and can take on several roles. Props and costumes are simple and minimal. The plot comes to life through movement, mime and expressive voice. This form of theatre lends itself to the Orff approach very effectively. The narration can be done by a single voice or chorus of voices. Songs, dances and rhythm instruments can be easily slipped in at appropriate moments to elaborate the dramatization.

The Snow Child

This Russian folktale lends itself easily to story theatre. Because of our Canadian winters the setting of this story is also meaningful in our culture. The dialogue interwoven with narration created for this story can be done in the same way with most short tales. Included are the characters, performers and a list of possible musical moments that can be part of the re-enactment. The text then follows.

CHORUS/NARRATOR: Once upon a time, there lived an old man and his wife.

MAN AND WOMAN: They were unhappy because they had no children. One cold winter day, the old couple stood at the window watching the children of the village playing outside.

CHILDREN: (*song and dance.*)

CHORUS/NARRATOR: When the children had gone, the old man turned to his wife.

MAN: Why don't we go outside and build a snow child?

WOMAN: We can make a little girl!

CHORUS/NARRATOR: So they went out to the garden, and set out to work. (*Dramatization.*) The snow child was as perfect as she could be.

MAN: The snow child is so beautiful!

WOMAN: How I wish she were real!

CHORUS/NARRATOR: The wife kissed the snow child, and suddenly she came to life.

SOLO 1: First she moved her head …

SOLO 2: Then her arms …

SOLO 3: Then her legs …

MAN: Look!

WOMAN: She's alive!

SNOW CHILD: I am a child of the snow. I come to you as the cold winds blow.

MAN: Our wish has come true.

231

WOMAN: Yes, at last we have a little girl of our own.

CHORUS/NARRATOR: The old man and his wife wanted to take the snow child into the cottage.

WOMAN: Come, it is time to go to sleep.

SNOW CHILD: I cannot sleep here. I must always sleep outside.

WOMAN: You will be too cold.

SNOW CHILD: Oh no! I can never be too cold.

CHORUS/NARRATOR: So every night she slept there on a bed of snow. Every night the old couple looked out of the window at their snow child.

CHILDREN: (Lullaby song.)

CHORUS/NARRATOR: During the cold winter the snow child played with the village children.

CHILDREN: (*Repeat song and dance: "It's snowing".*)

GROUPS 1 AND 2: At last spring came. The children of the village were glad as they jumped and skipped in the sunlight.

SOLO 1: Come, come and play with us too!

SOLOS 1 AND 2: But the snow child would not go.

SOLO 3: She hid from the sun.

MAN: What is wrong?

WOMAN: Are you ill?

CHILDREN: The snow child grew sadder and sadder. She seemed thin and weak.

SNOW CHILD: I must leave you now. I am a child of the snow. I must go where it is cold.

MAN: No! No! You cannot go!

WOMAN: Come back! Come back to us! (SNOW CHILD *leaves*.)

CHORUS/NARRATOR: The old couple were sad. All summer long, as the children played, they thought they would never see their little girl again. When the first snow fell again, the old couple looked out of the window. In the garden stood the snow child.

SNOW CHILD: I am a child of the snow. I come back to you as the cold winds blow.

CHORUS/NARRATOR: The snow child stayed through the winter. When the spring came, she left once more. The old man and his wife were no longer sad. They knew that their snow child would return to them for ever after.

Performers

The Snow Child; the couple; 6–8 children; a narrator and/or a chorus of speakers/singers; 6–8 percussionists, playing Orff instruments.

Musical moments

1   THE CHILDREN'S SONG

The couple are watching the children play in the snow, longing for a child of their own. The movement consists of six to eight children skipping in a line sideways with a great deal of energy and joy. The last child is waving a scarf up in the air. The line circles and weaves with some of the children falling over at the end of the third phrase. On the fourth phrase, the children stand up and pause to observe the beauty. The song is repeated a second time as the children resume their original energy skipping off a winding line.

words Hania Krajewski
music and arrangement Alice Brass

It's snow - ing, It's snow - ing, It's white all a - round, It's blow - ing, It's drift - ing with bare - ly a sound, It's snow - ing, It's snow - ing on tree - tops a - round and soon all the flow - ers will ne - ver be found.

2 MIME SEQUENCE

The couple build a snow child. A mime sequence involves two students as the couple, unfolding a third student, the snow child who is rolled up on the floor. Each limb is opened up very slowly and precisely in slow motion. The snow child is totally passive and is helped to an open standing position by the couple. Awareness and isolation of the joints is required.

3 ACCOMPANYING SOUNDSCAPE

An accompanying soundscape can be provided with metallophones and glockenspiels to support the movement. Set up the instruments in C pentatonic by removing the F and B bars. In a metre of four, one student plays any two low notes then moves up the instrument every four beats thus creating an ascending cascade, taking four bars to complete the phrase. Every four bars another instrument joins in to emphasize a build-up, as the snow girl gradually takes shape. End with glockenspiels. An alto metallophone and/or a bass xylophone can sustain a tremolo on a C and G throughout.

Introduction

Chimes plus tremolo on G bar of bass xylophone.

4 SOUNDSCAPE AND MIME

The snow child comes to life with a soundscape and mime. This is accompanied by a rhythmic layering, with each section coming in every four bars. The snow child starts to move each body part, with each new sound layer, moving every half note. Percussive motion becomes flowing in the end, when the snow child is fully alive.

5 THE SNOW CHILD'S SONG

Four children rub hands slowly over four hand drums. Another plays a soft tremolo on a large cymbal.

words and music Hania Krajewski

6   LULLABY

As the couple watch the snow child sleeping a lullaby may be played. Existing sources can be used, for example, "Eskimo Lullaby" (chapter 3) or "Acadian Lullaby" (chapter 5).

7   THE CHILDREN'S SONG

Repeat the song, as the children this time sing and dance with the snow child.

8   LAMENT

The couple grieve over the departure of the snow child in the spring. A recorder could play the melody a second time alone as a group of three performers dressed in black do an abstract, flowing movement sequence involving simple arm mirroring (in a triangle formation) to represent the couple's grief.

words and music Hania Krajewski

9   THE SNOW CHILD'S SONG

Repeat this song as the snow child returns to the couple the following winter.

10   FINALE: THE CHILDREN'S SONG

The children's song is repeated for the closing with the snow child and the couple looking on.

(Contributed by Hania Krajewski)

235

Musical Treatments of Stories and Fables

Joanne Kirkham

After working for many years as a music specialist and therefore being concerned with the total school music programme, including productions, I found myself suddenly a classroom teacher with very different priorities and responsibilities. I was working with far fewer children but was responsible for their growth in many more ways. I quickly discovered that my music teaching techniques were very useful in the regular classroom. Singing or rhythm breaks are great for gaining everyone's attention. Along with physical "energizers", these musical classroom breaks are critical to keeping children focused. We are all aware that listening skills have to be taught these days. However, until I worked as a classroom teacher I was not aware that a whole class of children are *better* listeners when there is melody or rhythm involved. Hence I felt totally justified in using lots of singing and rhythm work in my programme even though my children were lucky enough also to have music classes from a specialist.

Besides listening, another critical skill, on which we seem to have to focus more and more, is that of co-operation. Co-operative learning, group work, values education and "heart to heart" discussions all have their place. But I believe there is nothing as valuable for bringing a class together as working on a group production, no matter how simple. If the production is musical as well as dramatic, you have all the more need for class co-operation. What takes more concentrated effort from everyone than "in-tune" singing?

The many wonderful musicals which are fine for school productions are not really suitable for a classroom project where every child has to feel important. There can't be any "potted plants" or "trees" if each child is to gain self-esteem from the effort. A mini-musical suited to your particular group is the answer and it's easy to develop.

Elements

- A story that is a favourite of the class, or a theme, such as celebrating the environment.
- Singing (chanting) can be used to tell much of the story. The chant melody is mostly stepwise, using leaps for expressive purposes. Children find chants easy to sing in tune.
- Dialogue and narration should be used sparingly. They are adapted as the children practise. The way it comes out the first time is often the best.
- Develop drama and movement with the children.
- Use minimal costumes and/or sets.
- Instrumental parts (pitched percussion) should be kept to the bare bones – I and V chords, with an occasional IV. The orchestration usually has to be taught quickly and the class may have little Orff training.

If the mini-musical is developed during the last term it can be a "drawing together" of the class for a common purpose. Kids with few exceptions love to perform! Although the learning process is the main emphasis, performance of the product is invaluable.

236

The First Corn

Ojibwa legend: an easy mini-musical for the whole class

Retold by Patronella Johnston, adapted by Joanne Kirkham

Characters

Nokomis (grandmother), Bedabin (boy), Tawa (girl), Indian brave, many Indians, three or more corn, narrator.

Instruments

autoharp (accompanies chant), recorder(s), alto glockenspiel, alto metallophone, alto xylophone, bass xylophone, hand drum, maracas.

Introduction (Interlude)

(During the introduction Indians enter and assume a scatter formation. Nokomis and the children form a group downstage. As the music ends, everyone freezes, and the Indians fold their arms.)

NARRATOR: The story of how corn came to the Indians is a favourite of many tribes of the First Nations. The Ojibwa people have their own special version, which Nokomis passes on to her grandchildren, Tawa and Bedabin.

ALL INDIANS:

Chant A

(Repeat the melody to the syllable "ah" or hum, doing a "corn mime". Some Indians cut corn, some husk it and some stir it in a cooking vessel.)

NOKOMIS: We are so lucky to have the corn. Indian corn is beautiful. It is sweet and good.

BEDABIN: It smells wonderful. I love to eat Indian corn. We make sleeping mats from the corn husks, so none of the corn is wasted.

TAWA: I am very hungry. Nokomis, while we are waiting, will you tell us the story of the corn? How did corn come to us?

NOKOMIS: Many moons ago, long before there were any white men in our land, we received the corn from one of our young braves.

BEDABIN: Tell us how it happened.

NOKOMIS: When a brave is ready to become a man he must spend some time by himself. He must fast and do some deep thinking. This young man went by himself into a small wigwam.

(Steady drum beat as Nokomis, Bedabin and Tawa move downstage and the Indians change position. The Indian brave moves to centre stage. Three Indians surround the brave, arms raised to represent the wigwam.)

ALL INDIANS:

Chant B

yah ___ ah ___ yah   Ah   yah ___ ah ___ yah.

(The Indian brave sits in deep contemplation within the wigwam.)

Recorder solo

(As the last note, B♮, is held, the Indian brave stands, and emerges from the wigwam.)

ALL INDIANS:
Chant C

What   vi - sion   has   ap - peared   to   you?

INDIAN BRAVE: I have seen a wondrous vision. I don't know what it means, so you will have to help me. A great warrior came and challenged me. We fought for a long time. Finally I was able to defeat him, and he fell apart, into many little pieces.

(Glockenspiel plays randomly. All Indians' hands are raised, fingers flutter to represent the defeat.)

ALL INDIANS:
Chant D (Recitative in style)

This   is   not   the   whole   vi - sion.   Go   a -
- gain   in - to   your   wig - wam.   The   vi - sion   will   come   a - gain.

(Brave returns to the wigwam and sleeps.)

Interlude

(Recorder and instruments repeat the introduction, during which First Corn appears at back, and with sinuous, "corn-like" movements comes to stage centre front.)

(Brave wakes and steps forward to receive Corn. Wigwam disbands.)

CORN: I am Corn. I give myself to you because you have defeated me. Go! (*Corn points to back of room or stage.*) Go away with your people for the summer. When you return we will be flourishing!

(Recorder and instruments repeat the interlude as the Indians, a group at a time, turn, move to the rear of the stage and freeze, facing away from the audience.)

   (The three corn appear and, using "corn" movements, come to centre stage.)

   (Silence. The Indians return, a group at a time.)

CORN:

Chant E

ALL INDIANS: (*use actions to illustrate the words*) There are fields of tall green stalks as far as the eye can see. The stalks carry golden ears, wrapped in green husks and soft brown silk.

SOLO INDIAN:

Song and dance: The Song of the Corn

A The Indians sing, the Corn moves to represent growth;

B the interlude is repeated by the recorder and instruments; some Indians dance, the rest of the Indians form a semicircle around the dancers;

A repeat the song and movement.

NARRATOR: Ever since that day the Indians have had corn. When the white man came, it was one of the many gifts that he received from the people of the First Nations.

Coda

(*The musicians and semicircle of Indians sink to their knees and lower their heads. The dancers sink slowly down, lowering the maracas.*)

Recorder

Mortimer

Lesson plan by Sharon Smith-Miller

Mortimer is one of many delightful picture books by Robert Munsch. It tells the story of a little boy who has difficulty going to sleep. Each time he is left alone, he sings his signature song. First his mother, then his father, then his seventeen brothers and sisters and finally, the police go upstairs in turn, telling Mortimer to "be quiet!" After each has returned to the bottom of the stairs, Mortimer again sings his familiar refrain. At the conclusion, his parents, brothers and sisters, and the police, get into a big fight, during which time Mortimer gets so tired of waiting for someone to respond, he falls asleep.

The use of repetition throughout the book lends itself well to an Orff interpretation. Mortimer's song is repeated four times while a recurring passage about people going up and down stairs ("thump, thump, thump, thump, thump, thump, thump") can be adapted to vocal glissandi and/or body percussion. Visually, the words are placed to show ascending and descending motion to enlarge the child's attention (visual aid). The consistent repetition provides heightened anticipation, especially in young children, where focused attention is often difficult!

By means of extensions, the song and story can be used from Kindergarten to Grade 3.

Concepts

- Musical, literary experience;
- creating sound effects;
- body percussion;
- canon (grades 3–4);
- listening skills;
- math skills;
- experience of syncopation;
- gross motor skills.

words Robert Munsch
music Sharon Smith-Miller

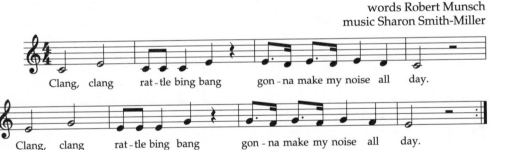

Process

1   Introduce the story, discussing the key words (the recurring "thump").

2   Count the "thumps". Stamp them and speak with voices going higher and lower.

3   Transfer them to a drum (Grades 2–3).

4   The students clap a steady beat while the teacher performs the song.

5   Teach song by echo imitation, one phrase at a time, then the whole song. The song could be simplified for very young children by repeating just the first four measures instead of adding the second half of the song.

6 Read the story using body percussion and/or vocal glissandi on the recurring key word "thump".

7 Sing the song each time it occurs; finish the story.

Extensions (Grades 2–4)

- Transfer key words of the song to unpitched percussion of the students' choosing: "clang, rattle, bing-bang, noise".
- In Grades 3–4 try the song in canon.
- In Grades 2–3 add movement. Form several circles. Step left, patsching at the same time; close with right foot while shaking hands over head. Do this a total of four times. Reverse, stepping to the right, patschen and shaking hands over head a total of four times.
  Try this movement with several circles in canon.
- With some classes it might be best to leave out the involvement of the policemen. We want to foster a positive image of the police and having them come at night to quiet a child might be misunderstood by some children. It might also be best to have Mortimer's mother put him to bed, not "throw" him in bed.

Robert Munsch has written many books that would be suitable for treating dramatically. One in particular, "The Paper Bag Princess", is a great favourite with children.

Canadian Books and Stories for Dramatization and Sound Effects

This is just a small selection of the books available.

Allinson, Beverly and Barbara Reid, *Effie*. Richmond Hill: Scholastic, 1990. A wonderful tale of an ant who had a big voice. Barbara Reid's plasticine illustrations are delightful.

Caduto, Michael J. and Joseph Bruchac, *Keepers of the Earth: native stories*. Saskatoon: Fifth House, 1991

Cameron, Anne, *How the Moon Lost Her Voice*. Madeira Park: Harbour, 1985

Clark, Ella Elizabeth, *Indian Legends of Canada*. Toronto: McCelland and Stewart, 1960

Gilmore, Rachna, *Lights for Gita*. Toronto: Second Story, 1994. A story of a little girl's first celebration of the festival of Divali in her new home in Canada.

Johnston, Basil, and Dale Ashkewe, *How the Birds Got Their Colours*. Toronto: Kids Can, 1978

Keens-Douglas, Richard, *La Diablesse and the Baby*. Toronto: Annick, 1994. A Caribbean folk tale.

Martin, Rafe (ed.), *Dear as Salt*. Richmond Hill: North Winds (Scholastic), 1993. A retelling of the universal, old tale.

Mollel, Tolowa M. (ed.), *The Flying Tortoise, an Igbo tale*. Toronto: Oxford, 1940

Moore, Yvette (ill. Jo Bannatyne-Cuguet), *A Prairie Alphabet*. Montréal: Tundra. The alphabet re-created and illustrated with scenes from life on the prairies.

Mother Goose; a Canadian sampler. Toronto: Groundwood / Douglas and McIntyre, 1994. Canadian illustrators are used to bring the old poems and chants alive.

Norman, Howard, *Northern Tales: traditional stories of Eskimo and Indian people*. New York: Pantheon (Random House), 1990

Paré, Roger, *Winter Games*. Toronto: Annick, 1991. Translated from *Plaisirs d'hiver*.

Penner, Fred, *The Bump*. Winnipeg: Hyperion, 1990. The book has wonderful illustrations. Use the song at the back of the book or have the children create their own.

People of the Trail. North Vancouver: Douglas and McIntyre, 1978. A series of books about the First Nations by different authors and illustrators. Includes: *People of the Trail, Sea and Cedar, People of the Buffalo, The Red Ochre People, How the Northwest Coast Indians Lived*.

Reid, Barbara, *Two by Two*. Richmond Hill: North Winds, 1992. A delightful retelling of the Noah story with magical illustrations done in Plasticine.

Taylor, C. J., *Bones in the Basket*. Montréal: Tundra, 1994. Native stories of the origins of people.

Thornhill, Jan, *Crow, Fox and Other Animal Legends*. Toronto: OWL, 1993

CHAPTER EIGHTEEN

Students' Work

The First Song Ever Sung

"The First Song Ever Sung" was written by three Grade 5 students at Forest Hill Public School in Toronto (Lauren Davies, Alana Geller and Evelyn Leong). It was based on a poem of the same name by Laura Krauss Melmed, with illustrations by Ed Young.[1] The students felt that they could write a poem that better expressed their feelings of the equality between men and women, and groups in the class wrote several versions. This one was picked to be used first at the Mosaic/Mosaïque conference of Music for Children – Carl Orff Canada – Musique pour enfants, and also in the Toronto Board of Education Festival Concert.

Various musical selections were interspersed throughout the presentation – songs with Orff accompaniments, dances and recorder pieces. Suggestions have been given here and many also appear in other sections of this book. Feel free to substitute your own material.

The children enter skipping and singing "Lachen" ("Laughing Singing") using the adapted words found in chapter 14. They all move into groups, ready to dance, or to instruments, ready to play.

ALL: The miracle begins!

The Narrator(s) speak(s) the first three verses,

> A child stood and
> gazed on high,
> A child stood and
> pondered the sky.
>
> "Who?"cried the child,
> "Who am I?
> Is the music in me
> the music out there?
>
> Are the notes the same everywhere?
> Where do the notes and the songs come from?
> What was the first song ever sung?"

> "The first song ever sung,"   followed by "African Children's
> said the mother to her child,   Clapping Song" (chapter 14)
> "Was a strong song, a wondrous song,
> a willing to be equal song."

---

1 New York: Lathrop, Lee and Shepard, 1993

"The first song ever sung," said the stars to the moon, "Was a twinkling song, a candle song, a light over the world song."	"Morning Mist" (chapter 21)
"The first song ever sung," said the husband to his wife, "Was a passion song, an honest song, a seeking growth and changing song."	"Rise up, O Flame" (chapter 14)
"The first song ever sung," said the father to his child, "Was a caring song, a loving song, a kind, feeling, gentle song."	"Lullaby" (chapter 2)
"The first song ever sung," said the ocean to the fish, "Was a vast song, a deep song, a soaking through the sand song."	"Bonavist Harbour" (chapter 3)
"The first song ever sung,' said the trees to the sky, "Was a reaching song, a stretching song, a leaf falling to the ground song,"	Instrumental piece #8, Allegro (*Music for Children*, vol. II)
"The first song ever sung," said the light to the darkness, "Was a bright song, a vibrant song, a searching freedom in the night song."	"Rundadinella", (*Music for Children*, vol. III)

Everyone skips off stage singing "Laughing Singing".

The entire work was conceived and directed by Angela Elster and fellow teachers from the Toronto Board of Education.

The next two pieces are compositions of students from Mont-Jésus-Marie school in Montréal. Their teacher is Francine Bellerose.

The first, "La Grenouille", was written by an eight-year-old student. "Mon champ d'amitié" is a harmonization for melodic percussion instruments of a familiar tune and was written by eleven- and twelve-year-old students as part of a project in which 60 Grade 5 students created their own compositions. These young composers have said that the piece represents to them "the joy of life". Most study violin or another instrument privately and enjoy table tennis, tennis and other sports. One wants to be an astronaut when he grows up.

La Grenouille

paroles, musique et harmonisation
Amélie Bellerose (8 ans)

- V1 could be played on a soprano recorder in this range. If sung by students it might be best to sing an octave lower.

Mon champ d'amitié

musique Francis Boulva, Pascal Charboneau,
Jean-Philippe Simard et Vincent Guibord

Mon pa-ys ce n'est pas un simpl' et grand pa-ys où nous vi-vons c'est l'a-mour

248

2   Ma province ce n'est pas une province comme les autres provinces c'est un rêve.

3   Montréal ma ville natale n'est pas une ville comme toutes les villes c'est festivals.

4   Oh mon champ d'amitié et d'intensité et grand bonheur où je vis chaque jour.

Original Poems and Songs by Students

The Grade 5 students at Claude Watson School for the Arts in North York, Ontario, under the direction of their Orff teacher Alice Brass were set the task of writing their own poems.

After this was done the students divided into groups and chose poems (not necessarily their own) to set to music with melody and accompaniment.

Some of the results follow. These are just a sampling of the many poems and songs that were created. Several poems, such as "Humfry Dumpty", "Little Miss Fool" and "The Telephone", had three or four versions. Choosing among these was very difficult.

Many thanks to the entire class and all the students involved for allowing us to publish their work.

The Windmill

I saw a tree on a distant hill,
It grew beside the old windmill.
I saw a bird flying by,
Passing the windmill in a clear, blue sky.
No soft, white flour is ground there now,
It's used as a storehouse for a plough.
Soon the windmill will be no more,
It's to come down; it's rotten – all but the door.

Meaghan Burford

Two Bad Ants

Two bad ants, crawling up my pants,
Up and down, round and round,
Up and down, round and round,
Those bad ants, crawling up my pants.

Heidi Smith

Stars

The stars are so beautiful, clear and white,
They shine like angels all through the night.
They shimmer so strongly, they shine so bright,
I wish I was a star. They're such a pretty sight.

Charissa Zoetmulder and Carys Montgomery

My Dream

Last night I had a dream about a place far above,
A place where everybody had someone to love.

There was no poverty or hatred anywhere in sight,
All the people that lived there didn't understand the word "fight".

I prayed no one would realize I wasn't one of them,
They would find out I came from earth and send me back again.

I loved the place, wherever it may be,
My favourite time was watching horses gallop through the sea.

But dawn broke and the sun came up, it was time to go back home.
I woke up early in the morn and found I was alone.

I never went back to that place where there was so much love,
But I know that it is still alive, in our sky above.

Kathryn Robson

Humfry Dumpty

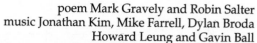

poem Mark Gravely and Robin Salter
music Jonathan Kim, Mike Farrell, Dylan Broda
Howard Leung and Gavin Ball

Hum — frey Dump — ty sat on a wall,

But this time he did — n't fall, He grabbed a rope and

swung a - way and clung to the clothes - line, where he would stay.

2 Then he was thrown into the wash
   And poor, poor Humfry he got squashed
   When the maid hung out the wash that day
   All she found was egg soufflé.

Little Miss Fool

words and music Charissa Zoetmulder, Carys Montgomrey,
Wing Sum Tang, Jenny Chang, Jeremy Freed

The Telephone

poem Ashley Storms
music Ashley Storms, Daniel Buchman,
Linda Wyles, Andrea Feder and Tina Ferluck

2   My sister loves to tease and play.
     She drives me crazy every day
     So when her friends call on the phone
     I tell them all that she's not home.

Split-Pea Soup

poem Stephanie Erb
music Kay Naito, Beatrice Fantoni
Alika Hendricks, Denise Ho, Kaori Yamagami

254

grue - some ha - bit I just hope I don't _ get hooked on - to rab - bit.

2   I was at a restaurant late one day
    And they had split-pea soup on the menu – yea!
    So I kept on ordering soup of split pea
    'Till the cook got angry and dumped some on me.
    As the yucky green mush poured down my head
    I yelled to the waiter, "I'll have pizza instead!"

Shake the Papaya Down

This arrangement was created by students in the Royal Conservatory of Music Orff Ensemble. This is a group of students who meet once a week under the direction of Alison Kenny-Gardhouse.

1   The group was first taught the song and then they created their own movements using the actions suggested by the text.

2   The teacher then explored the tonic–dominant, followed by having the students hear the song accompanied by the bass xylophone, using the root notes of F (tonic) and C (dominant). The students discovered where the accompaniment should change in order to sound well harmonically.

3   Other possibilities were introduced. Would it be possible to use a G on the accompaniment?

4   The final accompaniment pattern that was decided upon was F–G–C–F.

5   They were then shown the chords that these four notes suggested and the final result was the following accompaniment.

●   Add unpitched percussion instruments *ad lib*. Maracas, claves, tambourines and cabasas, playing the beat or the calypso rhythm would be very effective.

Ma - ma says no play, This is a work day.

Up with the bright sun, get all the work done. If you will help me,

Climb up the tall tree, Shake the pa - pa - ya down.

CHAPTER NINETEEN

Move and Dance

Beginning Movement Experiences

The following are some ideas for beginning experiences in movement, and some movement "warm-ups". These activities involve careful listening and show an awareness of tempo, dynamics, spatial awareness and different movement levels. As with all movement experiences these ideas develop the natural rhythmic sense and co-ordination. They aid memory – a skill learned with the whole body is remembered better – and are physically invigorating and fun.

Awareness of own space

1   Find a space on the floor. Make that space yours in some way: jumping in and out of the space; moving in and out slowly; twirling around, and many other ways.

2   Explore the space. How high is it? How wide? How low? Where is the middle?

3   Every time my drum beats make a statue that fills the space in some way.

4   Make three statues to the drum sound, one high, one low and one medium.

Awareness of others in space

1   Make a "space bubble" by defining the space all around you. This is your own space bubble and you are going to take it with you as you now move from your own space out into the larger space with others. You must be careful not to bump into anyone else's space bubble so leave lots of room between you as you move.

2   Start walking to my drum beat and fill up all the empty spaces in the room. Change direction when the drum sound changes.

3   Change tempo. Find a different way to walk: backwards, low down, up high, on the edge of your feet, like a crab, and so on.

4   Have the group sit and discuss the ways they moved. A chart can be made that lists the different movements.

A warm-up

1   Walk to the beat of the temple blocks. Walk and listen. Stop when the sound stops.

2   Explore walking and skipping, accompanied by the blocks.

3   Listen to the highest sounding block. How can you show this with your body as you walk? Repeat with the lowest sounding block and the one in the middle range.

4   Come to an agreement on three movements that show these three levels and have everyone do these. Increase the speed of changing from one sound to another to encourage quick reaction time. These are locomotor movements.

5   The children stand in one spot to try the same idea. (The reaction time is shorter.)

6   Sitting down, have the children echo rhythmic patterns played on one of the three blocks. They respond by clapping over their heads, at chest level or by patschen for the lowest level. (Stand where the children cannot see which temple block is playing.)

(Ideas contributed by Saundra Osborne, Alison Kenny-Gardhouse and Lois Birkenshaw-Fleming)

My Head and My Shoulders

Some children from Uganda taught this song to their classmates in a Toronto school. It became an instant hit and like true folklore it spread rapidly from child to child and school to school.

Grades

K through 3

Concepts

☐ Body awareness;
☐ co-ordination.

Process

1   Sing and touch the body parts referred to, slowly at first, gradually getting faster and faster each time it is repeated.

258

Let's Take a Walk

Ages

3 through 6

Concepts

- ❑ Spatial relationship;
- ❑ visual awareness;
- ❑ language development;
- ❑ stepping on the beat with the group.

words and music Donna Wood

Let's take a walk, take a walk, take a walk. To

see what we can see now.

Process

1 When the children are ready to move as a group, they are ready to try this game. The children stand along a wall in a line, holding hands. The leader takes the hand of the child at the end of the line and asks all to follow "so we can sing and walk in a long line". It is best if everyone turns their faces and bodies a little bit so they can see where to go.

2 The younger children are led through the room as the song is sung several times. They then sit down and talk about what they saw. If it is possible, lead them out into the hall, into the play yard, or some place where there are many things to see and talk about.

3 The older children, hopefully, can step to the beat. The leader takes them around the room, then leads them into the circle like a spiral. When all are "wound up" the leader turns and goes the other way, unwinding the group.

4 Try many other patterns. Can one of the children lead the group?

Special learners

- Walking in a line with children on either side can give a great feeling of security to most children who have special needs. This formation might, however, cause problems for visually impaired children. They often do not like to have both hands held, as they use their hands to detect things they cannot see. Try placing such a child at the end of the line.

- The "energy" created by going into a spiral might be overwhelming for students with emotional problems.

On the Mountain

Grades

K through 2

Concepts

☐ *so–la–so–mi* and *mi–re–do* patterns;
☐ rondo form.

music traditional
arrangement Joanna Robertson

On the moun-tain stands a la - dy, Who she is I___ do not know
All she wants is gold and sil - ver, All she wants is an ice-cream cone.

Process

1 For very young children, teach them the song and perform the dance. Older children can play the accompaniment, perform the movement rondo and work with the *sol–fa* note names.

2 Ask the older group to listen carefully as you sing the song and identify the *so–la–so–mi* motif each time it occurs in the song. Invite them to perform the hand signs as you sing the song. "How many times did you find the pattern?"

3 Repeat the procedure with the *mi–re–do* pattern.

4 Sing the song and, using alternate hands, patsch the beat.

5 Using imaginary mallets, play the alto xylophone part in the air.

6 Transfer the part to alto xylophones and sing the song with this accompaniment.

7 Repeat with the metallophone part.

8 The bass xylophone part is optional as some Grade 1 children may find it too difficult to play.

9 Sing the song with the full accompaniment.

Dance

Formation: the children form a circle, joining hands, with elbows bent.

Measures 1–2	take four steps clockwise;
measures 3–4	left patsch, right patsch, clap, snap;
measures 5–6	take four steps counterclockwise;
measures 7–8	repeat measures 3–4.

Movement rondo

A the song with accompaniment and dance;

B one child performs a skipping pattern while the children sing the song on the syllable "loo";

A as before;

C a different child performing a different pattern;

A as before.

The rondo form can be shown visually by using coloured shapes of a lady (A), a skipping rope (B) and a mountain (C), or just different shapes.

Sitting on a Tin Can

Grades

K through 1

Concepts

☐ Beat;

☐ movement;

☐ creativity;

☐ names.

> Sitting on a tin can,
> Who can? We can!
> Nobody else can
> Yay————

Process

1 One child sits in the middle of a circle of the other children, preferably on a large tin can, an overturned pail or a wash tub. S/he makes up an action which keeps the beat. The others copy and chant the little poem inserting the name of the child at "Yay".

2 The child in the middle stands up after "Yay" and chooses a new person to be in the middle. The game repeats.

(Collected from Palmerston School playground, Toronto, by Catherine West)

Soyons copains

Clientèle

1e année

Pologne: arrangement Monique T. Armand et Chantale Parent

Re - cule - toi, re - cule - toi, J'te con - nais pas, Re - viens, mais

re - viens, mais J'te con - nais bien. Donn' moi ta droite, Donn' moi ta

gauche Donn' moi tes mains, Soy - ons co - pains! - pains!

Démarche pédagogique

Formation: deux par deux, face à face, des couples disperses

Partie A
Danse "Soyons copains"

Recule-toi, recule-toi, J'te connais pas,	*L'enfant recule de quatre pas en faisant le geste de repousser l'autre;*
Reviens, mais reviens, mais J'te connais bien,	*faire les mouvements contraires;*
Donne-moi ta droite	*se donner la main droite. Dans le jeu, on nommera d'autres parties du corps;*
Donne-moi ta gauche	*se donner la main gauche;*
Donne-moi tes mains Soyons copains	*se redonner les deux mains et faire un demi-tour avec son partenaire.*

Répeter une autre fois la danse à partir de "Donne-moi ta droite".

Partie B

Les enfants marchent les pulsations rapids ♩♩♩, frappées au tambour de basque par le professeur. Après huit mesures, le tambour de basque est secoué: c'est le signal d'arrêt et chacun se replace face à face avec un nouveau partenaire afin de reprendre la partie A. (Une nouvelle partie du corps est nominée ou montrée: marionnette, tableau … et la danse est reprise avec cette nouvelle partie du corps.)

Forme

A pied;

B déplacement pendant huit mesures;

A genou;

B déplacement pendant six mesures;
A hanche;
B déplacement pendant quatre mesures;
A main;
B déplacement pendant deux mesures;
A coude;
B changement de partenaire immédiat sans mesure de transition;
A joue.

J'ai vu le loup, le renard et la belette

Clientèle

Maternelle et 1e année

Concepts

☐ Co-ordination;
☐ schéma spatial.

mélodie traditionelle
modifiée par Virginia K. Barteluk

Démarche pédagogique

Jeu 1

Comme le jeu "London Bridges". Deux élèves forment un pont avec tes bras. Un élève est le loup et l'autre est le renard. Les autres élèves marchent à la file en-dessous du "pont". Quand la chanson est finie, les deux élèves du pont attrapent le dernier élève et demandent "le loup ou le renard?" L'élève va derrière celui qu'il choisit.

Jeu 2

Quand la chanson est finie, l'élève qui est dans les bras des deux élèves, va choisir un instrument de bois comme les cuillers, les bâtons, les claves. Les élèves avec les instruments font un rythme précis pendant qu'ils chantent. Le professeur donne le rythme précis pour la leçon.

Can You Clap Your Hands?

Grades

K and 1

Concepts

☐ Body awareness; ☐ timbre of instruments;
☐ inner hearing; ☐ creativity.

words and music Diane Shieron

2 I can clap my hands, I can clap my hands,
   Big claps, little claps, I can clap my hands.

Process

1 The leader sings the first verse, the question. The children answer with the second verse. Everyone claps for the third time (just the beat or rhythm pattern) while singing verse 2 in their heads.

2 Change the words and actions to: snapping fingers, stamping feet, patting knees, rubbing stomach, popping cheeks, patting head … What else can the children think of to do?

3 Transfer the rhythm to unpitched percussion instruments.

4 Perform the same as above, but change the words to:

   1 Can you tap the bell (*metals*) … ?
   2 Can you play the wood block (*woods*) … ?
   3 Can you tap the drum (*skins*) … ?

Incorporate other instruments into the song to explore their sounds.

Special learners

● This little piece is excellent for children who have learning difficulties: it explores many different actions and thus develops body-awareness skills; it incorporates different sounds made by instruments, thereby developing listening skills; it encourages inner hearing; it encourages creativity by asking the children to think of different actions and instruments to use in the song. If you are working with children who have physical challenges, be sure to incorporate actions that everyone can do, such as nodding the head or blinking the eyes.

Here Are Grandma's Spectacles

Grades

K and 1

Concepts

☐ Body percussion transferred to instruments.

traditional finger-play
arrangement Susan Hall

V — Here are Grand-ma's spec-tac-les, And here is Grand-ma's hat.

△ snap
◻ patsch
○ stamp

Here's the way she folds her hands and puts them in her lap.

2   Here are Grandpa's spectacles,
     And here is Grandpa's hat,
     Here's the way he folds his arms
     And takes a little nap.

Process

1 Recite the poem, doing the actions (making "spectacles", a "hat", putting the hands in the lap, and so on).

2 Teach the body percussion part and combine these with the poem.

3 If it suits the needs of the children, transfer the body percussion parts to the instruments suggested.

Final form

1 Recite the poem (both verses), performing the actions.

2 Recite the poem, accompanied by body percussion.

3 Divide into three groups: one says the poem with the actions, one says the poem accompanied by body percussion, the third says the poem accompanied by instruments.

265

Old Dog

Grades

K and 1

Concepts

❏ Socialization;

❏ movement.

trad arr Lois Birkenshaw-Fleming

Process

1 Teach the song and perform the movement, having someone playing a woodblock during the "hopping" part.

2 If it suits the needs of your children, add the tambourine and xylophone parts.

Movement

Formation: scatter, standing back to back. Decide who is to be the flea and who the dog.

 Part 1   the children rub their backs together;

 Part 2   the "flea" hops off to find another dog and the game is repeated.

Keep repeating "hop, hop, hop" until everyone has found a new dog.

Change who is the flea and who the dog after a few times.

One Two Three / Un deux trois

Grades

1 and 2

Concepts

☐ Rhythm pattern;   ☐ body percussion.

trad arr Ada Vermeulen

Un, deux, trois,

267

Process

1   Sing the song in English and/or French.

2   Clap the rhythm pattern. Play it on a drum. Say the time names.

3   Have the children create a body percussion ostinato to go with the song. One example might be:

> clap three times (rest);
> patsch three times (rest);
> roll hands or snap fingers four times;
> clap three times.

4   Teach and play the instrumental accompaniment with the song.

Movement game

> Formation: in one circle form pairs, with partners beside and facing one another.
>
> measure 1   clap three times;
> measure 2   clap partner's hands three times;
> measure 3   hold partner's hands and turn a half circle with four steps;
> measure 4   the children turn their backs to their partners and each faces a new partner. (They may clap three times during this.)
> Repeat *ad lib.*

Special learners

●   Standing beside one's partner in a circle is a difficult formation for some children. They cannot remember which person is their partner. The movement game could be made simpler by having the children stand in pairs in random formation. The first three measures are the same. In the fourth the children stay facing their partners and simply clap three times. The game is repeated with the same partners.

Little Robot

Grades

2 and 3

Concepts

❏ Creative movement;   ❏ sound exploration.

> I'm a Little Robot,
>   Wires make me talk.
> I'm a Little Robot,
>   Wires make me walk.
> I'm a Little Robot,
>   Wires bend my knees.
> I'm a Little Robot,
>   Wires make me sneeze.
>   AAAACHOOOOOO!

I'm a Little Robot,
   Wires make me work.
So if you ever cross them,
   I'll probably go BERSERK!

ZOING ZOING BOINK!
ZOING ZOING BOINK!
ZING!

Robert Heidbreder

Process

1   Read the poem to the children and discuss what a robot is.

2   Ask the children questions, such as
      "how would a robot move?";
      "what would a robot sound like when it talked?";
      "what would it sound like when it moved?"

3   Let the children experiment freely with different forms of movement and with different sounds they make themselves.

4   Combine the suggested actions in the poem with the creative ideas of the children.

Instruments

Perhaps in another lesson, experiment with sounds to find those that would describe the sounds a robot would make. Some of these might be: woodblocks, slide whistles, temple blocks; log (or slit) drums, tin cans rattled together; drums smacked with the palm of the hand; xylophones played with wooden mallets.

Special learners

● This is an excellent activity for children who have special needs because there is no prescribed way to move and no "accepted" standard by which they will be judged. Their suggestions and ideas will be accepted readily.

Copycat

Grades

1 through 3

Concepts

❏ Creative movement;   ❏ copying movement from someone else.

Copycat, copycat,
Shadow's a copycat!

Out in the sun
Whenever I run,
   It runs.

269

Whenever I twirl,
    It twirls.
I curl up small,
It curls up small.
I stand up tall,
It stands up tall.

Copycat, copycat,
Shadow's a copycat!

Whenever I hide,
    It hides.
I spread out wide,
It spreads out wide.
I pat my head,
It pats its head.
I fall down dead,
It falls down dead.

But when I go inside to stay,
Copycat, copycat goes away!

Robert Heidbreder

Process

1 Read the poem and discuss the concept of shadows with the children. They will quickly realize that a shadow has to copy the actions of its "person" exactly.

2 Each child stands, facing a partner. They decide who will be the shadow first.

3 Give time for everyone to explore different movements – creating and shadowing. Reverse roles.

4 Read the poem very expressively, pausing often to give the children time to create and react to the movement.

5 Have the partners change places and repeat.

6 Can the children think of other motions to incorporate into the poem?

> I touch my knee,
> It touches its knee.
> I blink my eyes,
> It blinks its eyes.   … and so on.

Special learners

- Many children who have poor spatial-awareness skills will need a great amount of free-movement exploration first before attempting this activity.
- This is a useful poem to use with children who are visually impaired, because it describes each movement clearly in words.
- For children who have restricted movement, concentrate on motions they can perform.

270

Shake My Sillies Out

Grades

1 through 3

Concepts

☐ Co-ordination; ☐ language development.

words and music Raffi
arrangement Joy Reeve

shake my sil - lies out, And wig - gle my wag-gles a - way.

2   Gotta, clap, clap, clap my crazies out
    Clap, clap, clap my crazies out,
    Clap, clap, clap my crazies out,
    And wiggle my waggles away.

3   Gotta jump, jump, jump my jiggles out,
    Jump, jump, jump my jiggles out,
    Jump, jump, jump my jiggles out,
    And wiggle my waggles away.

4   Gotta yawn, yawn, yawn my sleepies out,
    Yawn, yawn, yawn my sleepies out,
    Yawn, yawn, yawn my sleepies out,
    And wiggle my waggles away.

Process

1   Sing the song and perform the actions suggested. Verse 4 should be performed much more slowly.

2   Teach the accompaniment if this suits the needs of your group.

3   Have the children create other verses, incorporating different actions they might do.

4   "Swing" the ♩♪ rhythm so it sounds more like ♪·♪ .

5   If no C♯ is available for the alto glockenspiel, use an E instead.

Danse des Foulards

Concept

☐ Forme: ABA.

musique et chorégraphie Marie-José Timperley

273

Démarche pédagogique
Jeu instrumental (ABA)

Partie A

1 Apprentissage de la mélodie à la flûte: d'abord par imitation, puis doigtés muets en solfiant les notes (flûte appuyée sur le menton).

2 Apprentissage de l'accompagnement instrumental: montrer la ligne de xylophone basse et métallophone basse aux percussions corporelles. A la troisième mesure, faire remarquer l'octave et le changement de notes.

3 Jouer aux instruments.

4 Jouer avec la mélodie aux flûtes.

5 Pour le xylophone alto, le rythme est identique à celui des XB et MB.

6 Faire jouer la ligne du carillon aux percussions corporelles. Faire jouer la mélodie à la flûte et y insérer la partie des carillons. Faire remarquer les octaves.

7 Percussions: pour les bongos et aussi les blocs sonores, faire jouer aux percussions corporelles d'abord, ensuite avec instruments.

Partie B

1 Apprentissage de la mélodie à la flûte: le même procédé qu'à la partie A.

2 Apprentissage de l'accompagnement de percussion: pour les bongos et blocs sonores, les cymbalettes et tambourins utiliser le même procédé que pour la partie A.

Danse (ABA)

Partie A
Formation: en cercle, un derrière l'autre

1 Foulards dans la main droite (vers l'extérieur du cercle).

2 Les pas suivent le rythme des XB et MB.

3 À la boîte 1, les foulards vers le bas.

4 À la reprise, les foulards au-dessus de la tête.

5 Essayer sur place avec les pas et les foulards avant de le faire en cercle.

Partie B

1 À la boîte 1 faire l'improvisation corporelle avec foulards, en se promenant dans la salle.

2 À la reprise reprendre la formation en cercle pour le retour de la partie A.

A-Hunting We Will Go

Grades

K through 3

Concepts

☐ 6/8 metre;   ☐ movement patterns.

Allegretto   traditional arr Doreen Hall

then we'll let him go.

Process

1. Teach the song by rote.

2. If the children are very young, teach a simple bordun accompaniment of G/D played on each beat (two beats to a measure). The notes might be played alternately.

3. Children in Grades 1 and 2 can learn the basic accompaniment as shown and by Grade 3 the introduction should be manageable.

4. Divide the timpani part between the hands (see chapter 24, "Tips for Teachers").

Movement

There are many different movement patterns that are commonly used with this song. Choose the one that most suits the needs of your children or create your own. Excellent for children in wheelchairs.

Easiest

The children line up in pairs at one end of the room. When the music begins they march to the other end and divide with the right-hand persons going back down the right side of the room and the left going down the left. They reform their original pairs at the other end and repeat the pattern.

More difficult

Four couples face one another in two lines. The head couple holds hands and skips eight counts down the middle of the line and eight counts back to the starting position. The song is repeated (with no introduction) while the head couple leads his/her line right or left down to the bottom of the original line. The head couple makes an arch with its hands and the rest pass under to form new lines with a new head couple. Repeat four times to give everyone a turn to be head couple.

276

Play the introduction before repeating to make sure each child is in position before starting again.

Tinikling

"Tinikling" is a dance from the Philippines that is a great test of co-ordination. It is performed with two long sticks, usually made of bamboo, that are moved in and out by two people while the dancer hops in and out of the space in the middle. The form of the dance has been used here and a little recorder melody has been composed for it. Add as many percussion parts as are suitable for your group.

Grades

5 and 6

Concepts

- ☐ Accelerando;
- ☐ co-ordination;
- ☐ ABA form;
- ☐ very secure beat sense;

- ☐ developing sense of trust;
- ☐ listening;
- ☐ group co-operation.

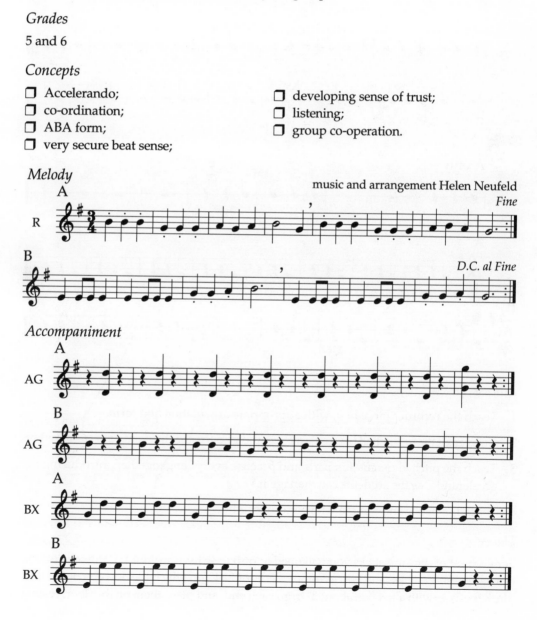

277

Percussion parts

These are to be added with each repetition in any order.

A and B

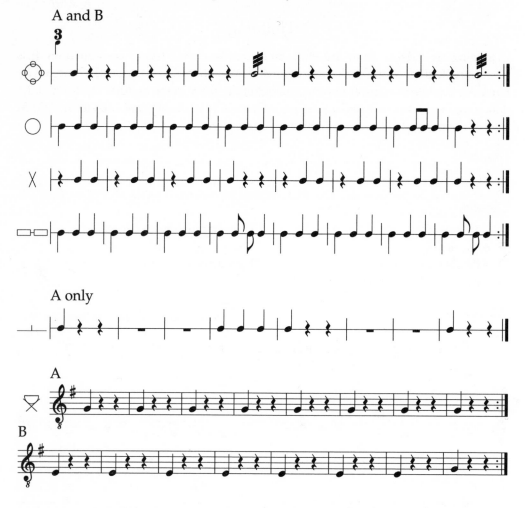

A only

A

B

Process

1 Teach the recorder piece first, with appropriate articulation and form.

2 Go over all the unpitched percussion parts and practise the different patterns together.

3 Teach the pitched percussion parts and practise everything together, introducing the accelerando, as the students can manage it.

4 Teach the dance and put the whole piece together.

Dance

For each set of dancing sticks you will need to purchase two ten-foot 1¼" dowels (or you can use bamboo sticks) and two two-foot pieces of 2×4", on which the dowels could slide. Mark the 2×4s with a felt pen about 3" from each end, and place them on the floor, resting

278

the dowels on them. With a child at each end of the dowels to click them together, begin the practice. For beat 1 click the dowels together in the middle. Tap the dowels on the wood for beats 2 and 3. From two to four dancers can dance with each set, depending on the level of their accomplishment and whether or not they dance as partners.

For the dance, keeping the body weight centered, alternate feet must step out of way to avoid the click of the dowels. Begin from beside the dowels. First step outside with the right foot, then, as the dowels move apart, shift inside, first with the left foot, then with right. For the next measure, step outside with the left foot on the first beat, then inside on the followi two, firs   t with the right foot, then the left. Dancers say "out, in, in" as they dance to memorize the pattern. To avoid ankle injuries, when you begin the practice, do not click the dowels together on beat 1. When dancers are adept at stepping out on beat 1, begin the regular dowel pattern of "together, click, click" for the three-in-the-measure pattern. Caution the students to lift feet well off the floor when dancing to avoid interference with the dowels. The stick holders must keep dowels sliding on the 2×4s without lifting them.

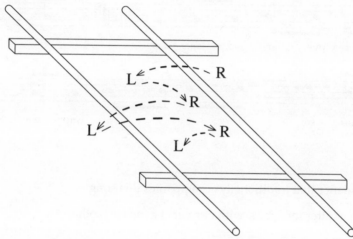

As the dancers become more secure, they may try a half-turn on the two steps between the dowels, or dance holding hands, facing a partner, moving in the same direction, or in opposite directions. When students have all had the opportunity to learn the dance, they may choose to be recorder players, accompanists, dancers or stick holders so that the whole thing may be put together.

Form

The song is in ABA form, and with each repetition add a pitched or unpitched percussion instrument – as many as can play together exactly on the beat. Slightly increase the tempo as the players and dancers become comfortable. The timpani and bass players especially must be very secure in beat and tempo as they control the accelerando.

Extensions

● Take the students to visit a multicultural festival to observe the dance being performed by experts.
● The music and the dance could form part of a unit on the Philippines.

The Shoemaker

Grades

1 through 3

Concept

☐ Non-locomotor and locomotor movement.

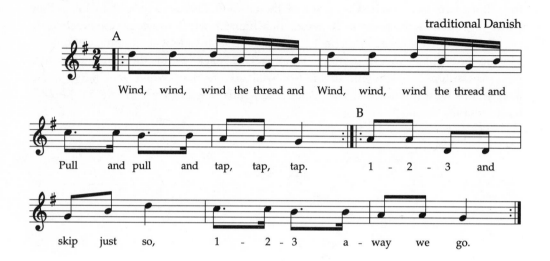

traditional Danish

Wind, wind, wind the thread and Wind, wind, wind the thread and

Pull and pull and tap, tap, tap. 1 - 2 - 3 and

skip just so, 1 - 2 - 3 a - way we go.

Process

1 Teach the dance that traditionally accompanies this song

Formation: scatter into pairs, with partners facing each other
Part A
    Clench your hands and perform a winding motion away from and then towards the body.
    Pull your arms apart with two vigorous jerks and then do a hammering motion with the fists three times.
    Repeat the actions for the repeat of the song.
Part B
    Grasp your partner's hand and skip freely through the space.
    Repeat the movement for the repeat of the song, but on the words "away we go" separate from your partner and find a new one.

2 Have the students suggest different unpitched percussion instruments to accompany the words "wind", "pull" and "tap".

● The song could be correlated with the story of "The Elves and the Shoemaker".

(Contributed by Carolyn McMillan)

Dancing Is What I Will Do

The music for this piece is found in volume 1 of Carl Orff's and Gunild Keetman's *Music for Children*. This is an example of another way to use these beautifully crafted instrumental works.

Grades

2 through 4

Concepts

- ❑ Creating words to existing melodies;
- ❑ creative movement;
- ❑ rondo form;
- ❑ ostinati;
- ❑ speech rhythms.

words Linda Campbell
music adapted from *Music for Children*, vol. 1

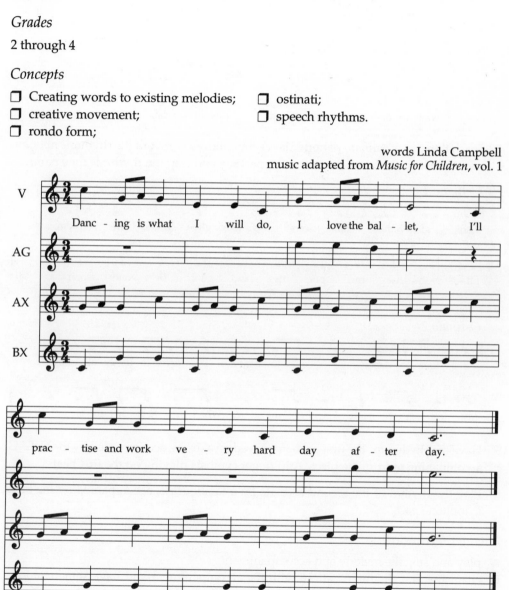

Process

1 Teach the melody. If possible, play the melody on recorders.

2 Teach the new words to the melody.

3 Teach the accompaniments (they are somewhat different than those written originally). Putting words to them will help to keep the rhythm steady:

BX   Danc - ing and danc - ing and danc - ing and danc - ing and

AX   Pi - rou - ette oh pi - rou - ette oh pi - rou - ette oh pi - rou - ette oh

G   I want to dance (*wait,* *wait*) I want to dance (*wait,* *wait*)

4 Teach the speech ostinato patterns. Have the children work out the rhythmic notation
and write it on the board or on chart paper. Say and clap the rhythmic time names.

Ostinato 1

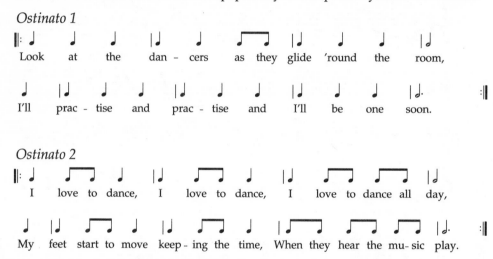

Look at the dan – cers as they glide 'round the room,

I'll prac - tise and prac - tise and I'll be one soon.

Ostinato 2

I love to dance, I love to dance, I love to dance all day,

My feet start to move keep - ing the time, When they hear the mu - sic play.

5 Have the rhythm for the first ostinato played on a drum, accompanied by the C–G–G
accompaniment from the piece. Add finger cymbals playing on the first beats.

6 Play the rhythm of the second ostinato on a tambourine, accompanied by the bass
xylophone part.

Final form (rondo)

A play and sing the melody and accompaniment;
B chant the first rhythmic pattern with the accompaniment and have some children
perform creative movement for these eight measures;
A play and sing as above;
C chant the second rhythmic pattern with accompaniment and movement;
A play and sing as above.

● This activity can be used with "The Camel Dance" in *Fables* by Arthur Lobel.

282

CHAPTER TWENTY

Instruments

Order of Instruments on a Score
with abbreviations and symbols

L'ordre des Instruments dans la Partition
avec les abbréviations et les symboles

F	Flute		F	Flûte

Voices

S	Soprano		S	Soprano
A	Alto		C	Contralto
T	Tenor		T	Ténor
B	Bass		B	Basse

Voix

SoR	Sopranino Recorder		Fl.So	Flûte à bec, Sopranino
SR	Soprano Recorder		Fl.S	Flûte à bec, Soprano
AR	Alto Recorder		Fl.A	Flûte à bec, Alto
TR	Tenor Recorder		Fl.T	Flûte à bec, Ténor
BR	Bass Recorder		Fl.B	Flûte à bec, Basse
SG	Soprano Glockenspiel		CS	Carillon Soprano
AG	Alto Glockenspiel		CA	Carillon Alto
SX	Soprano Xylophone		XS	Xylophone Soprano
AX	Alto Xylophone		XA	Xylophone Alto
SM	Soprano Metallophone		MS	Métallophone Soprano
AM	Alto Metallophone		MA	Métallophone Alto

Percussion*

Metals		Métal	
△	Triangle	△	Triangle
◎	Finger Cymbals	◎	Crotales
⌓	Jingle Bells	⌓	Grelots
⧖	Bell Tree	⧖	Arbre de Crotales
⊓⊓⊓	Chime Tree	⊓⊓⊓	Arbre de Carillon
◁	Agogo Bells	◁	Cloches Agogo
⌂	Cowbell	⌂	Cowbell
⊣⊢	Cymbals	⊣⊢	Cymbales
⊓	Cabasa	⊓	Cabasa
◁	Slide Whistle	◁	Flûte à Coulisse
◉	Tambourine	◉	Tambour Basque
⊓	Flexitone	⊓	Flexitone

Woods		Woods	
▭	Woodblock	▭	Blocs Sonores
⊓	Tic-toc Block	⊓	Tube Résonnant
⚲	Castanets	⚲	Castagnettes
⊐	Shakers	⊐	Hochet
✗	Maracas	✗	Maracas
⊬	Ratchet	⊬	Crécelle
∅	Rattle	∅	Rattle
▢▢▢	Temple Blocks	▢▢▢	Blocs Chinois
◁	Vibraslap	◁	Vibraslap
✕	Claves	✕	Claves
⊂▷	Guiro or Reco Reco	⊂▷	Guiro ou Reco Reco
▭	Log Drum	▭	Tambour de Bois
▦	Sand Blocks	▦	Blocs Sablés

Skins		Peau	
◯	Hand Drum	◯	Tambour
⬚⬚	Bongos	⬚⬚	Bongos
⬚	Conga	⬚	Conga
⬚	Snare Drum	⬚	Caisse claire
⬚⬚	Tumba	⬚⬚	Tumba

Large Percussion		Grand Percussion	
⊥	Hanging Cymbal	⊥	Cymbale Suspendue
⬚	Gong	⬚	Gong Japonais
◯	Bass Drum	◯	Timbale
⬚	Timpani	⬚	Timpani

* There is no particular order within families of non-pitched percussion
Aucun ordre spécifique pour les petites percussion

	Guitar		Guitare
BX	Bass Xylophone	XB	Xylophone Basse
BM	Bass Metallophone	MB	Métallophone Basse
BB	Bass Bars	CB	Note Contrabasse

Range of Barred Instruments
Le régistre des percussion mélodiques

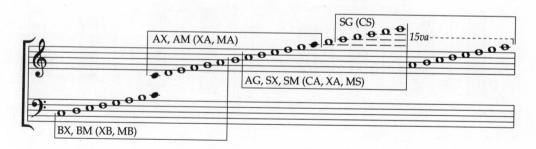

Set-up of Instruments for Pentatonic Scales

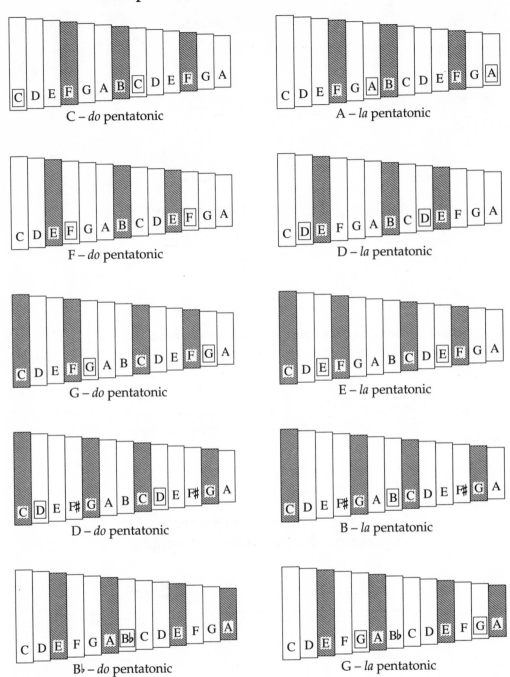

C – *do* pentatonic

A – *la* pentatonic

F – *do* pentatonic

D – *la* pentatonic

G – *do* pentatonic

E – *la* pentatonic

D – *do* pentatonic

B – *la* pentatonic

B♭ – *do* pentatonic

G – *la* pentatonic

- ● Remove the shaded notes.
- ● The main note of each scale is in a box.
- ● The above are possible using diatonic instruments.
- ● Replace Bs and Fs with B♭s and F♯s where needed.

Can You Play?

Grades

2 through 4

Concepts

❏ Instrumental technique;   ❏ listening.
❏ review of note values;

Diane Shieron

1. Can you play a lit - tle tune, lit - tle tune, lit - tle tune?
2. I can play a lit - tle tune, lit - tle tune, lit - tle tune?

Can you play a lit - tle tune, on your ins - tru - ment.
I can play a lit - tle tune, on my ins - tru - ment.

Process

Warm-ups

1 Set the instruments up in C pentatonic (remove all F and B bars).

2 The leader claps various rhythm patterns suitable for the capabilities of the children.

3 The group says the pattern using time names and then plays it on instruments, using any note(s). For example:

the leader claps ♫ ♫ ♫ ♩ ;

the children say ti–ti ti–ti ti–ti ta;

the children play ♫ ♫ ♫ ♩ (on any note).

4 Teach the song by rote, having the class clap the rhythm of the words.

5 After the class responds with the second verse "on my instrument" all the children who have instruments improvise a little melody, or a little rhythmic pattern (if they are playing unpitched percussion).

6 After each child has had a turn on an instrument in this ensemble form, the teacher directs the question to a specific instrument or family of instruments:

Can you play a little tune, little tune, little tune?
Can you play a little tune on your [xylophone/glockenspiel/percussion instruments]?

Sometimes words will have to be added or the rhythm will have to be changed.

7 The children playing those specific instruments respond as above.

Special learners

● This is a good activity for children who have special needs. It is creative and is designed for success.

Bartolo avait une flûte

Démarche pédagogique

Forme

Intro   mélodie à la flûte;

A   mélodie accompagnée;
         improvisation de mouvement avec banderoles de couleurs;

B   improvisation rythmique (avec les instruments fabriqués)
         accompagnée par le xylophone basse et les percussions
         corporelles;

A   idem.

(Activité préparée par Sylvie Guertin et Alain Croteau)

instrumentation Sylvie Guertin

* Percussion corporelle

288

Beginning Recorder

Beginning recorder practice can be made much more interesting by playing short tunes based on only the three notes B–A–G. Two of these follow, arranged for Orff instrumental accompaniment. They are from the Windsong series by Birthe Kulich and Joe Berarducci, published by Empire Music, Vancouver.

Other tunes you might try include "Hot Cross Buns", "Hop Old Squirrel", "Rain Rain Go Away", "A-Tisket A-Tasket", and "Hear the Bells Ring".

When the students can play high D you may add "Gramma Grunts" and "Merrily We Roll Along".

Bag Tune

music Birthe Kulich
arrangement Joe Berarducci

Polka Hop

music and arrangement Birthe Kulich and Joe Berarducci

Dance Time

words and music Priscilla Evans

Process

1 "Dance Time" can be sung first to learn the melody, then played on the recorder.

2 The piece itself is in ABA form, and the whole presentation could be made also in ABA form:

    A sing the song through (ABA);

    B play it on recorders;

    A one part of group sings, the other plays recorders.

290

No Money

Melody

trad. adapted Priscilla Evans

When you have no mo – ney, Life is not so fun – ny.

Life is not so fun – ny, When your purse is emp – ty.

Accompaniment

Process

1   The melody may be taught to beginning recorder players as it lies nicely under the fingers.

2   More advanced players may learn the accompaniment. It is in two parts, each can be played by soprano recorders. Combine it in various ways:

   with melody alone;

   melody with accompaniment;

   melody, accompaniment and hand drum playing:

Les petits oiseaux

This music is from a book of Métis songs and music. Music is a very important part of the social life of the Métis and when they come together, fiddlers gather and play long into the night.

"Les petits oiseaux" was played originally on the fiddle or mouth organ (when it is called "musique à bouche") but could also be played on a recorder.

The suggestion is to accompany with foot tapping. Try adding drums, playing in several rhythms.

Paul Proulx
St. Boniface, Manitoba

Tourbillon

Clientèle

4e année

Concept

☐ S'amuser tout en écoutant activement.

Démarche pédagogique

1 Apprendre la mélodie à la flûte par imitation du professeur (quatre mesures par quatre mesures).

2 Une fois la mélodie bien maîtrisée à la flûte, apprendre la partie instrumentale par le biais de percussions corporelles. Cette étape se fait par imitation des gestes du professeur tout en chantant sur des "la, la, la" la mélodie déjà apprise à la flûte.

Caroline Le May

Percussions corporelles

XB et MB

Partie A (bourdon croisé)

La main gauche sur le genou gauche, main droite sur genou droit, main gauche sur côté de jambe droite et main droite sur genou droit. Rythme de croches pour trois mesures, et une noire suivie d'un silence sur la quatrième mesure.

Partie B (bourdon en accord)

Les mains ensemble sur les genoux à chaque premier temps.

XA et tambourin

Partie A

Les mains ensemble sur genoux à la croche (sauf dernière mesure: deux croches, noire).

Partie B

La même chose qu'à la partie A mais avec le rythme noire deux croches.

Carillons

Parties A et B

Claquer des doigts.

Réalisation finale: une moitié de la classe joue la mélodie à la flûte tandis que l'autre moitié joue l'accompagnement sur les instruments Orff.

Activité de mouvement

Formation: deux par deux, debout et face à face pour la position de départ.

1 Un des deux prend la position d'arbre et l'autre sera "monsieur le vent".

2 L'enfant qui fait l'arbre place entre ses doigts trois feuilles d'arbre par main.

3 Au son de la musique, l'enfant qui fait le vent tourne doucement autour de l'arbre tout en bougeant légèrement ses bras.

4 Chaque fois que "monsieur le vent" entend le son des carillons (une fois à toutes les quatre mesures), il doit s'arrêter et souffler sur une des feuilles que l'arbre doit laisser tomber.

5 "Monsieur le vent", après avoir soufflé sur une feuille, tourne de nouveau autour de l'arbre jusqu'au prochain son de carillons, et ainsi de suite jusqu'à la fin de la pièce.

6 La pièce dans sa totalité contient six sons de carillons. Voilà pourquoi il y a six feuilles d'arbre par équipe de deux.

Two Instrumental Pieces

The following two instrumental pieces are by Keith Bissell and are found in his book *In the Modes; 15 modal pieces for percussion and recorder* (Waterloo: Waterloo Music, 1982).

In the book, each of the five modes is represented by three pieces.

Number III – Mixolydian

Number V – Lydian (uneven metre)

297

Ungaresca

This Hungarian folk dance from the early sixteenth century was arranged for recorders and Orff instruments by Carolyn Ritchey Kunzman and Ursula M. Rempel, and is taken from their book *A Medieval Feast: songs and dances for recorders and Orff instruments* (Waterloo: Waterloo Music, 1981). It should be played with energy and perhaps a controlled accelerando throughout. You might try a "Hai!" on the last beat of the final playing.

The solo interlude part may be simplified if necessary. For variety, use a different instrument for each repetition of the interlude. Choose from: timpani, woodblock, patschen, clapping, claves, and bass xylophone on G.

An interesting effect may be achieved by changing the rhythm of the dance to

Movement

The dance was choreographed (using traditional Renaissance step–close patterns) by Carolyn Ritchey Kunzman, Ursula M. Rempel and Carolyn's Junior High Orff Ensemble from Arthur A. Leach, Junior High, Winnipeg, Manitoba.

Formation: two concentric circles, girls forming the inner circle, facing their partners in the outer. Both circles begin to move to the left. Boys place their hands on their hips; girls, hands holding skirts.

Basic steps
Left (both circles)

Repeat the above pattern to the right, starting with the right foot.
Left

Repeat the above pattern to the right starting with the right foot and ending with a stamp instead of a step-touch.

Interlude

Repeat all the above steps.

Variations

Interlude steps may be improvised (with feet, patschen, clapping, and so on); boys and girls may exchange places on the second half (bar 2) of the interlude pattern. Appropriate "Hais" (with arms raised) may be added as desired!

Introduction

Hungarian folk song
arrangement Carolyn Ritchey Kunzman and Ursula Rempel

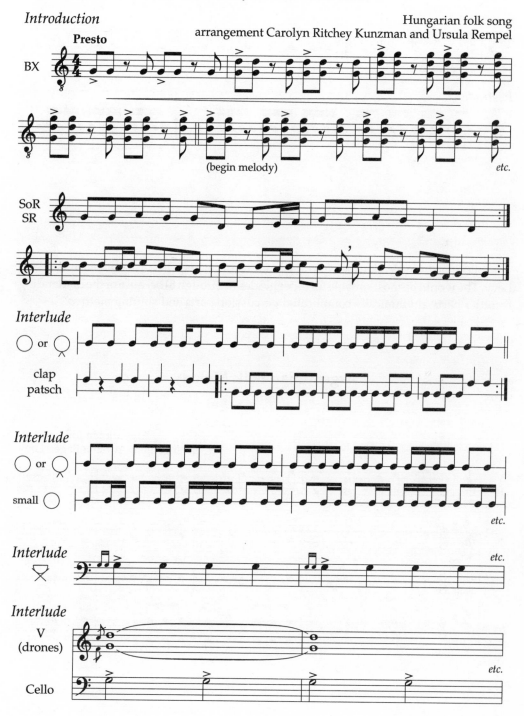

299

Interlude

The following two selections were arranged for recorder and Orff instruments by Adriana Levy. The would be most suitable for older grades (6 through 8) because of the demanding recorder parts, rhythmically complicated percussion parts and shifting metres.

Argentinian Folk Melody

Argentinian folk melody
arrangement Adriana Bages-Levy

Chacarera

Argentinian traditional dance
arrangement Adriana Bages-Levy

CHAPTER TWENTY-ONE

Listening Awareness and Music Appreciation

Sensory Awareness Exercises and Games

Hania Krajewskia and Lois Birkenshaw-Fleming

Everything humans learn in life comes through the five senses – hearing, sight, touch, smell and taste – th added information gleaned from the kinesethic sense (the knowledge the body has about its position in space). This vast daily input is sorted by the brain and translates into knowledge and experience.

Children need to develop *all* their senses.

An important part in any learning process is to spend the opening part of a lesson helping children to "centre" themselves physically and emotionally by isolating and exploring any one of the five senses. This kind of activity can bring a calmness to children and enable them to concentrate more readily on the skills to be developed. When children are put in touch with some aspect of their physical selves and their immediate environment they can focus and concentrate more easily and with more awareness.

The following activities are included for this purpose along with some suggestions on how to extend from these starting points. Choose those that suit the level and experience of the students with whom you work.

Sight / Looking

COPY-CAT

1   Students sit in a group formation and observe the teacher or leader perform a sequence of three to eight motions (the number depends on the age and experience of the students). For example, pat lap; clap hands once; touch chin, pat head; or sew with needle; prick thumb; suck thumb; bandage thumb. The students copy the patterns, combining the motions together.

Extensions

• Patterns following a theme can be used as a basis for story-telling. The teacher tells a story as the students re-enact, such as "I noticed a button was missing off my jacket and I began to sew another button onto it. All of a sudden I pricked my thumb … "

• Many possible themes can be developed by focusing on simple plots such as waiting at the doctor's, making a cake, or raking leaves. Each motion might have a different rhythm instrument accompanying it to enhance the mime and activate the imagination. This is a wonderful way to develop language by working with descriptive language.

OBSERVING DETAIL

1 In twos the students look at each other and then stand back to back.

2 Each student then chooses three items to change about their appearance, for instance, move a ring to another finger, or undo some button …

3 Students then face each other and try to identify the changes.

TRANSFORMATIONS

1 Students form themselves into groups of between six and ten.

2 Each group will have 90 seconds to transform an object through mime into others based on its shape. For instance, a pencil could become a toothbrush or a baton or a walking stick; a piece of cloth becomes a blanket, a veil, a belt or a monster cape.

3 When the group's time is up the rest of the students have turns miming with the object.

4 Change the object used (a drum, a small basket, a tin can, a rope …).

5 This activity encourages creativity and lateral thinking.

MUSICAL DETECTIVE

1 One student leaves the room while the rest of the group selects a leader who will keep a steady beat through a gesture that all the rest will copy, such as patting knees, clapping a pattern or nodding the head.

2 The group sits in circle formation. The "detective" returns and stands in the middle of the circle trying to guess who is leading as the leader changes from one action to another. Everyone must focus not to give the leader away.

3 This is an excellent exercise to help students internalize the beat and overcome inhibitions with movement (particularly with students who have special needs or with self-conscious adolescents).

PASS-A-MIME
Pass an action around a circle, for example, sharing an apple, carefully giving a lighted candle, planting a garden or eating spaghetti.

PASS-A-PRESENT
Each person passes a "present" around the circle. The person receiving the object changes it in mime and passes it on. It could be long and thin, transformed to fat and heavy to very small and light and so on. As the students become familiar with the game have them pass to people across the circle as well as to their neighbours.

DRAW WHAT YOU HEAR
Listen to the lyrics of a song or the words of a poem and have the students draw the detail given. By encouraging visualization, students will sing the song or dramatize the poem with more awareness.

304

1 Everyone mimes the action of putting on magic gloves that make the voice disappear. The leader's hands direct the other(s) to do things, such as stand up, take two steps in, turn around, jump up and down and so on. "Take the gloves off" at the end to restore voices. For some children, giving the leader a real set of gloves to wear would make the game easier to understand. If they were purple, pink, bright green or orange it would be more fun.

2 Play the game with one person leading the rest or in pairs. Change the leaders often.

GROUP SCULPTURES

1 Each group is shown a pattern or a picture. The task is to re-create the image by arranging the people in the group in ways that copy the picture.

2 Spell a words by arranging the body shapes of the group.

3 Re-create a rhythm pattern by joining people together. What do you do about the rests?

Smell

GUESS WHAT IS IN THE CAN

Put small amounts of spices and other "smelly" substances in jars or plastic containers. The children have to identify these by smell only – eyes shut – no peeking. Some ideas might be: cinnamon, garlic, crushed mint leaves, rotten eggs, talcum powder, perfume.

COLLECT SMELLS

"What did you smell on your way to school?" "What did we smell on our visit to the zoo?" Make a list. Put the items into categories of good smells and bad smells. Discuss that some people have different ideas of what is good and bad. Discuss how poor humans are in detecting smells in comparison to dogs and other animals.

Taste

WHAT IS IT?

Put a small amount of a variety of foods out on separate plates and have the students identify them by taste alone. Blindfolds should be used if the students can tolerate these. Include such items as ginger, cinnamon, salt, vinegar, chocolate, rice, carrots and so on.

Hearing / sound

SOUNDS AROUND

"Close your eyes, be still and listen. What do you hear? Tell us about the sounds you hear." Have the children "collect" sounds from their homes, on the way to school, in the play yard and, if possible, describe these in words.

SOUND DURATION I

Have the children put their hands in the air when a sound such as a gong, bell or cymbal begins and lower them when it can no longer be heard.

SOUND DURATION II

1 The children sit in circle formation with lowered heads, closed eyes and palms of hands resting in their laps.

2 The teacher or leader strikes a metal instrument, such as a chime or metallophone, letting its sound die out naturally.

3 When the children cannot longer hear any resonance they slowly and silently bring up their arms and heads, opening their eyes in the final position.

4 Each child is to respond independently according to their own hearing. The result is flowing group movement which, however, requires individual self-control.

5 This activity could be used as an opening to a dramatization of a legend or myth as a lead-in to a song of the people of a tribe. It is visually and aurally a powerful beginning.

SOUND TRACKING I

The students sit in scattered formation, eyes closed. Play a sound in a corner of the room. The students point to where they think the sound is coming from. Play up high, down low. Move around, silently, so the sound will come from different places.

SOUND TRACKING II

1 The children sit in a scattered formation in an open space. Eyes closed, heads down.

2 Two students walk around the space, each on their own, playing intermittently a rhythm instrument such as a woodblock, finger cymbal or guiro.

3 The children raise both hands and follow each of the two sounds with their fingers pointing. Sometimes both arms are moving, sometimes only one, depending on when a sound is being produced. This takes very careful listening.

CONTRAST SOUNDS

Make or find sounds that make sounds that are high/low, fast/slow, smooth, absolutely the most boring sound in the world, and so on.

INSTRUMENTS

Experiment with different instruments to produce many sounds. "How many sounds can you make with your cabasa, triangle, guiro?"

PARTNERS IN SOUND

Join with one or several classmates to create a mini-composition combining different sounds in many ways. The result could be a composition that had the form ABA or AABA, or a rondo ABACADAEA, or a piece that started with one sound and added all the others, one after the other. The possibilities are endless.

SWITCH: THREE WAYS OF BEGINNING

1   Have sets of "sound pictures" available. These can be made by you or the students.

2   Create these pictures with your sound maker (voice/found sound/instruments/body percussion). Create these sounds in movement.

3   Start with movement. Describe the movement by creating pictures and using instrumental sounds.

4   Start with a sound. Describe the sound in movement and by creating pictures.

SOUND EFFECTS

Choose instruments that will simulate sounds from a particular environment to introduce a theme or story. For instance, a woodblock can represent a woodpecker; sand blocks or a cabasa can be footsteps on a path filled with leaves (as part of a forest setting for a story). By visualizing, students will then move with more sensitivity through the imaginary bushes, over logs, stones and streams.

FOOTSTEPS

1   Children sit in scattered formation with closed eyes.

2   The leader taps from two to six children lightly on their heads or shoulders. Those tapped stand up very quietly. With a visual signal they begin to walk with heavy, slow footsteps as if they were only one person. They then return to their places and sit down.

3   The rest of the group guesses how many people were walking.

4   This exercise could be used to introduce the theme of bears or giants in terms of the quality of their movement, and to stimulate the imagination.

QUICK RESPONSE

1   The children sit up with eyes focused on the teacher or leader. They are in rows or scattered formation. A number of cued responses are explained (as many as your group would be comfortable with). The students are asked to respond to the cues which are given in mixed up order. This requires close attention.

Cue	Response
"hands like this" (hold hands in a particular way)	they clap one time
cymbal tremolo	breathe in to "ah"
cymbal stops	breathe out to "wow"
"one, two three"	"four"
"make this motion"	move head to steady beat of woodblock

2   This is an excellent way to start a choir rehearsal. The game promotes concentration and breathing.

Touch

SURPRISE

1 Sitting in any formation, children close their eyes and lower their heads. The teacher touches heads gently in random order.

2 When touched, students raise their heads in total silence until only one child remains.

3 On cue, all children together whisper, "Wake up ——", naming the last child who is still waiting to be touched.

4 This activity is a good way to create a relaxed atmosphere and to practise a projected whisper for choral speaking.

HAND SCULPTING

1 With a partner, one student makes a shape with his/her hands while the other student, with closed eyes, feels the shape made and tries to reproduce it. Take turns being the shape-maker.

2 This has to be done with no talking. Playing mood music in the background helps to reinforce the quietness and isolate the experience of the sense of touch.

PASSIVE/ACTIVE

1 In pairs, one student moves the limbs of the other student creating different shapes and formations. The student being molded must be totally passive in taking direction. A frozen gaze is important.

2 No talking! Total silence creates an illusion that one person is a mannequin. This activity is done very slowly and respectfully, requiring trust by the participants.

3 Use two students who have maturity to demonstrate for the group.

4 Have one molder work on a group of three or four students creating a tableau or group sculpture. If there is a theme present, the activity could be accompanied by recorded music depicting the same theme.

LEAD BY TOUCH ONLY

One blindfolded person is led around by a partner who puts one finger under his or her elbow. (Make sure that the students will accept wearing a blindfold. Some might panic.)

A MAGICAL STRING

Partners hold the ends of a three-foot string or rope and move around to music.

WONDROUS LYCRA

1 A strip, possible three or four feet across and four to five feet long (depending on the age of the group) is pulled and stretched between two or more students to make "sculptures." Some can get under the strip and push it out to make even more interesting shapes.

2 Lycra can be sewn into "bags". One or two people can get inside to make "ghostly" shapes or sculptures.

A few ideas for sound exploration

THAT'S MY VOICE

1 Experiment with voices: going up, down, sliding up and down, babbling, shouting.

2 Make a chart with squiggles, jagged sounds, rough sounds, smooth sounds and explosions! Have someone come and "play the piece", pointing to different pictures in turn, in different order and sequence, quickly, slowly, switching back and forth between two contrasting pictures and so on. The group interprets the sounds with their voices.

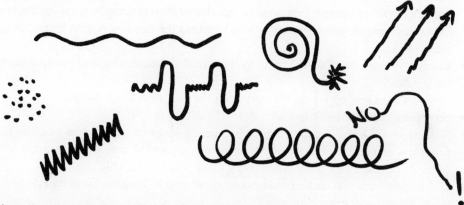

3 Have the children create their own "sound pictures".

4 Create a "singing space": a cushion, low stool or chair. When the teacher or leader goes there it is a sign for those who want to sing with him or her, to gather around.

BODY PERCUSSION

1 Experiment in a similar way with sounds that can be made by: clapping, patschen, snapping, stamping, patting cheeks with the mouth open, patting the backs of hands/arms, cupping hands together and squeezing the air out ... The children will be able to add many more "homemade" sounds.

UNPITCHED PERCUSSION

1 Experiment with these instruments, finding out how many sounds can be produced.

2 Combine these in different ways, perhaps using the "sound picture" ideas above.

DRUMS, DRUMS, DRUMS

1 Collect different sounding drums – large ones, small ones, those made by stretching rubber or drum skin over coconut shells or cut-off plastic drain pipe, bongo drums, cardboard mailing tubes (one end covered with several thickness of plastic), kitchen sealer, talking drums, many different ethnic drums.

2   Let the students experiment with all of these to see what different sounds they can produce by playing them in different ways.

3   Play two or three behind a screen. "Which ones did I use?" "In what order?" (a harder task). Add more drums as the students increase their listening ability.

EXPERIMENT WITH OTHER SOUNDS

♦ Egg slicer harp.
♦ Suspended ceramic flower pots.
♦ Suspended nails, spoons and other pieces of metal.
♦ A "growler": thread an old guitar string, an elastic band or a piece of thick string through a small hole in the bottom of a tin can, an empty plastic ice cream tub or other container, and tie a firm knot on the inside. Invert the container and pull along the string from the fixed end. This makes a wonderful growly sound – good for lion stories.
♦ "Whirlies": plastic ribbed tubes to whirl around the head, rub with a stick or speak into.
♦ Kazoos – sometimes the very thing to start children vocalizing, and particularly good for the deaf.
♦ Stainless steel mixing bowls: tap gently on the side with a soft mallet.
♦ Styrofoam cups rubbed together.
♦ Shakers – all kinds — made from beans, small stones or paper clips put into plastic film cans, empty tins and plastic bottles of all sizes and shapes. Make sure the lids are securely fastened especially when using these with young children.
♦ Old hockey-stick claves. Cut old hockey sticks into 8" lengths. Sand and paint if you wish. These make great claves.
♦ Fax paper rolls. The inside cone of fax paper rolls make good, soft-sounding claves when hit together. They can be decorated by the children using magic markers.
♦ Small bells sewn on to elastics or ribbons.

These are just a few ideas. Prowl through hardware stores, your own kitchen, a flea market or garage and jumble sales to discover wonderful sound-makers.

Experiment with different ways of producing sounds from these objects. Create little rhythmic patterns. Combine these sounds (either just the pure sound or rhythmic patterns) in different ways to create small forms (ABA, AABA, rondos, canons).

METAL WEEK

1   Occasionally organize a "metal week". The students bring in sound-producers that are made of metal.

2   Experiment with producing as many interesting sounds as possible with these objects. Classroom instruments or parts of these (the keys of glockenspiels or metallophones for instance) can be added to the metal "instrumentarium".

3   Combine the sounds in different ways to produce different forms.

310

4   Experiment with producing sounds that illustrate the basic music concepts – pitch/duration/tempo/timbre/dynamics.

5   Create a rondo. One person is A and creates a rhythm on his/her "instrument". The others create their own rhythms (in the same metre as A) for B, C, D, E, and so on.

6   Make a metal mobile in one corner of the room, hanging keys, bells of various kinds, metal wind chimes, old spoons, small metal bowls, glockenspiel keys and so on from a frame or the ceiling. The students can activate these by walking through and setting them in motion. They produce a wondrous sound.

During the year organize other kinds of weeks and encourage students to bring in interesting sounds that are produced from: paper (cardboard boxes, tissue paper, other paper to scrunch or tear), wood, (wooden boxes, notes from xylophones, doweling of various lengths, 2x4's, wooden bowls) or plastic (bottles, plates, drum heads, beads).

CONSTRUCT A "SOUND SPACE"

1   Make a private space constructed from hanging curtains, discarded packing crates or something similar. Put some colourful cushions in this to make it cozy, and also place in it an easily played, interesting sound-maker such as a "mbira" (finger piano), a xylophone, a drum, and so on. A child goes into this space and experiments with playing this sound maker.

2   Children who have feelings all bottled up inside will sometimes express these by "playing them out" on the instrument. Sometimes (not always) they will then begin to verbalize what is troubling them.

Special learners

● These experimental activities are excellent for students who have special needs. There is a great amount of learning about the properties of sound taking place and in addition, language is being developed in an almost subliminal way.
● There is no absolutely right or wrong way to perform the activities, so these children can have their contributions accepted and valued thus developing self-esteem.

Morning Mist

Grades

3 and 4

Concepts

❏ Creating sound effects.

When ⬚I awake in morning mist

the (sun) has hardly shown,

and everything is still asleep

and ⬚I am all alone ✗ ✗

The st✳ars are faint and flickering.

The (sun) is new and shy, ✗ ✗

and all the world sleeps quietly

except the (sun) and ⬚I.

anonymous

Process

1   Identify the important words, and mark them in some way.

2   Experiment with sound effects – vocal, body percussion, sounds from the classroom or from home, classroom instruments. Decide which sounds would be most effective to use to describe the mood of the poem and the key thoughts and words.

3   Say the poem and add the sound effects. One idea might be:

   Introduce and end the poem with the sound of a rain stick.

   ⬚   drum

   ◯   triangle or cymbal

   ✗ ✗   claves

   ～   glissando (glockenspiel or metallophone)

   〰   note clusters on glockenspiels / finger cymbals

   ✳   finger cymbals

(Contributed by Angela Elster and Ada Vermeulen)

This Is My Voice

Grades

K through 2

Concepts

☐ Sound recognition and differentiation.

Question

Answer

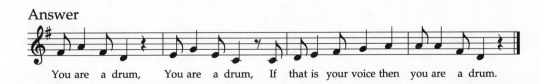

Process

1 This little game can be played with either instruments or children's voices. If it is played with instruments the teacher should ensure that the children are familiar with the names and timbres of the instruments before beginning the game.

2 Start with two or three instruments, gradually adding more as the children become more adept.

3 The teacher should ask the class to close their eyes and then s/he sings the "question". The children should respond with their eyes closed also.

4 If the game is played with children's voices, the teacher should quietly circulate through the room and gently touch a child who then sings the question. The class sings the response, guessing who the child was.

5 In the same manner the teacher could give various children instruments and have then sing the question while playing the instrument.

6 The class can respond individually or as a group as indicated by the teacher.

Special learners

● This is an excellent activity to encourage careful listening. Make sure that some of the voices of instruments are easy enough for everyone to guess.

(Contributed by Marianne Kennedy)

Pond Song

Grades

2 through 4

Concepts

☐ Combining speech patterns;
☐ pitch;
☐ listening awareness.

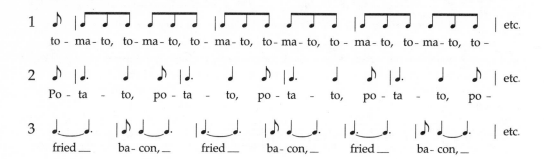

1 to - ma - to, to - ma - to, to - ma - to, to - ma - to, to - ma - to, to - ma - to, to -

2 Po - ta - to, po - ta - to, po - ta - to, po - ta - to, po -

3 fried __ ba - con, __ fried __ ba - con, __ fried __ ba - con, __

Process

1 Divide into three groups. Have a leader for each group.

2 Bring in the groups in sequence. Each group says its part four times, after which the next group comes in.

3 When all are performing together, the result sounds like the sounds of a pond.
   Number 1 is to be spoken with a high, squeaky voice;
   number 2 with a medium-pitched voice;
   number 3 in a very low-pitched voice.

Possible actions
   Number 1: stretch tall with fingers toward ceiling;
   number 2: sway back and forth while standing;
   number 3: kneel on the floor like a frog and do a little hop on "bacon".

● It would be possible to transfer the speech rhythms to unpitched percussion instruments. Choose those that would give the same pitch as the suggested voices (finger cymbals for number 1, hand drum for number 2, large timpani for number 3, for example).

(Contributed by Gwyneth Hughes-Penman)

314

In the Hall of the Mountain King

This is a piece from the *Peer Gynt Suite* by Edvard Grieg.

Grades

4 and 5

Concept

❏ Anticipating the length of question and answer phrases at an accelerating tempo.

Process

1 Tell the story of Peer Gynt. A précis follows.

> Once upon a time there was a young Norwegian lad named Peer Gynt. One day he met a troll princess sunbathing on a rock. They became friends and decided to get married. Peer followed the princess up the mountain to meet her father, the Mountain King. When Peer arrived in the Hall of the Mountain King, the King agreed to let Peer marry his daughter and become the next Mountain King if he agreed to behave like the trolls. First, Peer had to agree to stay in the dark caves for ever. Peer thought this would be easy enough. Also, he had to eat like a troll. This was less appealing to Peer, but he wanted to be the king so he reluctantly agreed to do that, too.
>
> The king then announced that he would certainly never allow his daughter to marry someone without a tail, so Peer submitted to having a tail tied to his back. The last thing Peer had to do to inherit the kingdom and gain his bride was to see as a troll, so a large group of trolls prepared to slit his eyes. Peer quickly changed his mind at this and tried to escape. He ran and the trolls followed. The faster Peer runs, the faster the trolls run.
>
> The ancient story has different endings. Some say the trolls overtake Peer and bury him in a rain of blows, some end with Peer making good his escape and running for his life over the hills.
>
> Ask the students to tell what they think happens at the end of the story as they listen to the music composed by Edvard Grieg.

2 Put the circle and triangle rhythms on the board. Have the students read and clap these. Discover where they are different.

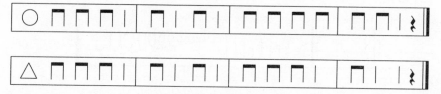

3 Draw an empty chart of nine boxes on the board. Listen to the entire selection, deciding where the "circle" rhythms and where the "triangle" rhythms are heard.

4 Fill in the boxes with a circle or square.

5 The part at the end – the coda – depicts the chase, getting faster and faster.

6 Let's act it out! The leader pretends to be Peer during the first four measures (creeping stealthily throughout the woods to avoid the trolls). Freeze at the end of this phrase.

All the students pretend to be trolls and move for the next four measures (trying in vain to find Peer). Continue in this way until the end of the piece, gradually getting faster and faster, thus experiencing the accelerando.

7   Now find a partner. One person is Peer and the other person is a troll. The above actions are repeated except that at the end of each eight measures, the troll must make one point of contact with his partner, such as touching elbows, shoulders or heads.

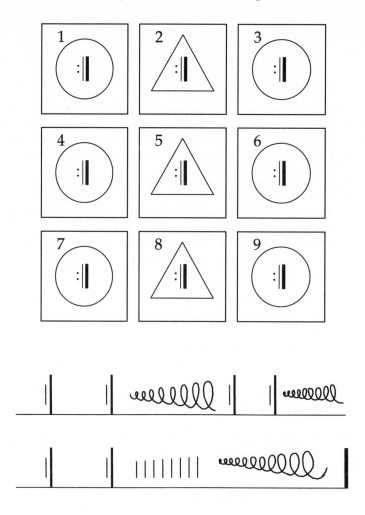

(Contributed by Joan Linklater)

Rondo for Bassoon and Orchestra

from Andante and Rondo, Op. 35

Carl Maria von Weber

Grades

3 and 4

Concepts

❏ Instrumental "families" of the orchestra;
❏ identification of bassoon sound;
❏ rondo form;
❏ "cadenza", "bridge", "coda" terms;
❏ awareness of composer's creativity with a simple form.

Process

1 Discuss the orchestra, defining the different families of instruments. Show pictures of orchestral instruments, particularly the bassoon.

2 Review rondo form (ABACADA).

3 The students clap the rhythm of the rondo (A) theme from a chart. Say the rhythm names or add a word pattern to help learn the rhythm. These could also be played on drums:

Lis - ten to the mo-tor-cyc-le hum-ming It can go and go a-long for e - ver

Lis - ten to the mo - tor - cyc - le hum, It can go and go all

day a - cross the coun - try and a - long the sun - ny prai - rie roads

Theme for "A"

4   The teacher sings the melody while pointing to the rhythms, the students echo the melody, phrase by phrase, until they can sing it securely. Sing fairly slowly, then increase the tempo to approximate the tempo of the theme on the recording.

5   Listen to the theme on the recording several times. The students can sing along with the music.

6   Put the notation for "A" on the board and explain that this is the theme we have learned. The students are asked to raise their hands every time they hear this theme when the recording is played.

7   Now ask the students to listen to the whole selection and give the parts of the rondo letter names as they hear them.

8   Explain that the orchestra and bassoon "quarrel" at the "bridge" passage and ask the students who they think wins.

9   Have them listen for the bassoon "show-off" part (the "cadenza") near the end.

10 The students discover two A sections at the beginning and the end. On second listening, ask who has the theme, the bassoon or orchestra. Help the students discover the form of the entire selection: AABACAD bridge AA coda.

11 Discuss how this rondo is different from the simpler form the students had learned previously.

(Contributed by Helen Neufeld)

CHAPTER TWENTY-TWO

Good-bye

Good-bye songs are very important for younger children and some students who have special needs. They give a sense of form to a lesson and mark the conclusion of an activity. The students can then ready themselves to move on to the next task.

Neesa

This beautiful song in the Seneca Indian language is not exactly a "good-bye" song but it gives such a peaceful feeling when it is sung. It is often used to bring a lesson to a quiet close. The words speak of honouring the creator.

Grades

5 and 6

Concepts

❏ Form: a round;   ❏ quiet, controlled singing.

Process

1   Teach the song using a phonetic translation.

2   When it is well learned, sing it in a two- or four-part round.

3   A very simple movement pattern can be created.

Movement

Formation: form a circle, with hands joined.

| Measures 1–2 | step right, left over right, right, left close, in half-note pattern: ♩ ♩ |♩ ♩ | |
| measures 3–4 | repeat the above but just touch left foot beside the right in the last step; |

319

measures 5–6	step left, right over left, left, right close beside left;
measures 7–8	step left, right, left, into circle ♩ ♩ ♩ ♩	bringing arms up slowly for eight beats;
measures 9–10	repeat the above pattern coming out of circle and bringing arms down slowly.

4 The song and movement may be performed in a two-part round. The formation would be two circles, one inside the other, and one smaller than the other to give room for the movement into the circle.

Good Night, Good Night

Grades

3 through 5

Concepts

☐ Moving bordun;
☐ rhythm pattern ♩ ♩ | ♩ ♩ ♩ | and ‡ ♩ ♩ ‡

words Dennis Lee
music Judy Sills

The dark is dream-ing, day is done. Good night, good night to

ev - ery - one. Good night to the birds and the fish in the sea, Good

night to the bears and good night to me. The night to me.

Process

1 Teach the melody to a neutral syllable then add the words.

2 Add the orchestration.

3 Clap the two rhythm patterns of ♩ ♩ | ♩ ♩ ♩ | and 𝄽 ♩ ♩ 𝄽 then transfer these rhythms to the bass xylophone/metallophone and the finger cymbals.

4 Use two measures of the accompaniment for an introduction and a coda. "Starlight, Star Bright" and "Twinkle Twinkle Little Star" may be used to extend this piece into a rondo, such as

    A   Good Night, Good Night

    B   Starlight, Star Bright

    A   Good Night, Good Night

    C   Twinkle Twinkle Little Star

    A   Good Night, Good Night

Bonsoir

A beautiful song for saying goodnight.

trad arr Lois Birkenshaw-Fleming

Le ruis - seau dans la plai - ne mur - mu - re fai - ble - ment, L'oi -

- seau sur le grand chê - ne chan - te bien douce - ment "Bon - soir, bon - soir, pe -

322

V: - tit en - fant, bon - soir! Bon - soir, bon - soir, pe - tit en - fant bon - soir.

SR

G

BX

2 L'ombre descend et l'ombre,
   Chasse l'onde qui fuit.
   Al'heure où tout est sombre,
   Enfant, gagne ton lit.

3 Petit enfant, repose!
   Que l'ange du sommeil,
   Sur ta paupière rose,
   Jette un rayon vermeil.

1 The brooklet in the valley,
   Murmers quietly,
   In the oak tree all the night birds
   Are singing beautifully.

2 The shades of night are falling
   And they chase the waves at play.
   This hour all is quiet,
   Rest now at end of day.

3 My child may you sleep well,
   With angels watching o're.
   On your eyelids closed and rosy
   There's a light of purest gold.

The following two songs are for quite young children and are sung to familiar tunes.

It's Time to Say Good-bye

It's time to say good-bye,
It's time to say good-bye,
We'll see you all tomorrow (the next time),
It's time to say good-bye.

(To the tune of "The Farmer in the Dell")

This could be followed by singing good-bye to each child individually and by name if there were not too many in the group. This could be done on a two-note chant (*so–mi*).

Everybody Wave Good-bye

Everybody wave good-bye,
Wave good-bye, wave good-bye.
Everybody wave good-bye,
We'll sing another day.

(Adapted from the tune of "London Bridge")

CHAPTER TWENTY-THREE

Glossary

This is not a complete glossary of musical terms, but rather one that pertains more particularly to the teaching of the Orff approach.

Aeolian mode
> One of the scales used in early music. This one corresponds to the white notes of a piano played from A to A. It is a minor mode.

aleatoric music
> Chance music. Much of the composition is left up to the performer although certain indications may be given as to the general form the composer might want.

antiphonal singing
> Singing in which groups and individuals alternate in performing.

atonal music
> Music that is not in any particular key.

augmentation
> A lengthening of the note values in a melody. Usually the length is doubled. The opposite is "diminution".

autoharp
> A stringed instrument that produces melodies and chords when strummed. The chords can be changed by depressing bars that are pre-set.

bar
> Also called a **measure**, particularly in the USA. The space between bar lines.

beat
> The basic unit of time in music. The beat is sometimes called the "pulse" and is present or implied in most music.

body percussion
> The sound made by snapping, clapping, stamping, patschen or with other parts of the body.

bordun
> An accompaniment that uses the first and fifth notes of the scale, rather like a drone in that it never changes.

cadence
> Several chords (most often two or three) that occur at the end of a phrase or piece and which give a feeling of finality.

call and response
> A form in which one person sings a short phrase and another person or group replies, usually using elements of the "call" in the "response". This links the two parts together.

calypso

Music from the West Indies with a particular rhythmic accompaniment and much syncopation.

canon

Similar to a **round**. The same song or activity is performed by two or more people or groups, but they start at different times. Canons can be performed using movement, song, body percussion, instruments and/or speech.

carillon

An instrument that produces a bell-like tone. It is usually played by a keyboard. "Carillon" is also the French word for glockenspiel.

castanets

Two small concave pieces of wood that fit in the hand and are clicked together.

chaconne

A set of melodic variations built over a repeating chord sequence.

chant

A short speech pattern said rhythmically.

chanty (shanty)

A work song sung by sailors in years past as they hauled in the anchors and worked on the sails.

claves

Two short pieces of very hard wood that are tapped together to produce a sound.

coda

The ending part of a song or musical composition.

counter melody

A secondary melodic part that blends well and enhances an existing one.

counterpoint

Two or more melodies that are played or sung together. This creates harmony but each melody is important and complete on its own.

cross rhythms

Conflicting rhythm patterns sounding together.

D.C.

Italian abbreviation for *da capo* which means "from the top", that is, repeat the music from the beginning. *Da capo al fine* indicates that you should repeat the music from the beginning until you come to the word *fine*.

D.S.

Italian abbreviation for *dal segno* which means repeat from the sign 𝄋.

drone

A note or notes of fixed pitch that sounds throughout a piece, for example, in bagpipe music.

dominant

The fifth note of the scale; also used for describing the chord on the fifth.

Dorian mode

One of the scales used in early music. The Dorian mode corresponds to the white notes of a piano from D to D. It is a minor mode.

elemental style

An approach using very simple rhythms, pitch sequences, movements, speech and forms. It is easily grasped by children.

fine

The Italian word for "the end".

finger cymbals

Very small cymbals played in one hand like castanets or by lightly touching the edges together.

gamelan

An ensemble of percussion instruments (xylophone-like instruments and gongs) from Indonesia.

glissando

A sliding passage of notes moving very quickly up or down a scale.

glockenspiel

Small, tuned metal bars arranged in a scale and played with mallets.

gong

Large, suspended metal disk, struck by a mallet.

guiro

A notched gourd or hollow piece of wood that is scraped with a stick.

handbells

Tuned bells or tubes that have the clapper fixed inside. They are played by a downward motion of the wrist and hand.

harmony

Sounds that are heard together. The results are usually pleasing.

homophonic music

A single melody line with or without accompaniment.

idiophone

A percussion instrument that is played by striking, shaking or scraping. Some examples are guiros, log drums, rattles and xylophones.

improvisation

Music that is created while it is being performed.

instrumentarium

The "orchestra" of Orff instruments: xylophones, glockenspiels, metallophones, timpani, drums and other untuned percussion.

interval

The distance in pitch between two notes.

Ionian mode

A scale found originally in early music. It consists of the white notes of a piano, from C to C. It therefore corresponds to our C major scale.

irregular metre

Groupings of beats in a measure that cannot be divided by two or three, for example, 5/4 and 7/8 metres.

kettledrum (timpani)

A large, circular-based instrument that is tunable. The membrane on top is struck with mallets.

krummhorn

An ancient wind instrument that has a curved end. It is often played with recorders.

Lydian mode

An ancient scale corresponding to the white notes of the piano, from F to F. It is a major mode.

major scale

The arrangement of notes that follows the pattern of intervals: tone, tone, semitone, tone, tone, tone, semitone.

maracas

Wooden tubes or round gourds filled with seeds or small pebbles that rattle when shaken.

measure

Also called a **bar**, the segment of music that is found between two bar lines.

metallophone

An instrument with flat metal bars arranged in a scale and played with mallets. It has a lower range and a louder sound than the glockenspiel.

metre (US: meter)

The grouping of beats and accents within a **measure**. The time signature at the beginning of the piece indicates what the metre is.

minor scale

The arrangement of notes that follows the pattern of intervals: tone, semitone, tone, tone, semitone, tone, tone. This gives the natural minor scale.

Mixolydian scale

An ancient scale corresponding to the white notes of a piano from G to G. This is a major mode.

modal music

Music based on the old modes developed by the Greeks and used in the Church for centuries.

modulation

Changing from one key to another during a piece of music.

monophonic music

Music consisting of a melody line only, with no accompaniment.

motif (motive)

A short rhythmic or melodic fragment of a theme.

Orff instruments

The pitched percussion instruments (xylophones, metallophones, glockenspiels) developed to be used in teaching the Orff approach.

ostinato

A short repeated pattern. It can be rhythmic, melodic, or a speech or movement ostinato.

pentatonic scale

A five-note scale. The most common (and the one usually used in the Orff approach) is based on notes 1, 2, 3, 5 and 6 of a scale.

percussion instruments

Those played by hitting, shaking or scraping. Percussion includes drums, maracas, guiros, claves, metallophones and xylophones.

Phrygian mode

An ancient scale that corresponds to the white notes on a piano from E to E.

pitched percussion instruments

Barred instruments that have definite notes so they may be used to play melodies.

polyphonic music

Music that has several melodies playing at the same time. These weave in and around each other. **Counterpoint** is polyphonic music.

polytonal

Music that uses notes from several scales, all playing at the same time.

recorder

A family of woodwind instruments (although most of those used in schools are plastic); also known as an end-blown flute. Most common are soprano, alto, tenor and bass.

refrain

The part of the song that comes after each verse. It usually repeats the same words and melody and is often called the "chorus".

resonator bells

Individual tuned wooden or metal bars mounted on hollow blocks (the resonators) played with a mallet.

retrograde

A melody or rhythm played backwards, from the last note to the first.

rhythm

Musical tones or sounds that are organized according to duration.

rondo

A composition in which there is a recurring theme with contrasting parts between. The form is usually represented as ABACADA.

round

A song in which the same melody is sung but the parts start at different times (see **canon**).

slit drum

Also known as a log drum. A hollow, wooden box with slits cut in the top to give different pitches when struck with a mallet.

steel drums

Made from the tops of discarded oil drums that have been hammered into sections to give varying pitches. Found most often in the West Indies.

tambourine

A flat drum with metal discs mounted around the side so they will jingle when it is struck.

tempo

The speed a piece is played, fast, slow, moderate, and so on.

texture

The overall sound of a piece. Are there many or few instruments? Chords with many notes or few? **Polyphonic** or **monophonic**? Is it a rich, full texture such as an organ or a thin texture such as a recorder?

tonal centre

The note of a tune or piece around which it is based or towards which it proceeds. Also known as the tonic.

tonality

The key in which a piece is written, sung or played. It can also refer to whether the piece is in a **major** or **minor**.

tone (note)

The pitch or duration of a sound.

tone cluster

Adjacent notes in a scale sounded together.

tonic

The first or most important note of a scale.

triad

A chord consisting of three notes.

unison

At the same pitch or played together.

variation

A version of a piece or a section whose rhythm or melody has been altered slightly.

xylophone

A percussion instrument which has tuned wooden bars arranged in a scale. It is played with felt mallets.

CHAPTER TWENTY-FOUR

Tips for Teachers

This chapter outlines some of the more central processes that are part of the Orff approach. The ideas presented here are in no way inclusive and are not intended to replace formal Orff-Schulwerk teacher training. They are included only to assist teachers in understanding the material contained in the book.

Carl Orff and Gunild Keetman felt that music education should be a unity of speech, movement and music, and that all this should be taught in a way that involves the creativity of the child at every point. They also felt that basic, elemental concepts should be used – those that were suited to the child's stage of development. These concepts include borduns, ostinatos, simple forms such as AB, ABA, folk-song form and rondos, chants, nursery rhymes, and the simple songs of childhood.

Through the use of this elemental approach all concepts of music (tempo, pitch, duration, dynamics, timbre and form) are taught in a holistic way. The whole body experiences each concept and this helps the mind understand and retain the information.

Notation is introduced as needed but always after the concept has been presented in an experiential way. Music literacy is an important goal towards which to strive but there must be whole-body understanding first before the abstract symbol is introduced.

This chapter includes some basic "Orff" teaching techniques.

Imitation / Echoes

Imitation is the basis of learning. Young children learn language, behaviour, morals – indeed almost everything – by imitating their parents and other adults. So too, music is learned in the beginning by imitation and rote learning.

Echo activities are at the basis of the Orff approach. Students are invited to copy movement patterns, rhythm patterns, melodic motives and phrases. Accompaniments are also learned at first by imitation.

Sometimes children need a vocal and gestural prompt to understand whose turn it is. One idea is to point to yourself and say "my turn", then to the group and say "your turn".

Here are two little verses that also work well:

> Fiddle dee dee, fiddle dee dee,
> Do the same thing, after me.

> Let's play copycat – that's the game.
> Whatever I do – you do the same.

Body percussion (sound gesture)

1   Clap a short phrase; the children echo.

2   Perform a short phrase using other body percussion, for example

patsch, clap clap snap   rest.

3   Depending on the age and abilities of the child, work with phrases that are very simple, then proceed to those that are longer, more complicated, and use different metres, such as 3/4, 7/8, 5/4. Always challenge the students, to maintain their interest.

With very young children echoes of one measure and in 4/4 time are appropriate. By Grade 1 the students should be ready for two measures. Introduce 3/4 metre in about Grade 2, and by Grades 3 and 4, 6/8 metre and four-measure phrases should be appropriate. By Grades 5–6 most students should be able to work in uneven metres.

At the beginning, keep the tempo moderate, the body percussion used uncomplicated and within the competency of the children (for example, beware of using snapping with Kindergarten children), and have a rest on the last beat in the measure. The rest ensures that the children can relax and assimilate the pattern before trying to repeat it.

In 3/4 metre the last two beats should be rests.

Unpitched percussion

The rhythmic echo activities described above can be transferred to unpitched percussion instruments. Choose those that have fairly definite sounds for both the leader and students. Drums, claves and woodblocks are preferable to maracas and jingle bells. If the class is large have only four or five students echoing on instruments at a time. Otherwise the noise level will be so great that no-one will listen.

Pitched percussion

Begin with just one note for the leader and the person (people) echoing. Use a note that can be played as a *so* (G, C or D would be good choices).

Gradually add notes in the following order: *so–mi / so–mi–la / so–mi–la–do / so–mi–la–do–re*. This gives the pentatonic scale which is so useful in working with children. Later add *fa* and *ti* to give the full diatonic scale.

Students might find it helpful to sing the notes first to hear the tonic *sol–fa* before playing them on an instrument.

Movement and vocal echoes

Echoes can be given in movement and also vocally. When using the voice, work with a few notes at a time, possibly *so–mi* or *so–mi–la*, and gradually add until first the pentatonic scale and then the diatonic scale is reached (see "pitched percussion" above).

Perform these to neutral or to tonic *sol–fa* syllables.

Creativity

Right from the earliest, creativity is encouraged as the children invent their own ways of moving, their own accompaniments, and their own speech and rhythmic patterns. Later they can perform activities such as changing the words to songs or poems such as "Down by the Bay", "Aiken Drum", "Davey Dumpling", "Pink" (chapter 16), "What Shall We

Do?" (chapter 10). Indeed students quickly learn to write entirely new songs, creating both lyrics and melodies.

A more formal way of encouraging creativity is through "question and answer" or "phrase completion" (also known as "call and response").

Question and answer / phrase completion

1 This activity begins the same way as "echoes", but instead of copying the student responds with something different.

2 The sequence of starting with one measure, gradually using longer patterns, introducing more and more difficult rhythms, and more advanced metres, is also the same as "echoes".

3 The first answers given are often longer or shorter than are needed to produce a balanced phrase. Often too, they are in the wrong metre. Nevertheless, these should be accepted because they are the students' creations. Later, by example and perhaps through the introduction of speech patterns, the students will reply with phrase completions of the appropriate length and metre.

4 Questions and answers can be done in movement, with unpitched percussion instruments, and pitched percussion. They also can be worked out vocally. These again follow the same sequence as has been outlined for "echoes".

5 At first the teacher or leader "asks the question" and the students "give the answer" (the second part or completion of the phrase). Later, two students can take these roles, and later still, one student can create both the first and second parts of the phrase.

6 These phrases can be combined in different ways to create small compositions, using simple forms: AB, ABA, AABA, ABCA, or rondo, ABACADA. This exercise leads to an immediate understanding of form and is equally successful when worked out vocally or by using body percussion, unpitched percussion, melodic percussion (xylophones, glockenspiels, tone bells) or in movement.

Speech and Poetry

The use of speech patterns, chants and short poems encourages the development of vocal rhythm and inflection and gives a good foundation for learning to read.

In any speech work be sure to preserve the original integrity of the speech and not change the natural rhythm and accents for the purposes of making the speech fit into a set rhythmic pattern of, say, an accompaniment. For example, the word "Karen" should not be used with a steady quarter-note pattern because the natural rhythm is ♫ 𝄾 not ♩ ♩ – this point is especially important when working with children's names.

Present and repeat the words until they flow rhythmically. Interest can be sustained by repetition, change of volume, change of tempo, use of different pitches and quality of voice, and so on. The result is that the words will be said with greater inflection, interest and feeling.

Body percussion

The use of body percussion to accompany speech leads to greater interest, better developed co-ordination and rhythmic sureness. Throughout the book these patterns are written out, according to the following scheme. Up to four lines are usually used. The bottom one is for stamping, and the stems on the notes go up for the right foot, down for the left, and both ways for a jump. The second line from the bottom is for patschen (slapping the top of the knees), and again the stems go up for the use of the right hand, down for the left, and both ways when both hands are to be used. Clapping is shown on the third line and these notes need only one stem – you cannot clap with one hand! The top line is for snapping. Again, an upstem means the right hand, a downstem the left, and two stems for both hands.

Often there is an additional line for a specific purpose, such as clapping a partner's hand. See "Up Like a Rocket" (chapter 12) for an example of body percussion notation. The body percussion patterns in the book are suggestions only. The students are encouraged to create their own.

Body percussion patterns can be transferred to unpitched percussion instruments. Usually those with the lowest sounds are reserved for the stamping line (large drum) and the highest sound (finger cymbals) reserved for snapping.

Speech patterns

Speech ostinatos are effective when used to add interest to poems. A good example is "Diddle Diddle Dumpling" (chapter 16).

Speech patterns are used to keep the rhythm of accompaniments steady. This is more interesting and often more effective than counting. See, for instance, "November Round" in chapter 10.

Poems that are metric may be accompanied by a rhythmic pattern worked out with body percussion, unpitched percussion or speech patterns.

Sound effects can be created that will enhance the meaning of poems that are non-metric. Sometimes these take the form of a "cushion of sound" (see "The Elders are Watching", chapter 13); sometimes sound effects are used to heighten the meaning of individual words in poems ("Morning Mist", chapter 21); and sometimes the sound effects describe the action taking place in the poem ("Neighbourhood Noises", chapter 13).

All these techniques give many opportunities for students to contribute their ideas in creative ways.

Accompaniments

For pentatonic songs and melodies

BORDUN

These accompaniments are based on notes that are the first and the fifth notes of the diatonic scale (tonic and dominant) in the same octave (C and G, in the C–*do* pentatonic scale). They serve to establish the tonal centre. The characteristic of pentatonic melodies is that they can be accompanied by just one chord (the chord on I) and borduns are commonly used for this purpose.

There are several kinds of bordun but they are all easily played. The simple bordun has both notes played simultaneously. The level bordun plays the chord in one register and then in the register above, alternating between the two. The arpeggiated bordun plays the notes in an arpeggiated form.

OSTINATOS

The word comes from the same root as "obstinate" and is a constantly repeated pattern using the same notes. Ostinatos (the plural is also "ostinati") can be rhythmic, melodic, they can use speech, be vocal or instrumental, or use body percussion. They can also, of course, use combinations of the above.

The repetition of the pattern enables very young children and those with special needs to participate in playing accompaniments – even melodic percussion.

Students can, from an early age, be encouraged to create their own melodic ostinatos in the pentatonic scale. In 4/4 metre, they choose four notes that they repeat over and over. Of course, some ostinatos sound better than others when played with a melody. Those that move in contrary motion to the melody are usually best and it often helps to suggest that one of the notes be the tonic or first note of the scale.

The ostinato can become more complicated and involved as the students' competency develops. Obviously, writing an ostinato that sounds well is an art that takes time to master, and mastery for the teacher will come with experience and formal study of the principles of Orff-Schulwerk.

For changing chord accompaniments

If used before Grade 5 or so these accompaniments should just be taught by rote. If using a two-chord harmony – I and V – the pattern can be memorized by moving the hands high and low and saying the pattern out loud at the same time. "I'se the B'y" (chapter 3) is a song that requires an accompaniment on I and V. It can be learned in this way:

high   low   high   low   high   low   low   high

For this particular song, the children can transfer this pattern to the two notes G and D. Stickers can be used on the notes to indicate which ones to play on high (H) – G – and low (L) – D – if this aid is needed.

In Grades 4 or 5 the ability to hear and understand harmonic concepts is usually developed enough for the concept of harmonic accompaniments to be studied with understanding.

1   Have the students sing the song while you accompany it with a bordun. They put their hands up when it does not sound correct.

2   Play the correct chord when it is appropriate and ask if this sounds better.

3   Sing the root of the chords while the class sings the song.

4   Teach the progression using tonic *sol-fa* syllables, I, V, and/or the letter names of the notes.

5   Transfer this to melodic instruments.

6   Add the other notes in the chords in musical ways.

7   Embellish the basic chord progression with passing notes or rhythmic variations to create interest.

Iconic representation

If the students you work with cannot process note representation and if the use of chord symbols such as I–V or C–G is also too difficult, use iconic representation.

For example,   for I or C, and ● for V or G.

A typical example of an accompaniment would look like this ("I'se the B'y"):

The beauty of this approach is that stickers with the appropriate symbols can be placed on the corresponding keys of xylophones or notes of a piano. The representations are shape- *and* colour-coded in case students you are working with are also colour-blind.

Teaching accompaniments

All accompaniments should be taught through patschen at first – left hand for the low notes, right hand for the high. Use the outside and inside of the knees as well to show the melodic movement of the notes. This method clearly shows the spatial relationship of the notes and helps the students play the accompaniments accurately when it is their turn.

When children are young, teach in mirror fashion (always telling them exactly what you are doing). This method is easier for most youngsters to grasp.

Alternating hands

When playing melodies and accompaniments on melodic instruments it is usually best to alternate the hands. In some books the hands to be used are indicated by the stems of the notes going up (right) or down (left). This is very clear but leads to problems in writing the music on the staff. Other books (this one included) write the instrumental parts in the conventional notational manner and leave the alternating pattern up to the player (or teacher) to decide. This probably works best because people have decided preferences for which hand to begin with. The important thing to remember is that both hands should be used whenever possible. (See the timpani part in "A-Hunting We Will Go" in chapter 19.)

Cross-over patterns

Work these out carefully on the knees first. Begin by resting the hand to be crossed on one knee just wiggling the fingers when it should be "playing" a note. The other hand plays on one side then the other. When this is secure, allow the resting hand to play the notes but always have this hand positioned below the crossing-over hand.

Appendixes

A Canadian Bibliography

General books on music and music education

Green, J. Paul and Nancy F. Vogan, *A History of Music Education in Canada*. Toronto: University of Toronto Press, 1990

Elliot, David J., *Music Matters – a new philosophy of music education*. New York: Oxford University Press, 1995

Kallmann, Helmut, Gilles Potvin and Kenneth Winters (eds), *Encyclopedia of Music in Canada* (2nd edn). Toronto: University of Toronto Press, 1992. (Includes many references to the Orff approach and its teaching.)

McGee, Timothy J., *The Music of Canada*. Markham: Penguin, 1985

Schafer, R. Murray, *Creative Music Education: a handbook for the modern music teacher*. New York: Schirmer, 1976

Schafer, R. Murray, *Ear Cleaning: notes for an experimental music course*. Don Mills: BMI, 1967

Schafer, R. Murray, *The Tuning of the World*. Toronto: McClelland, 1977

Shand, Patricia Martin, *Canadian Music: a selective guidelist for teachers*. Toronto: Canadian Music Centre, 1978. (Contains lists and description of Canadian vocal and instrumental compositions including a list of choral compositions based on Canadian folk songs. Part of the Adaskin Project. There are several other volumes in this project.)

Upitis, R., *This Too is Music*. Portsmouth: Heinemann, 1990. (An excellent book that makes a plea for allowing more creativity in music education.)

Orff-Schulwerk

Bissell, Keith, "Carl Orff's Music for Children: a reply to the critics", *Recorder*, vol. 6, Oct 1993

Doloff, Lori-Anne, *Das Schulwerk: a foundation for the cognitive, musical and artistic development of children*. Lee R. Bartel (ed.), Research Perspectives in Music Education, Monograph #1. Toronto: Canadian Music Education Research Centre, University of Toronto, 1993

Hall, Doreen, *Music For Children*. Mainz, Germany: Schott, 1960. (A short manual for teachers that would be helpful for anyone working with Carl Orff's approach to music education.)

Hall, Doreen, "Music for Children's Past, Present and Future", in *Music for Children – Carl Orff Canada – Musique pour enfants*, vol. 4, Feb 1976

Hall, Doreen, (ed.), *Orff Schulwerk in Canada: a collection of articles and lectures from the early years (1954–1962)*. London, UK: Schott, 1992

Orff, Carl and Gunild Keetman, *Music for Children*, edited by Doreen Hall and Arnold Walter, 5 vols. Mainz, Germany: Schott, 1956–61

Otto, Donna (ed.), "Orff Schulwerk and the B.C. Elementary Fine Arts Curriculum", *B.C. Music Educators*, vol. 29, Summer 1986

Walter, Arnold, "Elementary Music Education: the European approach", *Canadian Music Journal*, vol. 2, Spring 1958

Wuytach, Jos and Judy Sills, *Musica Activa*. New York: Schott Music Corporation, 1994

See also the many articles in *Ostinato*, the journal of *Music for Children – Carl Orff Canada – Musique pour enfants*.

Collections of songs with Orff accompaniments

Asplund, David and Donna Otto, *Let's Do It Again*, 3 vols. Jenson, 1984. (Collections of songs with Orff accompaniments that are very useful in the classroom.)

Bissell, Keith, *Carols for Singing and Playing*. Waterloo: Waterloo Music, 1980

Bissell, Keith, *International Folk Songs and Singing Games*. Waterloo: Waterloo Music, 1976

Bissell, Keith, *It's Fun to Sing and Play*. Waterloo: Waterloo Music, 1976

Bissell, Keith, *Let's Sing and Play – for primary grades*. Waterloo: Waterloo Music, 1976

Bissell, Keith, *Let's Sing and Play – for junior and intermediate grades*. Waterloo: Waterloo Music, 1978

Bissell, Keith, *Singing and Playing for Primary Grades*. Waterloo: Waterloo Music, 1978. French version is called *Chantons et jouons*.

Bissell, Keith, *Songs for Schools*. London, UK: Schott, 1963

Bissell, Keith, *Songs for Singing and Playing*. Waterloo: Waterloo Music, 1980

Dubois, Chantel, *Musique en Fête*. Montréal, 1992

Dubois, Chantel, *Nations en Fête*. Montréal, 1992

Les Éditions l'Image de l'art. 1991. (Un recueil de répertoire de chansons des plus grands auteurs–compositeurs du Québec. Cet ouvrage est accompagné d'une cassette et d'un cahier avec les arrangements pour instruments Orff.)

Hall, Doreen, *Canons and Rounds*. Waterloo: Waterloo Music, 1980

Hall, Doreen, *Singing Games and Songs*. Mainz, Germany: Schott, 1963

Ladendecker, Dianne, *Oh Canada*. St. Louis and St. Paul, USA: Misty Isle, Dunvegan House, 1994. (Dianne is an American, but it is included here as the book is a collection of Canadian folk songs with Orff accompaniments.)

Nugent, N. et Michèle Leblanc, *Arc-en-sons*, édité par la Maison Beauchemin. Montréal.

Sills, Judy, *Canadiana*. Edmonton: Black Cat, 1995. (A collection of Canadian folk material arranged in the Orff style.)

Vermeulen, Ada, *Songs to Play, Games to Sing/Chansons pour s'amuser*. Don Mills: Gordon V. Thompson/Warner Chappell, 1988

Vermeulen, Ada, *More Songs to Play and Games to Sing/Chansons pour s'amuser ... encore!*. Don Mills: Gordon V. Thompson/Warner Chappell, 1991. (This book and the one above give many examples of bilingual singing games with precise instructions and suggested instrumental accompaniments.)

Wuytack, Jos and Judy Sills, *Can You Canon?* Waterloo: Waterloo Music, 1994

Wuytack, Jos and Judy Sills, *55X Funtastic*. Waterloo: Waterloo Music, 1993

Early childhood

Cass-Beggs, Barbara, *To Listen, To Like, To Learn*. Toronto: Peter Martin, 1974

Cass-Beggs, Barbara, *Your Baby Needs Music: a musical sound book for babies up to two years old*. North Vancouver: Douglas and McIntyre, 1978

Cass-Beggs, Barbara, *Your Child Needs Music: a complete course in teaching music to children*. Oakville: Frederick Harris, 1986

Kulich, Birthe, *Friendly Bear's Song Book. Songs and music activities for young children, their families and teachers*. Vancouver: Empire, 1989

Martin, Elaine, *The Joyful Guide to Children's Play from Birth to Three Years*. Toronto: Stoddart, 1988

Panabaker, Lucile, *Lucile Panabaker's Song Book*. Toronto: Peter Martin, 1968

Wood, Donna, *Move, Sing, Listen, Play* (2nd edn). Don Mills: Gordon V. Thompson/Warner Chappell, 1995

Books for classroom teaching

Birkenshaw, Lois, *Music for Fun, Music for Learning* (3rd edn). Toronto: Holt, Rinehart and Winston, 1982

Birkenshaw, Lois, *Musictime K–3*. Agincourt: Silver Burdett & Ginn, 1985 [teacher's book and recordings]

Birkenshaw, Lois and Joan Clarke, *Musictime 4–6*. Agincourt: Silver Burdett & Ginn, 1986 [teacher's book, student book and recordings]

Birkenshaw-Fleming, Lois, *Come On Everybody Let's Sing*. Don Mills: Gordon V. Thompson/Warner Chappell, 1989 [book and recordings]. (A book for regular classroom use that contains many ideas about working with students who have special needs.)

Corneille, Marcelle, C. N. D., *Épanouissons-nous par la musique*. Don Mills: Gordon V. Thompson/Warner Chappell, 1995 [translation and adaptation of Lois Birkenshaw-Fleming, *Come On Everybody Let's Sing*]

De Frece, Robert, *Canada: Its Music*. Don Mills: Collier Macmillan, 1989. (A book of Canadian music, art and biographies of Canadian artists, composers and performers, specifically designed for the classroom. Many Orff arrangements.)

Fallis, Lois, *Seasons and Themes*. Waterloo: Waterloo Music, 1982. (Songs, activities and musical playlets.)

Fallis, Lois, *And a Glass Slipper*. Waterloo: Waterloo Music, 1984

Gauthier-Houle, Gertrude, *Apprenons par la musique*. Montréal: Éditions HRW, 1981 [translation and adaptation of Lois Birkenshaw, *Music for Fun, Music for Learning*]

Mason, Elaine and Marilyn Hardy, *Music Builders*. Agincourt: Berandol/Ginn, 1981. (Songs, poems, activities and listening selections (played by Canadian artists) for each grade, K to 6. Excellent material; should be part of every music program.)

Mason, Elaine and Marilyn Hardy, *Musique s'il vous plait* [M–3e et 4e–6e]. Agincourt: Berandol/GLC/Ginn, 1998–93. (Similar to above, but in French.)

Watts, David W., *Exploring the Joy of Music*. Richmond Hill: Scholastic, 1991

Specifically for special needs

Allin, Nan, Lois Birkenshaw and Lloyd Queen, *Music is Special, Children are Special.* Toronto: A Curriculum Guideline from the Ministry of Education, Ontario, 1981

Birkenshaw-Fleming, Lois, *Music for All. Teaching music to people with special needs.* Don Mills: Gordon V. Thompson/Warner Chappell, 1993. (Written for teachers of individual students in the school setting or the private studio.)

Bunch, Gary Owen (ed.), *The Curriculum of Hearing-Impaired Students, Theoretical and Practical Considerations.* Boston, USA: College-Hill,/Little, Brown, 1987

Estabrooks, Warren and Lois Birkenshaw-Fleming, *Hear and Listen! Talk and Sing!* Toronto: Arisa, 1994 [book and recording, distributed by The Alexander Graham Bell Association for the Deaf, Washington DC]. (Songs for young children who are hearing-impaired and others who need help in learning to talk.)

Herman, Fran and James Smith, *Accentuate the Positive.* Toronto: Jimani, 1988

Herman, Fran and James Smith, *Creatability.* Tucson, USA: Communication Skill Builders, 1992. (This book and the one above give excellent ideas for fostering the creative arts for children with special needs.)

Page, Berthé, et al., *L'épanouissement de tous par la musique.*Toronto: A Curriculum Guideline from the Ministry of Education, Ontario, 1983 [translation and adaptation of Nan Allin, Lois Birkenshaw and Lloyd Queen, *Music is Special, Children are Special*]

General song collections

Cass-Beggs, Barbara, *A Musical Calendar of Festivals.* London, UK: Ward Lock, 1983

Fowke, Edith, *Sally Go Round the Sun.* Toronto: McClelland and Stewart, 1969. (The "best ever" book of nursery rhymes and children's songs.)

Fowke, Edith and Bram Morrison, *Canadian Vibrations.* Toronto: Macmillan, 1972. (A good collection of Canadian songs for older students.)

Sharon, Lois and Bram Sharon, *The All New Elephant Jam.* Toronto: McGraw-Hill Ryerson, 1989

Walden, David E. and Lois Birkenshaw, *The Goat with the Bright Red Socks.* Toronto: Berandol, 1980. (A song book and recording for language learning.)

Canadian folk songs

Barbeau, Marius, *Jongleur Songs of Old Quebec and New Brunswick.* Toronto: Ryerson, 1962

Barbeau, Marius, Arthur Lismer and Arthur Bourinet, *Come A-Singing.* Ottawa, 1947

Bray, Kenneth, Nancy Telfer and Gerhard Wuensch, *Reflections of Canada*, 3 vols. Oakville: Frederick Harris, 1985. Two-part arrangements of Canadian folk songs.

Cass-Beggs, Barbara, *Canadian Folk Songs for the Young.* Vancouver: J. J. Douglas, 1975

Cass-Beggs, Barbara, *Seven Métis Folk Songs of Saskatchewan.* Toronto: BMI (Berandol), 1967

Canadian Folk Music Journal. Toronto: Canadian Society for Musical Traditions, 1973–

Centre franco-ontarien de ressources pédagogiques, *Musique Vocale*, 6 vols. Ottawa, 1986. (A very useful, graded collection of French folk songs which includes many games.)

Cook, D. F., *Sing the Sea*. Waterloo: Waterloo Music, 1986. (A collection of songs from Newfoundland.)

Cook, D. F., *Twelve Songs of Newfoundland*. Waterloo: Waterloo Music, 1986

Creighton, Helen, *Maritime Folk Songs*. Toronto: Ryerson, 1962

Creighton, Helen, *Songs and Ballads from Nova Scotia*. Toronto: Dent, 1932 (reprinted New York: Dover, 1966). (Helen Creighton was one of the foremost collectors of folk material in the Maritimes.)

Dibblee, Randall and Dorothy Dibblee, *Folksongs from Prince Edward Island*. Summerside: Williams and Crue, 1973

Evans, Robert, *Song to a Seagull: a book of Canadian songs and poems*. Toronto: Ryerson, 1970

Fowke, Edith, *The Penguin Book of Canadian Folk Songs*. London UK: Penguin, 1973

Fowke, Edith, Alan Mills and Helmut Blume, *Canada's Story in Song*. Toronto: Gage, 1960. (A book combining our folk-song tradition with our history. Good for Integrated Studies.)

Fowke, Edith and Carole Henderson, with Judith Brooks, *A Bibliography of Canadian Folklore in English*. Downsview: York University, 1976. (A remarkable source of folk material.)

Fowke, Edith and Richard Johnston, *Chansons de Québec*. Waterloo: Waterloo Music, 1957

Fowke, Edith and Richard Johnson, *Folk Songs of Canada*. Waterloo: Waterloo Music, 1954

Fowke, Edith and Richard Johnson, *More Folk Songs of Canada*. Waterloo: Waterloo Music, 1967. (This book and the two above are the most complete and useful sources for Canadian folk songs available.)

Gabriel Dumont Institute of Native Studies and Applied Research Inc., *Métis Songs: visiting the Métis way*. Regina Sask: Saskatchewan Music Educators Association, 1993

Gledhill, Christopher, *Folk Songs of Prince Edward Island*. Charlottetown: Square Deal, 1973

Gordon, Shelly, *Songs to Sing and Sing again*. [Available from 25 Belsize Dr., Toronto ON or from World Around Songs Inc., Burnsville, NC 28714, USA], 1984. (A handy pocket book containing well-known folk songs.)

Grant, Catherine (ed.), *Touch the Pioneers. A Tanglefoot song book*. Waterloo: Waterloo Music, 1984

Greenleaf, Elizabeth B. and Grace Y. Mansfield, *Ballads and Sea Songs of Newfoundland*. Cambridge, USA: 1963

Johnson, Richard, *Folk Songs North America Sings*. Toronto: E. C. Kirby, 1984

Karpeles, Maud, *Folk Songs from Newfoundland*. London, UK: Faber, 1971

Lemieux, Germain, *Chansonnier franco-ontarien*, 2 vols. Sudbury: Université de Sudbury, 1974–5. (Germain Lemieux is one of the most distinguished collectors of folk material in Canada and is known around the world for his books and many articles on the subject.)

Manny, Louise and James Reginald Wilson, *Songs of the Miramichi*. Fredericton: Brunswick, 1968

Peacock, Kenneth, *Folk Songs of Newfoundland*. Toronto: Berandol, 1969

Peacock, Kenneth, *Songs of the Newfoundland Outports*, 3 vols. Ottawa: National Museum, 1965

Pottie, Kaye and Vernon Ellis, *Folksongs of the Maritimes*. Halifax: Formac, 1992. (An excellent collection of folk songs designed to be used in the schools.)

Saskatchewan Music Educators Association, *Songs of the Northern Plains*. Regina Sask: Weigl, 1992

Sing Silverbirch Sing: a collection of Canadian folk songs, analysis by Ilona Bartalus. Toronto: Boosey and Hawkes, 1980

Movement and dance

Boorman, Joyce, *Creative Dance in the First Three Grades*. Don Mills: Longmans, 1967

Boorman, Joyce, *Creative Dance in Grades Four to Six*. Don Mills: Longmans, 1971

Boorman, Joyce, *Dance and Language Experiences with Children*. Don Mills: Longmans, 1973. (Three books with a wealth of ideas to use in movement programs.)

Bourque-Moreau, France, *Je dance mon enfance*. Montréal: privately published, 1979

Bourque-Moreau, France et Michel Landry, *La danse d'inspiration traditionnelle au primaire*. Montréal: privately published, 1983

Morin, Francine L., *Psychological and Curricular Foundations for Elementary Dance Education*. Edina: Bellwether, 1988

Choral

Ashworth Bartle, Jean, *Lifeline for Children's Choir Directors*, (revised edn). Don Mills: Gordon V. Thompson/Warner Chappell, 1993. (An excellent and practical guide to directing children's choirs.)

Rao, Doreen, *We Will Sing!* New York: Boosey and Hawkes, 1993

Telfer, Nancy, *Successful Sight Singing*, 2 vols. San Diego, USA: Neil A. Kjos, 1992–3

Instruments

Bissell, Keith, *In the Modes: 15 modal pieces for percussion and recorder*. Waterloo: Waterloo Music, 1982

Bissell, Keith, *Musical Portraits For Children*. Waterloo: Waterloo Music, 1976. (For Orff instruments only.)

Duschanes, Mario, *Mario Duschanes' Method for the Recorder*. Toronto: Berandol, 1957

Evans, Priscella, *Piping Songs: a first recorder workbook*. Halifax: McCurdy, 1981

Gaizauskas, Barbara R., *Castle to Classroom. The recorder in music history: a method for adults*. Toronto: Berandol, 1981

Kulich, Birthe and Joe Berarducci, *Windsong Series*, (revised edn). Vancouver: Empire, 1993. Included in the series are the following titles: *Windsongs, Ho Ho Wataney, Go Tell Aunt Rhody, I'se the B'y, À la claire fontaine*, and *Alto Odyssey*.

Orr, Hugh, *Basic Recorder Technique*. Toronto: Berandol, 1961. (One of the most popular methods for learning the recorder.)

Orr, Hugh, *Canons*. Waterloo: Waterloo Music, 1980. (Written on the notes D to G for beginning recorder students.)

Rempel, Ursula M. and Carolyn Ritchey, *A Medieval Feast: songs and dances for recorders and Orff instruments*. Waterloo: Waterloo Music, 1981

Rempel, Ursula M. and Carolyn Ritchey, *A Medieval Feast II: Children's menu: songs and dances in easy arrangements for voices and Orff instruments*. Waterloo: Waterloo Music, 1984

Drama

Booth, David, *Games For Everyone*. Markham: Pembroke, 1986. (This book has many ideas to stimulate the dramatic imagination through games.)

Booth, David and Catherine Lundy, *Improvisation, learning through drama*. Toronto: Academic, 1985. (Contains co-operative games, sensory awareness, role-playing and sources appropriate for Grades 2–8).

Goulding, Dorothy-Jane, *Play-Acting in the Schools*. Toronto: Ryerson, 1970 Press. (Filled with excellent, practical ideas.)

Ministry of Education, Ontario, *Drama in the Formative Years*. 1984. (An excellent document that gives a theoretical overview of what drama is and includes practical ideas.)

Swartz, L, *Dramathemes*. Markham: Pembroke, 1988. (Excellent for elementary grades with all the activities organized into ready-made thematic units.)

Poetry

Booth, David, *'Til All the Stars Have Fallen*. Toronto: Kids Can, 1989. (A selection of Canadian poems for children.)

Booth, David, Robert Barton and Agnes Buckles, *Brown is the Back of a Toad* and *Yellow is the Colour of a Lemon Tart*. Don Mills: Longman, 1974. (Two books of poetry that were part of a language arts program called "Colours".)

Downie, Mary Alice and Robertson, Barbara, *The New Wind Has Wings*. Toronto: Oxford University Press, 1984. (Excellent poems and illustrations.)

Dunn, Sonja, *Butterscotch Dreams*. Markham: Pembroke, 1987. (Simple structures on a variety of themes that enable even primary children to create their own chants. Sonja Dunn has written other books of poetry, including *Primary Rhymerry* and *Crackers and Crumbs*.)

Heidbreder, Robert, *Don't Eat Spiders*. Toronto: Oxford University Press, 1985. (Original poems with good illustrations.)

Lee, Dennis, *Alligator Pie, Nicholas, Knock, Garbage Delight, Jelly Belly, The Ice Cream Store*. Toronto: Macmillan/Harper Collins, 1974–92. (Books of wondrous poems for children. They are well illustrated and have enchanted children for years.)

Newman, Fran, *Round Slice of Moon*. Richmond Hill: Scholastic, 1980. (An excellent collection of poems for children.)

Index

* These are poems or chants

** Plays, Stories, Legends, Sayings, Speech, Chants